T0320144

CONSTRUCTIVE
INTERCULTURAL
MANAGEMENT

CONSTRUCTIVE INTERCULTURAL MANAGEMENT

INTEGRATING CULTURAL DIFFERENCES SUCCESSFULLY

CHRISTOPH BARMEYER
University of Passau, Germany

MADELEINE BAUSCH
University of Passau, Germany

ULRIKE MAYRHOFER
IAE Nice, Université Côte d'Azur, France

Cheltenham, UK • Northampton, MA, USA

Cover image: Ulrike Haupt.

Published by
Edward Elgar Publishing Limited
The Lypiatts
15 Lansdown Road
Cheltenham
Glos GL50 2JA
UK

Edward Elgar Publishing, Inc.
William Pratt House
9 Dewey Court
Northampton
Massachusetts 01060
USA

A catalogue record for this book
is available from the British Library

Library of Congress Control Number: 2021936861

MIX
Paper from
responsible sources
FSC® C013056
www.fsc.org

ISBN 978 1 83910 453 4 (cased)
ISBN 978 1 83910 455 8 (paperback)
ISBN 978 1 83910 454 1 (eBook)

Printed and bound in Great Britain by TJ Books Limited, Padstow, Cornwall

CONTENTS

FIGURES

1
What this book is about and why it is worth reading

1.　WHY ORGANIZATIONS MUST DEAL WITH INTERCULTURALITY

Organizations are increasingly permeated by interculturality, and their actors are becoming more intercultural in their work and practices. Although globalization has, to some extent, led to harmonization and standardization in social, cultural and economic spheres, cultural diversity remains present in organizations. These differences can neither be denied nor minimized, as illustrated by longstanding debates on the convergence and divergence of values and practices or on the theses of *culture bound* and *culture free*. With internationalization, digitalization and migration, interculturality plays a central role within and between organizations, and actors need new approaches of how to deal with cultural diversity.

Interculturality emerges from cultural diversity and reflects the processes and outcomes of diverse groups. If not managed in an appropriate way, interculturality can be irritating and conflicting due to diverging values, expectations, norms, meanings and interpretations of actors. *Critical incidents* might then absorb organizational resources, such as human and financial resources. Interculturality can lead to misunderstandings, which hinder organizational goal attainment. However, such misunderstandings can also be reduced or even avoided. This book assumes that cultural diversity can also lead to synergy and complementarity, in the form of creativity and innovativeness. Far too often, the positive effects of interculturality remain hidden due to the predominant 'negative bias' of scholars and practitioners. In contrast to the prevailing *problematizing* approach in intercultural research and practice, we consider interculturality and cultural differences as a *resource* and take an explicit *constructive* approach to cultural diversity. We call this new approach *constructive intercultural management*.

Constructive intercultural management relies on several decades of the authors' own research and consulting experience in the field of interculturality. It is also inspired by works on cultural synergy (Adler, 1983) and positive organizational scholarship, which focuses on the positive aspects of organizational life such as employees' strengths and motivations, as well as a collaborative spirit, virtuousness and purpose (Cameron, 2017; Cameron & Spreitzer, 2011). *Constructive intercultural management* considers cultural differences as strengths, which, combined in an appropriate way, open the path to creative and innovative collaboration. It assumes that cultural diversity can be enriching and complementary, leading to new practices, innovation and well-being among employees (Barmeyer & Mayer, 2020). This assumption is the leitmotiv of this book and can be found in all chapters.

The development and persistence of organizations depend on whether they are able to generate, apply and establish good practices for problem-solving. This rule affects all organizations that act internationally – whether they are large multinational companies, small- and medium-sized enterprises (SMEs), start-ups, non-governmental organizations (NGOs) or public institutions. With internationalization, organizations bring together people from different cultural backgrounds and meaning systems. Such meaning systems arise through socialization, providing guidance and orientation (d'Iribarne et al., 2020), and they are reflected in different ways of thinking and working.

Cultural differences thus affect intercultural cooperation in daily work: actors constantly negotiate meanings, practices, ways of working and problem-solving. Organizations, departments and teams that are particularly affected by interculturality show special interest in creating effective, target-oriented and constructive work processes and solutions. Theoretical and practical research on *constructive interculturality* has developed in recent years, but remains still limited (Adler & Aycan, 2018; Stahl & Tung, 2015). Bearing in mind the desirability of intercultural synergy as a *positive* output of intercultural interaction (Barmeyer & Franklin, 2016; Mayrhofer, 2017), we have chosen a *constructive* perspective on interculturality in this book, and highlight the *complementary* and *synergetic* sides of cultural diversity in organizations. We aim to contribute to the conceptual foundations of constructive interculturality and help organizations to build on positive effects of cultural diversity.

2.   WHY THIS BOOK IS DIFFERENT AND HOW IT IS STRUCTURED

This book attempts to highlight the *constructive* aspects of *interculturality* and *complementarity* in organizations. We claim that a merely problem-oriented approach does not advance intercultural management research and practice, even if we consider that the understanding, analysis and explanation of problems related to interculturality remain important. This book therefore addresses the complementary side of cultural differences through the lens of resource and solution orientation. Our approach is based on the humanistic, idealistic and normative conviction that humans, whether in their functions as managers or consultants, are able to learn and develop. Consequently, we assume that they can actively influence the social environment of their organizations, such as teams and departments, in a *constructive* and *creative* way. In this perspective, intercultural competence is of particular importance. Constructive interculturality can thus serve many different areas of organizations.

Furthermore, the book focuses on *organizations*, and more specifically on companies. Organizations are an important and widespread form of social systems, which are subject to internationalization, digitalization and migration. They are not only places where strategic goals are defined, tasks are fulfilled and added value is created; above all, organizations are places of professional socialization, learning, meaning and identity creation. They are thus places of intercultural interaction.

This book emphasizes the *dynamic* aspects of culture and interculturality, which represent unpredictable processes of mutual rapprochement, social negotiation and development. Actors in intercultural situations are not 'machines' or 'robots' with determined cultural ways of thinking and behaving. Indeed, they gradually adapt their behaviours to contexts and inter-action partners, and actively influence and shape the course and outcome of interaction situations. These intercultural dynamics can be found everywhere in organizations, for example, in leadership and management practice transfers.

Moreover, we take into account the multiple dimensions of culture in the sense of cultural pluralism, and therefore consider regional, sectoral, organizational and professional cultures, as well as gender and generation. Nevertheless, the focus is on national culture, in line with common contents of intercultural management courses that take place in bachelor and master programmes at universities and business schools.

In keeping up with the tradition of the University of Passau (Germany), the orientation of the book is interdisciplinary in nature, which means that interculturality is analysed and interpreted from multiple perspectives and disciplines such as cultural anthropology, social psychology, sociology, organizational and management research, and communication science. This diversity enables a multi-perspective understanding of intercultural realities.

This textbook presents current and innovative topics, theoretical frameworks and empirical findings. We add value by considering studies from multiple regions including emerging economies and developing countries, and thus counteract the ethnocentric worldview, contexts and themes of dominant US and Western discourses (Barmeyer et al., 2019a).

We also adopt a *contextualized* perspective on intercultural interaction, taking into account socio-historical, political, institutional, functional and actor-specific elements such as power relationships, language and conflicts of interest.

Last but not least, this book reflects a *systemic approach*. 'Systemic' means that we do not only consider the inherent characteristics of a social system such as an organization, but also the options for design, which actively transform the system. To achieve a certain objectivity and neutrality in perception and analysis, we often take a *meta-level* position and aim to provide a holistic view of phenomena in cultural and social systems, considering contexts, actors and their mutual relationships.

Because of the strong empirical interplay between interculturality and management, this textbook integrates *research and practice*: theoretical foundations and empirical findings are enriched by practical experience. Examples from everyday work in organizations serve to illustrate and apply concepts and frameworks. In the sense of *constructive intercultural management*, we also provide recommendations for managing interculturality.

This book provides a comprehensive overview of the multiple approaches, frameworks and practices in intercultural management, and highlights the systemic character of cultures and contexts. We build on the extensive work conducted in *intercultural* and *cross-cultural* management. According to Nancy Adler, one of the pioneers of research and practice in the field, *cross-cultural management* describes organizational behaviour 'within countries and cultures, compares organizational behaviour across countries and cultures, and, perhaps most importantly, seeks to understand and improve the interaction of co-workers, clients, suppliers, and alliance partners from different countries and cultures' (Adler & Gundersen,

2008, p. 13). Building on Adler's definition, intercultural management opens up options for designing and shaping intercultural cooperation in organizations. *Intercultural management* (from Latin *'inter'* for 'between') considers all the processes that emerge between actors from different cultures. While comparing cultures, it also considers the underlying dynamics and outcomes of intercultural interaction, whether positive or negative. It thus takes into account both the interaction of individuals and the evolutionary character of social systems. Therefore, *constructive intercultural management* deals with the positive and constructive design of interculturality in its multi-layered dynamics. The field comprises three steps (Table 1.1), which are reflected in the structure of the book and the chapters.

Table 1.1   Overall framework of constructive interculturality in organizations

Step		Objective	Concretization	Content
1.	Awareness and understanding of culture and cultural differences	Theorizing and acquiring knowledge about intercultural reality and possible interpretations	Conscious perception, reflection and understanding of cultural characteristics and differences	Concepts and frameworks for structuring and classifying intercultural situations
2.	Experiencing through examples and practices	Illustrating and experiencing intercultural reality in different contexts	Experience of functions, roles and situations in organizations	Research findings and practical examples
3.	Design and options for strategic action	Achieving the ability to influence intercultural reality	Development and implementation of options for strategic action	Methods, instruments and practices for developing constructive interculturality

3.   FOR WHOM THIS BOOK IS WRITTEN AND ACKNOWLEDGEMENTS

Due to its interdisciplinary and systemic nature, this textbook addresses several target groups.

First, the book is relevant for students in business and management, cultural studies, intercultural communication and study areas with an international focus. We provide an important number of frameworks and examples which explain cultural behaviours within and across organizations and which can be used for learning and (personal) development. We encourage students to experience cultural differences on their own to profoundly value the contents of this book.

Second, the book addresses researchers in intercultural and cross-cultural management, organization studies, international business and related fields with an interest in cultural issues. We offer a comprehensive overview of theoretical concepts and frameworks, illustrated by numerous examples, case studies and surveys, which might inspire ideas for future research.

Third, the book is interesting for practitioners who are facing the challenges of a complex and diverse society and workforce within and across organizations. They can be executives, leaders, managers, employees and consultants, but also other individuals who wish to find solutions for the constructive design of cultural diversity within and across teams and organizations. This book delivers ideas on how to leverage the richness of multiple perspectives and resources, to lead employees constructively and to create an enjoyable atmosphere, with the aim to achieve complementarity and synergy in the form of creativity and innovation.

Lastly, this book may serve all people who are interested in the effects and consequences of culture on (work) behaviours and who wish to learn more about the reasons, dynamics and possible outcomes of interculturality.

This book is based on a wide variety of disciplines, languages and cultures, but also on numerous conversations and projects conducted with students from many countries and scholars, managers, consultants, trainers and friends who are personally or professionally affected and fascinated by interculturality. Many thanks to all these people!

We would like to thank the following organizations for providing enriching insights into their intercultural management practices: Airbus, Alleo, ARTE, Audi, Boehringer Ingelheim, Bosch, Continental, Faurecia, Institut Mérieux, Liebherr, Merck, Mixel Agitators, Publicis, Siemens-Matra, Swarovski, Volkswagen, Weleda and Wilo.

We recognize fruitful discussions and debates at the annual conferences of several academic associations: AIB (Academy of International Business), Atlas AFMI (Association Francophone de Management International), EGOS (European Group of Organizational Studies), EIBA (European International Business Academy), EURAM (European Academy of Management), GEM&L (Groupe d'Etudes Management & Langage), IACCM (International Association for Cross-Cultural Competence and Management) and SIETAR (Society for Intercultural Education Training and Research).

We acknowledge the insightful suggestions and advice from Volker Stein, holder of the Chair of Human Resources Management and Organization at the University of Siegen (Germany), for key suggestions and advice. The three authors had intensive working meetings to discuss the book contents in Nice (France) and in Passau (Germany). These meetings were financially supported by BayFrance (Centre de Coopération Universitaire Franco-Bavarois); we want to give our thanks to Axel Honsdorf.

We would also like to thank our colleagues whose ideas and contributions have inspired our work: Nancy Adler, Katia Angué, Hanane Beddi, Milton Bennett, Jean-Sylvestre Bergé, Jürgen Bolten, Mary Yoko Brannen, Ludivine Chalençon, Jean-François Chanlat, Sylvie Chevrier, Ana Colovic, Christoph Czychon, Jacques Demorgon, Silvia Didier, Eric Davoine, Noémie Dominguez, Marion Festing, Peter Franklin, Jean-Christophe Gessler, Pervez Ghauri, Edoardo Ghidelli, Martin Heidenreich, Sylvie Hertrich, Geert Hofstede, Philippe d'Iribarne, Björn Ivens, Elias Jammal, Jacques Jaussaud, Allain Joly, Olivier Lamotte, André Laurent, Jean-Paul Lemaire, Hana Machkova, Antonio Majocchi, Christopher Melin, Vincent Merk, Pierre-Xavier Meschi, Eric Milliot, Emna Moalla, Alois Moosmüller, Bernd Müller-Jacquier, Sophie Nivoix, Claude Obadia, Hannes Piber, Claire Roederer, Laurence Romani, Sonja Sackmann, Eberhard Schenk, Stefan Schmid, Jean-Pierre Segal, Alexander Thomas, Dora Triki, Sabine Urban, Jean-Claude Usunier, Stefano Valdemarin, Alfredo Valentino, Philippe Very, Matthias Walther and Antonella Zucchella.

We appreciate the support provided by our colleagues from IAE Nice Graduate School of Management, GRM (Groupe de Recherche en Management), Université Côte d'Azur, and the University of Passau, especially the student assistants Anna Ibrahim, Julian Fischer and Maike Grömping who helped in formatting the references of the manuscript. Special thanks go to Ulrike Haupt who kindly provided us not only with conceptual input, but also with the front image of this textbook with her creative talent. We are grateful to Günter Presting from Vandenhoeck & Ruprecht for the consistently pleasant and professional cooperation for the German version of this book. Last but not least, we thank the team of Edward Elgar, and in particular Fiona Briden and Francine O'Sullivan, for their constructive advice in editing the textbook.

PART I
UNDERSTANDING CONSTRUCTIVE INTERCULTURAL MANAGEMENT

2
Interculturality in a global context

In this chapter, we will highlight that intercultural management is framed by the context of internationalization and globalization: people and organizations from different countries and continents interact in the political, social and economic field of a global world. Foreign activities, increasing mobility and digitalization have considerably intensified interactions between actors, shaped by divergent cultural backgrounds. We will explain major characteristics associated with globalization, digitalization and migration (macro-context), the internationalization of organizations (meso-context) and intercultural individuals (micro-context).

CHAPTER LEARNING OBJECTIVES

1. Understand that intercultural management is embedded in internationalization and globalization processes.
2. Be aware of globalization, digitalization and migration trends (macro-context).
3. Identify intercultural challenges associated with the internationalization of organizations (meso-context).
4. Define cultural identities, intercultural individuals and boundary spanners (micro-context).

1. MACRO-CONTEXT: GLOBALIZATION, DIGITALIZATION AND MIGRATION

Internationalization concerns the expansion of activities beyond national borders. Globalization is an ongoing process connecting people, cultures, organizations and nations. Based on the principles of free trade and liberalization, globalization leads to the interdependence of a growing number of actors (companies, consumers, citizens, public institutions, etc.) around the world (Cavusgil et al., 2019; Hill & Hult, 2020). Internationalization and globalization intensify cross-border contacts and socio-cultural diversity in societies and organizations. On the one hand, it seems that the world is becoming 'smaller', with countries and regions being increasingly more interlinked through politics and trade. On the other hand, the world is becoming 'bigger', since nations and societies continuously develop and find different answers to the challenges of globalization, digitalization and migration. These answers might differ across nations, leading to cultural, economic and institutional distance. To bridge the distance, nation states establish rules and institutions on the supra-national level, such as the

European Union or the World Trade Organization (WTO), facilitating international activities and mobility (Bergé et al., 2018; Czinkota et al., 2021).

1.1 Global Investment Trends

Over the past few decades, trade and investment flows have significantly increased and diversified. 'North–South' investment flows (for example, Western companies investing in BRIC – Brazil, Russia, India, China – countries), but also 'South–North' (for example, emerging market multinationals investing in mature economies) and 'South–South' (for example, Chinese companies investing in Africa) investment flows have gained considerable importance in the global economy (Bandeira-de-Mello et al., 2015; Cuervo-Cazurra & Ramamurti, 2015).

Foreign direct investments (FDI) – greenfield subsidiaries, joint ventures, mergers and acquisitions – have accelerated the globalization process and contributed to the establishment of global value chains (Gereffi, 2018; Pananond et al., 2020). Many organizations thus have to manage activities in culturally distant markets, which can represent new challenges for their workforce. Table 2.1 shows the geographic distribution of FDI across the world. In 2019, FDI inflow investments amounted to $1.54 trillion, with Asia (30.8 per cent), Europe (27.9 per

Table 2.1 FDI flows by region in 2019

Geographic region	FDI inflows (billion dollars and per cent)	FDI outflows (billion dollars and per cent)
Developed economies[1]	800 (52%)	917 (69.8%)
Europe	*429 (27.9%)*	*475 (36.1%)*
North America	*297 (19.3%)*	*202 (15.3%)*
Developing economies[2]	685 (44.5%)	373 (28.4%)
Africa	*45 (2.9%)*	*5 (0.4%)*
Asia	*474 (30.8%)*	*328 (24.9%)*
(East and South-East Asia)	*389 (25.2%)*	*280 (21.3%)*
Latin America and the Caribbean	*164 (10.7%)*	*42 (3.2%)*
Oceania	*1 (0.1%)*	*-1 (-0.1%)*
Transition economies[3]	55 (3.6%)	24 (1.8%)
World	1,540 (100%)	1,314 (100%)

Notes:
[1] Developed economies: the member countries of the Organisation for Economic Co-operation and Development (OECD) (other than Chile, Colombia, Mexico, the Republic of Korea and Turkey), plus the new European Union member countries which are not OECD members (Bulgaria, Croatia, Cyprus, Malta and Romania), plus Andorra, Bermuda, Liechtenstein, Monaco, San Marino, Faeroe Islands, Gibraltar, Greenland, Guernsey and Jersey.
[2] Developing economies: all economies not specified in (1) and (3). For statistical purposes, the data for China does not include those for Hong Kong Special Administrative Region (Hong Kong SAR), Macao Special Administrative Region (Macao SAR) and Taiwan Province of China.
[3] Transition economies: South-East Europe, the Commonwealth of Independent States and Georgia.
Source: Adapted from UNCTAD (2020, p. 13).

cent) and North America (19.3 per cent) being the most attractive territories. In the same year, FDI outflow investments reached $1.31 trillion, with Europe (36.1 per cent), Asia (24.9 per cent) and North America (15.3 per cent) being the most important investing regions.

Following the COVID-19 pandemic, global FDI inflows are projected to decrease by up to 40 per cent in 2020 (bringing FDI below $1 trillion for the first time since 2005), by 5 to 10 per cent in 2021 and to recover in 2022 (UNCTAD, 2020). The pandemic has led policymakers, organizations and individuals to question global economic integration and global value chains. Globalization could be partially reversed, with a stronger regional focus on international activities (Rosa et al., 2020).

1.2   Digitalization and the VUCA World

Globalization is marked by ongoing changes, which are also linked to digitalization and the VUCA (Volatility, Uncertainty, Complexity and Ambiguity) world.

Digitalization refers to the increasing use of digital technologies, which allows transforming manual into digital processes and solutions. Digital technologies enable organizations to increase their efficiency and to improve their communication and innovation processes. They have led to what is called Industry 4.0 (or the Fourth Industrial Revolution), with the ongoing automation of traditional manufacturing and industrial practices through large-scale machine-to-machine communication and the Internet of Things. The development of smart machines enables organizations to analyse and diagnose issues without human intervention and facilitates the monitoring of global value chains. The digital transformation has accelerated the internationalization and globalization processes. It has changed economic, social, cultural and human interaction (Barmeyer & Mayer, 2020; Schwab, 2017).

At the same time, we can observe new pressures from the VUCA world, an acronym for Volatility, Uncertainty, Complexity and Ambiguity (Bennett & Lemoine, 2014). Originating from the US military, the concept is used as a contextual framework, capturing the challenging environment for organizations: 'The VUCA world is all about change, including both dangerous ruptures and positive innovation. Inspiring strategies are hidden in the volatilities, uncertainties, complexities, and ambiguities' (Johansen, 2007, p. 46). To gain competitive advantage, organizations must therefore align their strategic orientation and management with VUCA conditions.

1.3   International Migration and Mobility

Over the past five decades, economic, social, political and technological transformations have led to a significant increase of international migration and mobility. The number of migrants has tripled from 1970 to 2019 worldwide: in 2019, 272 million people were living in countries other than their countries of birth (against 153 million in 1990 and 84 million in 1970). This represented 3.5 per cent of the world population (7.7 billion). The majority of people have migrated for work, family and educational purposes, even if migration due to political unrest, religious or political persecution and natural disasters has increased during the last decade.

Table 2.2   Top 10 countries of origin and destination for international migration in 2019

Top 10 countries of origin	Top 10 countries of destination
India: 17.5 million	United States: 50.7 million
Mexico: 11.8 million	Germany: 13.1 million
China: 10.7 million	Saudi Arabia: 13.1 million
Russian Federation: 10.5 million	Russian Federation: 11.6 million
Syrian Arab Republic: 8.2 million	United Kingdom: 9.6 million
Bangladesh: 7.8 million	United Arab Emirates: 8.6 million
Pakistan: 6.3 million	France: 8.3 million
Ukraine: 5.9 million	Canada: 8 million
Philippines: 5.4 million	Australia: 7.5 million
Afghanistan: 5.1 million	Italy: 6.3 million

Sources: International Organization for Migration (2019); United Nations (2019).

The global refugee population amounted to 25.9 million in 2018 (International Organization for Migration, 2019).

In 2019, the top ten countries of origin accounted for one third of international migrants, and the top 10 countries of destination hosted about half of international migrants (Table 2.2). The two major regional corridors (region of origin to region of destination) accounted for about 25 per cent of international migrants: (1) Europe to Europe (41.9 million) and (2) Latin America and Caribbean to North America (26.6 million) (International Organization for Migration, 2019; United Nations, 2019).

The growth of international migration and mobility presents major challenges for intercultural management. Even if the large majority of people continue to have a monocultural background, we can observe the increasing importance of intercultural individuals, that is, persons who integrate two or more national cultures. In 2019, one out of 30 people has a migration background (International Organization for Migration, 2019). International migration and mobility leads to the diversification of national societies and organizations who must deal with an increasingly diverse workforce.

1.4   Convergence or Divergence of Cultures?

A central question in intercultural management concerns the *convergence* versus *divergence* debate (Barmeyer & Mayrhofer, 2008). Do global transfer and diffusion processes lead to the gradual approximation of people and organizations across the world, that is, are they becoming more uniform? Or do specific nations and cultures come up with their own ways of dealing with cultural diversity, maintaining their uniqueness?

(1)   The *convergence* thesis predicts a global alignment of cultural and institutional characteristics. It assumes that organizations and management exhibit rational patterns for solving operational problems and that the pursuit of efficiency does not leave room for different cultural solutions.

(2)   The *divergence* thesis predicts the maintenance or increase of unique cultural and institutional characteristics. It assumes that solutions must be adapted to the respective context and that organizations and management therefore need to consider cultural specifics to be successful (Table 2.3).

Table 2.3   Convergence and divergence in intercultural management

Characteristics	Convergence	Divergence
Assumption	Differences are likely to disappear.	Differences are likely to remain or increase.
Consequence	Cultural homogeneity.	Cultural heterogeneity.
Management	Management methods are universal and can be transferred and applied in other societal contexts.	Management methods are marked by their culture of origin and encounter resistance when applied in other societal contexts.
Risk	The negation of culture may cause misunderstandings and conflicts.	The overestimation of culture may cause misunderstandings and conflicts.
Organizational change	Cultures can change over time; therefore, it is possible to develop and implement new corporate values and practices.	Cultures resist change; consequently, adjustments and compromises are necessary.

Source: Adapted from Barmeyer and Mayrhofer (2008, p. 31).

Corresponding to the convergence thesis, an ethnocentric attitude tends to underestimate cultural differences in management and assumes similarity. In particular, organizations that appear geographically or culturally close are likely to adopt the perspective of convergence. However, the more intensive the engagement with another culture, the greater the awareness of differences, as supported by the divergence thesis: 'many cultures that appear quite similar on the surface, frequently prove to be extraordinarily different on closer examination' (Hall, 1983, p. 7).

In the sense of *constructive intercultural management*, rather than seeing convergence and divergence as opposing concepts, Ralston (2008) proposes the concept of *crossvergence* as a synergistic solution. Crossvergence 'advocates that the combination of socio-cultural influences and business ideology influences is the driving force that precipitates the development of new and unique value systems among individuals in a society owing to the dynamic interaction of these influences' (Ralston, 2008, p. 28). Thus, individuals are influenced by the two mechanisms of alignment *and* differentiation as well as the convergence *and* divergence of cultural influences, which lead to value changes in society (Witt, 2008).

2.   MESO-CONTEXT: INTERNATIONALIZATION OF ORGANIZATIONS

Organizations are social entities which are characterized by interpersonal, professional and intercultural interaction. An organization can be defined as a social system of actors who unite resources and competences and who contribute to the achievement of goals under certain structural and strategic conditions (March & Simon, 1958). Organizations have a formative role in human societies. In other words, humans live in an 'organizational society' (Kieser & Walgenbach, 2010). Organizations determine our education at school and university, our work life and available products and services that we buy. So, organizations are an inevitable part of our life, shape our behaviours and have far-reaching implications for society.

In this respect, organizations do not only refer to companies, but also to educational institutions, hospitals, public authorities, international organizations and non-governmental organizations (NGOs). Although all organizations must deal with issues regarding objectives, strategies, structures, processes and culture, this book focuses primarily on profit-oriented organizations, and namely companies who internationalize their activities.

2.1   Internationalization of Companies

In the context of globalization, companies have increasingly developed their business activities on international markets (Buckley & Ghauri, 2015; Johanson & Vahlne, 2009). This trend concerns nearly all companies whatever their industry, geographic origin or size – start-ups, small and medium-sized companies (SMEs) and multinational companies (MNCs). Companies who internationalize are confronted with intercultural challenges, which can concern both their internal organization and their external relationships with customers, suppliers, distributors and other stakeholders (Dominguez & Mayrhofer, 2017, 2018a). Companies with a strong international orientation are embedded in intra- and inter-organizational networks with a variety of actors marked by different cultural backgrounds (Buckley, 2014). When expanding into foreign countries, companies can use and combine three types of market entry modes: (1) export activities, (2) strategic alliances and (3) wholly owned subsidiaries (Box 2.1). The internal organization and established relationships with external stakeholders, and thus the importance and complexity of intercultural issues, vary according to the chosen market entry modes.

BOX 2.1   CLASSIFICATION OF FOREIGN MARKET ENTRY MODES

- Export activities concern the selling of products and services abroad. Companies can sell their products and services directly to their foreign customers (direct exporting) or to intermediaries (for example agents) who then sell them to wholesalers or end users.
- Strategic alliances can take the form of cooperation contracts (for example franchising agreements), minority equity investments and joint ventures. They allow sharing resources with foreign partners and can concern several elements of the value chain (research and development – R&D, production, sales).
- Wholly owned subsidiaries are subsidiaries whose capital is fully controlled by the company. They can take the form of greenfield subsidiaries, mergers and acquisitions.

Source: Mayrhofer (2013).

2.1.1   Intercultural challenges in cross-border operations

Companies need to deal with intercultural issues whatever their market entry mode choices, but such issues are particularly challenging in the case of strategic alliances, mergers and acquisitions as well as wholly owned subsidiaries.

Despite their proliferation, cross-border alliances, mergers and acquisitions are characterized by high failure rates, mainly for cultural and organizational reasons. When companies decide to collaborate or to merge, it appears that differences in national and organizational cultures, as well as interculturality experienced by managers and employees, are often perceived as major obstacles to effective collaboration.

The objective of establishing strategic alliances, mergers and acquisitions with foreign companies is to achieve synergy effects, which means that cultural differences and expertise are leveraged to achieve cost advantages. However, developing synergies with companies from other countries remains a difficult task (Chalençon & Mayrhofer, 2018; Triki & Mayrhofer, 2016). In practice, the associated companies often prioritize strategic and financial considerations and tend to neglect cultural issues. It often happens that culture is only taken into account when conflicts arise and when the level of distress of managers and employees becomes too high. Only then – and usually too late – it becomes apparent that it is not companies that cooperate and merge, but *employees*. It is *people* with specific culture-dependent values, desires, goals, expectations, standards and behaviours who shape management and work in organizations. It is therefore necessary to pay more attention to the 'human side' of cross-border operations, particularly to their actors, their skills, emotions, sense-making and actions, which are shaped by multiple cultural and social influences (Sarala et al., 2019).

Cross-border cooperation and integration processes reveal a higher degree of complexity than domestic ones, because employees with different cultural backgrounds and organizational cultures meet, but also because of different institutional contexts, with specific laws and regulations (Chalençon et al., 2017; Hassan et al., 2018). Nonetheless, there are also strategic alliances, mergers and acquisitions where the associated companies have succeeded in dealing *constructively* with intercultural challenges. Examples are provided by the Airbus group, where three companies with different national (French, German and Spanish) and corporate cultures merged to create the European leader in the aeronautic, defence and space industry, or the strategic alliance formed by Renault (French), Nissan and Mitsubishi (Japanese), which has become the world's leading automotive partnership (Chapter 10).

The establishment of wholly owned subsidiaries abroad affects different fields of action in multinational companies (Moore, 2016; Schmid et al., 2016):

(1)   Organizations coordinate their actions – and also those of their actors – across borders (transnationalization). In doing so, they consciously control their cross-border integration.
(2)   The complexity of managing multinational companies increases with the diversity of headquarters–subsidiaries relationships.
(3)   Resource acquisition involves different cultural and institutional contexts, especially in terms of human resources.
(4)   Internationalization strategies develop in tension between process design, implementation (headquarters) and adaptation (subsidiaries).

(5) The multinational company has become the central organizational unit of the globalized economy.

Box 2.2 illustrates how the Italian company ATOM faces these challenges.

BOX 2.2 ATOM, A SMALL MULTINATIONAL COMPANY

ATOM is an Italian SME that has developed internationally to become the leading supplier of cutting systems for leather, soft and semi-rigid materials. Located in Vigevano, a mechanic-shoe district in Lombardy (North-West of Italy), the company has established four production units – three in Italy and one in China – and ten sales subsidiaries in Europe (France, Spain, Germany and the United Kingdom), the United States, Brazil, China (Shanghai and Guangzhou), India and Vietnam. They employ 300 people and export activities account for 80 per cent of their sales. The family owned company has succeeded in managing subsidiaries in different cultural and institutional contexts. The managers attach particular importance to the coordination of foreign subsidiaries to avoid tension with the Italian headquarters. ATOM has a strong customer orientation, and foreign subsidiaries attempt to meet the requirements of their customers. The company favours local recruitment to facilitate relationships with local customers. The SME has learned from its international experience and is thus able to overcome cultural and institutional challenges linked to the management of foreign subsidiaries. Those challenges are particularly important in emerging markets, notably in terms of communication and protectionist policies. The company organizes regular meetings between headquarters and subsidiaries, so that managers can discuss local market characteristics and share their business practices.

Source: Magnani et al. (2018).

Cultural differences, which can be measured by cultural distance, are often viewed as an obstacle to cooperation and integration processes (Angué & Mayrhofer, 2010). Nevertheless, cultural diversity can also contribute positively to the performance of cross-border operations and lead to cultural attractiveness. Box 2.3 presents the concepts of cultural distance and cultural attractiveness.

BOX 2.3 CULTURAL DISTANCE VERSUS CULTURAL ATTRACTIVENESS

- *Cultural distance* measures the relation between two cultures through their differences, relying on the assumption of discordance, which often provoke liabilities of foreignness in cross-border interaction. More specifically, the more dissimilar two cultures are, the more likely disruption occurs during organizational interactions, thus causing failures in cross-border operations.
- In contrast, *cultural attractiveness* focuses on the positive perception of other cultures. It assumes that people see the exchange with other cultures as beneficial.

> In other words, cultural diversity can have a constructive effect on organizational interactions and thus on cross-border operations, especially when the other culture is considered as enriching.

Sources: Li et al. (2017); Stahl et al. (2016).

2.1.2 Diverging conceptions of organizations

We thus emphasize that organizations are not as universal as often portrayed. Organizational structures and processes exist and function through the subjectively shared ideas of the members of organizations. They construct a social reality (Berger & Luckmann, 1966) by communicating, interacting and interpreting behaviour. In this sense, organizations must not only be understood as functional bureaucratic machine-like systems, but also as a combination of social roles and behaviours with related attitudes, perceptions, values, experiences, and goals based on a collective memory (March & Simon, 1958):

> Organizations are cultural constructs and, at the end of the day, any social system is a set of relationships between actors. The essence of these relationships is communication. Communication is the transport of information and information is the carrier of meaning. Since culture is the system of shared meaning, the organization is essentially a cultural construct. (Trompenaars, 2003, p. 183)

There are different conceptions and expectations about organizations across countries. The functional view of organizations has been found to apply to most Anglo-Saxon, Germanic and Scandinavian contexts; the person-oriented view rather in Latin and East Asian contexts (Amado et al., 1991) (Table 2.4).

Diverging assumptions and ideas are thus likely to impact intercultural management. The functional and technical organization of the 'well-oiled machine' (Hofstede et al., 2010) works consistently and evenly when objectives and rules have been clarified. It is suitable for the equal circulation of knowledge and for efficient cooperation. This type of organization does not require the presence of a personalized authority, but it might lack flexibility in response to unexpected situations. Conversely, the hierarchical person-oriented organization reveals more irregular processes, but offers space for flexibility: the hierarchical model of the 'pyramid of people' (Hofstede et al., 2010) is then exemplified by the person-oriented view providing more agility. Fast and context-adapted decisions by top managers can thus compensate for delays and drawbacks associated with the bureaucratic system. The hierarchical person-oriented organization is then able to react more quickly to new situations.

2.1.3 International strategic orientations

Perlmutter (1969) and Perlmutter and Heenan (1979) propose the EPRG model, which allows to differentiate four strategic orientations of international companies: ethnocentrism, polycentrism, regiocentrim and geocentrism (Table 2.5). These enable different approaches to cultural diversity and interculturality.

Table 2.4 Functional versus person-oriented organizations

Characteristics	Functional organization	Person-oriented organization
Conception of the organization	System of tasks, functions and objectives	System of persons working together on a project
Metaphor	'Well-oiled machine'	'Pyramid of people'
Structures	Defining activities	Defining degree of authority and status
Position of actors in the structure	Functional	Social
Management coordination	Tasks and responsibilities: who is responsible for what?	Relationships between actors and definitions of authority zones: who has authority over whom?
Authority	Functional attribute: limited, specific and impersonal	Personal attribute: diffuse, all-encompassing and personalized
Achieving order and efficiency	Heterarchical distribution of functional responsibilities	Hierarchical structures of authority relationships
Management instruments	High degree of participation and personal responsibility: MBO (management by objectives), empowerment, 360° feedback, matrix organization	Hierarchy: paternalist leadership style, clear roles; 'open-door' policy

Source: Based on Amado et al. (1991, p. 82); Hofstede et al. (2010).

(1)   The *ethnocentric* orientation, also known as 'home country orientation', reflects the dominant position of headquarters who define strategies, processes and management practices and then transfer them to foreign subsidiaries, often in a top-down process. This approach favours standardization, but the requirements of local subsidiaries and cultural differences might not be sufficiently considered.

(2)   The *polycentric* orientation, also known as 'host country orientation', takes into account the differences – including cultural ones – between headquarters and subsidiaries. The parent company accepts different ways of thinking and working, so that subsidiaries can operate autonomously. This approach allows an adaptation to the local context but may result in a lack of uniformity within the headquarters.

(3)   The *regiocentric orientation* is similar to the *geocentric* orientation, but refers to smaller, homogeneous geographic areas. The company puts in place regional headquarters, which can operate autonomously and coordinate activities at the regional scale. This approach favours a strong regional integration but may result in a lack of uniformity between regions.

(4)   The *geocentric* orientation aims for the global integration of corporate activities. The most competent managers are assigned as decision-makers within the company, including subsidiaries, 'regardless of their nationality' (Perlmutter, 1969, p. 14). This approach facilitates the leverage of core competences within the company but increases the interdependence between headquarters and subsidiaries.

The four orientations of the EPRG model can coexist within the same organization. For example, research and development can be ethnocentric, marketing and sales polycentric and production geocentric. In the same way, the strategic orientation can change over time, for example, according to the degree of internationalization and the shared vision by senior managers.

Table 2.5 The EPRG model

Characteristics	Ethnocentrism	Polycentrism	Regiocentrism	Geocentrism
Organizational complexity	High complexity at headquarters, low complexity in subsidiaries	Varied across headquarters and subsidiaries	Rather complex, because of interdependency on a regional scale	Very complex, because of interdependency on a global scale
Decision-making	Mainly at headquarters	Mainly in subsidiaries	Mainly in regional headquarters	Joint decision-making between headquarters and subsidiaries
Evaluation and control	Home-country standards	Determined locally	Determined regionally	Universal standards
Communication	Top-down, from headquarters to subsidiaries	Limited between headquarters and subsidiaries, very limited between subsidiaries	Limited to and from headquarters, but strong to and from regional headquarters	Strong communication between headquarters and subsidiaries, and also between subsidiaries

Sources: Based on Perlmutter (1969, pp. 11-14); Perlmutter and Heenan (1979, pp. 18-19).

Companies often tend to ignore or trivialize the influence of culture on their international activities. Table 2.6 shows that a geocentric orientation favours *constructive intercultural management*. It enables the pluralistic, equal and complementary combination of different perspectives, strategies, options for action and resources.

Table 2.6 Dealing with cultural diversity

Characteristics	Ignoring cultural differences	Minimizing cultural differences	Utilizing cultural differences
Strategic orientation	Ethnocentric	Polycentric	Geocentric
Assumption of culture	Irrelevant	Problematic	Opening opportunities
Major challenge	Gaining acceptance	Achieving coherence	Leveraging differences
Major concern	Inflexibility	Fragmentation	Confusion
Expected benefit	Standardizing	Localizing	Innovating
Performance criteria	Efficiency	Adaptability	Synergy
Meaning for constructive interculturality	Dominance of *one* option	Multitude of *separate* options	Multitude of *combined* options

Source: Adapted from Schneider et al. (2014, p. 247).

Intercultural management takes place in organizations, which are embedded in specific contexts that shape the behaviour of actors and that lead to the emergence of certain norms, values and structures (d'Iribarne et al., 2020). National contexts may exhibit a certain degree of homogeneity due to the historical development and a dominant legal, linguistic and communication system (Hofstede et al., 2010; Whitley, 1999). They are marked by the development and consolidation of certain cultural characteristics and successful patterns of thought and action.

With increased internationalization and digitalization, hierarchical divisional and functional organizational structures often shift towards more dynamic, process-related network structures (Laloux, 2014), which can be characterized by temporary project collaborations with external partners located in different parts of the world. Intercultural cooperation plays a particular role in such projects. An example is provided by the French Danone group, which has adopted a network structure (Box 2.4).

BOX 2.4   DANONE, A FRENCH MULTINATIONAL ORGANIZED AS A NETWORK

The French Danone group has become a world leader in fresh dairy and plant-based products, packaged waters and nutrition. Their mission is 'to bring health through food to as many people as possible'. The company employs more than 100 000 people in over 55 countries. Danone is structured as an intra-organizational network, operating research and development, production and sales subsidiaries across the world. Foreign subsidiaries can thus adapt to local market conditions and develop inter-organizational networks with a variety of local stakeholders such as suppliers, distributors, customers, competitors and public institutions. They enjoy a high degree of autonomy. Subsidiary managers are therefore called 'entrepreneurs'. This flexible network organization has allowed the Danone group to seize global market opportunities and to enjoy profitable growth over several decades.

The Danone group has a geocentric orientation and the network structure facilitates the creation of a work environment where cultural differences are recognized, respected and leveraged. In 2017, they launched the 'Global Inclusive Diversity' roadmap, with the ambition to have culturally diverse teams representing the diversity of their markets. The company nominated 200 'Inclusive Diversity Champions' who are developing local 'Inclusive Diversity Roadmaps'. In 2019, they organized the first 'Global Inclusive Diversity Week', with cross-cultural workshops and celebrations taking place around the globe. As expressed by Emmanuel Faber, Chairman and CEO (Chief Executive Officer) of the Danone group: 'creating inclusive and diverse teams is at the heart of Danone's future. The diversity of our teams represents the diversity of our customers, and by creating an environment in which everyone is valued for their experiences and perspectives, we can serve our customers better.'

Source: Danone (2020); Hertrich et al. (2016).

The geographic diversification of value chains and the necessity to establish networks with local actors increase the organizational complexity. Companies thus need to strengthen headquarters–subsidiaries relationships and networks with external stakeholders such as customers, suppliers, distributors and public authorities to succeed in the global field. Consequently, interculturality becomes a key issue in both internal and external relationships.

2.2   New Organizational Forms

Internationalization and globalization have challenged the traditional view of coherent, stable and continuously growing organizations. In response to the fast-changing environment, companies have adapted their strategies, structures and processes to remain competitive and new organizational forms have emerged.

Given the business opportunities provided by international markets, we can observe the proliferation of *born global* companies across the world. Born global companies are organizations who internationalize within their first years of existence and who build their competitive advantage with resources located in several countries (Cavusgil & Knight, 2009). The companies are affected by multiculturality and diversity since their inception and emerge as intercultural organizations *per se*. They often function as network structures. Leadership and organizational structures in these companies are characterized by the delegation of responsibility, decentralized decision-making, empowerment and a high degree of employee autonomy (Chhotray et al., 2018). Famous examples of born global companies are Skype from Estonia, Spotify from Sweden, Deezer from France and Airbnb from the United States. There are also many smaller companies which are created as *born globals*. An example is provided by PocketConfidant, a French start-up targeting the global coaching market (Box 2.5).

BOX 2.5   POCKETCONFIDANT, A BORN GLOBAL PROPOSING DIGITAL COACHING

Created in 2016 by three entrepreneurs with international experience, PocketConfidant AI proposes digital coaching powered by artificial intelligence (AI). The start-up is characterized by the cultural diversity of the management team (British-American, French and Ukrainian) and the customers who are companies, higher education institutions and individuals from around the globe. Through their international experience and cultural diversity, the management team could successfully access financial resources through fund-raising in the United States, the United Kingdom, France and Australia. They decided to market the innovative self-coaching services in their home-countries and on international markets. PocketConfidant AI can therefore be considered as a born global. The company's mission is 'to create a solution for self-reflection and personal growth that empowers individuals and organizations in an ethical, flexible, scalable and inexpensive way'. The company was able to establish itself on the growing coaching market, which is characterized by a large number of players operating worldwide. PocketConfidant AI is thus able to observe major trends in the highly competitive coaching market and to seize growth opportunities in the digital coaching segment. The flat organization allows for quick responses to new customer expectations across the world, for example those linked to the COVID-19 pandemic.

Source: Mayrhofer et al. (2020).

Flat organizational systems such as *holacracy* have also gained in popularity in the last decade (Laloux, 2014). In contrast to classical hierarchical organizations, holacracy corresponds to decentralized management and organizational structures where authority and decision-making are distributed throughout self-organizing teams. In that case, organizations strive for meaningful business behaviour and action. They are characterized by flat, up to no, hierarchies (hierarchies without bosses). Authorities, roles and goals within the organization are defined by a corporate constitution, which can take the form of a handbook (Box 2.6) Holacracy structures enjoy a high degree of agility and can easily change their processes and adapt to external pressures and changes (Robertson, 2015). In such organizations, cultural issues are dealt with in autonomous teams at the local level.

BOX 2.6 VALVE AS AN EXAMPLE FOR HOLACRACY

The US company Valve is an emblematic example of a decentralized organization. Founded in 1996, the company is famous for the development, publication and digital distribution of video games such as Counter-Strike or Half-Life. The company employs 400 people. Its headquarters are located in Bellevue, Washington. When starting to work at Valve, employees are given the 'Handbook for new employees' which outlines the organizational characteristics of the company:

- There is no formal management and no hierarchies within the organization.
- The company in structured in 'Cabals', self-organized multidisciplinary project teams.
- There are no job titles, and nobody tells the employees what to work on. Rather, they must find their own roles within their team and within the organization. Employees decide on their own on which project they work.
- Every employee has access to Valve's source code, so that anyone can modify it. This shows a lot of trust in employees and transparency.
- Open error culture: nobody gets fired for making mistakes. Problem-solving is required.
- Evaluation of work occurs via peer reviews and stack ranking. Colleagues give feedback on 'how to best grow as individuals' and stack ranking serves as a method for adapting compensation and rewards based on the performance of each employee. Compensation results out of four factors: skill level or technical ability and knowledge, productivity output, group contribution and product contribution.
- Human resources are characterized by a 'Bring your friends' principle. The company values 'T-shaped people', that is, people who are both generalists and experts in their fields.

In general, Valve relies on personal responsibility, self-management, and the principle of spontaneous order (a principle coined by the philosopher David Hume). However, as remarked by Morgan (2015): 'For some this sounds like a dream for others, their worst nightmare.'

Source: Valve (2012).

3.   MICRO-CONTEXT: INTERCULTURAL INDIVIDUALS

Intercultural management primarily deals with the management of cultural diversity (Özbilgin & Chanlat, 2018). Management is then not only focused on strategic success and financial performance, but also on the sensitivities, competences and conditions of the people involved. Managers inevitably practise intercultural interaction but are often confronted with misunderstandings and irritations. In fact, individual behaviour in organizations is marked by cultural identity, but depends also on the situations in which people act (Yagi & Kleinberg, 2011; Vora et al., 2019). In order to deal with globalization, digitalization, human–machine interaction and increasingly diverse workforces, it is necessary to develop positive approaches and new leadership competences. Barmeyer and Mayer (2020) point to interculturally competent leaders, intercultural individuals and intercultural boundary spanning.

3.1   Cultural Identities of Individuals

The cultural identity of individuals is shaped by a variety of factors, which are linked to the different levels of culture (Sackmann & Philips, 2004; Vora et al., 2019):

- National, ethnic and 'societal' culture
- Regional culture
- Organizational, industry and professional culture
- Religious belonging
- Gender
- Age and generational culture
- Internet culture.

These different *spheres* of cultural belonging (Schneider et al., 2014) interact with each other and come differently to the forefront, depending on the intercultural situation in which individuals act. The result might be hybrid cultural identities of individuals, who make up organizations and society. The discourse on cultural identity has influenced politics and thus the legal framework in which organizations move. For example, the debate on the role of women in society has initiated debates on a variety of topics, such as career opportunities (some countries have introduced quotas for women in leadership positions), flexibilization of working times and home office opportunities, parental leave policies and language rules for gendering in official documents. Even food choices such as vegetarianism or veganism can influence the cultural identity of individuals and thus cultural interactions in organizations (Box 2.7).

BOX 2.7   ETHICAL VEGANISM IS PROTECTED BY LAW

In the United Kingdom, Jordi Casamitjana, 55, recently claimed that he was sacked by the animal welfare charity League Against Cruel Sports, because of his ethical veganism after disclosing that his employer invested pension funds in companies involved in animal testing. He informed the tribunal that 'when he drew his bosses' attention to the pension fund investments, they did nothing so he informed colleagues and was sacked as a result'. League Against Cruel Sports, Britain's leading charity that works to stop animals being persecuted, abused and killed for sport, responded that Jordi Casamitjana was dismissed for gross misconduct. The judge ruled that 'ethical vegans should be entitled to similar legal protections in British workplaces as those who hold religious beliefs'.

Source: BBC (2020).

Moreover, digitalization has facilitated a shift from physical work in offices to more virtual work in online spaces. This is reflected by the increasing number of *digital nomads* (Makimoto & Manners, 1997). Digital nomads are persons who work remotely from any part of the world, with the freedom to combine travel and leisure with work. They are often dedicated to online jobs such as programming, online marketing or web design. They work either for global companies or found their own businesses. Still characterized as a 'lifestyle movement' (Thompson, 2019), the number of digital nomads is likely to increase, especially among the young generations. Internet platforms such as Fiverr or Upwork enable global entrepreneurs to find online jobs and to employ people from around the world.

The cultural identity of individuals can evolve over time and be influenced by laws, norms and societal movements which transform societies across the world. Legal frames and social movements can thus affect the behaviours of actors. The cultural interactions of individuals with multiple identities can lead to misunderstandings and conflicts (Vora et al., 2019). For *constructive intercultural management*, the existence of multicultural identities can have positive effects, stimulate creativity and lead to new dynamics in organizations.

3.2   Intercultural Individuals

Today's organizations unite people from diverse backgrounds and with different intercultural experiences. Intercultural individuals concern people with a migration background (for example, expatriates and refugees), but also people who have been socialized interculturally (for example, through parents, partnerships and longer stays in foreign countries). These individuals identify themselves with *several cultures* because they have internalized different systems of values and meanings (Fitzsimmons, 2013). Examples are:

- *Third culture individuals* (or *third culture kids*) who are exposed to various cultural influences during their childhood or adolescence, for example due to frequent changes of residence and school attendance in several countries or the due to parents from different cultural backgrounds (Moore & Barker, 2012; Pollock et al., 2003).
- *Cultural marginals* who are both insiders and outsiders of a certain culture. They belong to more than one culture but neither identify fully with one nor the other culture (Bennett, 1993; Fitzsimmons et al., 2012).
- *Global cosmopolitans* who are highly educated and multilingual people with extensive study and work experience in several cultures: 'while their international identities have diverse starting points and experiences, their views of the world and themselves are

profoundly affected by both the realities of living in different cultures and their manner of coping with the challenges that emerge' (Brimm, 2010, p. 4).

Intercultural individuals present the following characteristics (Brannen et al., 2009; Brannen & Thomas, 2010). They:

- have access to several cultural knowledge systems,
- understand and speak several languages,
- are able to switch between different frames of reference (cultural frame switching),
- have a higher cultural mindfulness,
- reveal a high degree of empathy and flexibility,
- have the ability to integrate ideas in novel and more creative ways.

There exists a variety of intercultural individuals, which can be classified into four ideal types (Figure 2.1) (Brannen et al., 2009):

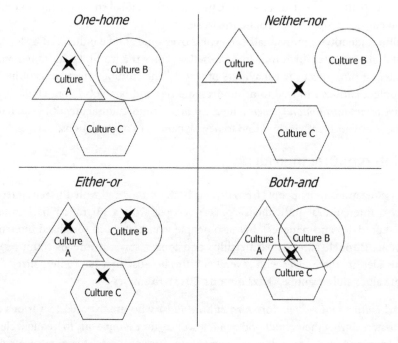

Source: Adapted from Brannen et al. (2009).

Figure 2.1   Types of intercultural individuals

(1)   *One-home* individuals usually identify themselves with one of the cultures where they have grown up.
(2)   *Neither-nor* individuals identify themselves with neither the one nor the other cultures; they are also called 'cultural marginals'.

(3)   *Either-or* individuals identify themselves with several cultures, but engage in cultural code switching depending on the context and the situation.

(4)   *Both-and* individuals identify themselves with several cultures and integrate them into something new; they either mix characteristics from these cultures (hybridization of cultural identity) or they develop a new cultural identity (cultural syncretism).

Interculturality can be seen as problematic and deficient, especially when intercultural people experience negative effects associated with cultural otherness. Different collective memories, languages and cultures can make their identity-building more difficult. In shifting between cultural frames, they might feel disintegrated and never 'at home'. They can become homeless 'cultural marginals' without a clear identity, who do not belong to any cultural system and encounter problems of acceptance. However, in the perspective of *constructive intercultural management*, interculturality is considered as an asset: people with diverse cultural backgrounds can combine different viewpoints and feel 'at home' in various cultural contexts. They can become highly qualified, flexible and sensitized 'global cosmopolitans', who view cultural differences as an opportunity for intercultural cooperation (Bennett, 1993).

Intercultural individuals have been shown to handle the challenges of cultural diversity, complexity and uncertainty constructively (Fitzsimmons et al., 2013):

Cultural diversity: international companies are marked by diverging values, norms and working styles, which are often associated with emotional and cognitive tensions, resulting in dissatisfaction and conflicts. Intercultural people belong to several cultures, thus holding different norms and values (cross-cultural perspective) and having more flexibility and freedom of behaviour. This makes it easier for them to switch between cultural groups, making them particularly suitable for leading intercultural teams.

Complexity: intercultural persons have a higher degree of cognitive complexity, which is due to experienced dissonance. They reveal a more complex worldview and identify themselves with multiple cultural groups, thus avoiding self-categorization. This allows them to better deal with complexity in terms of strategic thinking and problem-solving.

Uncertainty: intercultural individuals are undergoing an ongoing process of identity re-structuring since they do not identify themselves with one particular culture. They explore and integrate new situations instead of adopting a defensive attitude. They demonstrate a higher degree of flexibility and a higher tolerance of ambiguity, because they do not adopt a fixed cultural identity (constant in-betweenness) and include various opinions and standards in their identity development process.

For *constructive intercultural management*, it is interesting to note that intercultural people might reveal particular problem-solving strategies: they can be insiders and outsiders of two (or more) cultures at the same time, and present a behavioural repertoire that results from the access to several cultural knowledge systems. In this way, intercultural people can put themselves in the position of different meaning and action systems, understand the logic of various cultural reference systems and thus adopt neutral 'meta-positions'. This is why they are called 'cultural chameleons' (Szymanski, 2018): They can combine cultural differences in a complementary way. Through 'outside-the-box thinking', they perceive the world from different perspectives. 'Either-or'-thinking does not favour creative processes whilst 'as well as'-thinking does: apparently contradictory values, ideas and practices can be cognitively anchored at the same time and used synergistically.

Examples of intercultural individuals are the scientific entrepreneurs Uğur Şahin and Özlem Türeci, inventors of one of the vaccines against the coronavirus, and Mohed Altrad, a French businessman of Bedouin descent and 'Ernst & Young World Entrepreneur of the Year 2014' (Boxes 2.8 and 2.9).

BOX 2.8   UĞUR ŞAHIN AND ÖZLEM TÜRECI, INVENTORS OF THE VACCINE AGAINST CORONAVIRUS

The Turkish–German couple Uğur Şahin and Özlem Türeci, both scientists and entrepreneurs, are two of the heroes in the coronavirus pandemic: as one of the pioneers, they invented a vaccine against COVID-19. Both came to Germany as children of Turkish immigrants and pursued a career in medicine. Since 2006, Şahin has been Professor of Experimental Oncology at the University Hospital of Mainz. In 2008, the couple founded the company BioNTech together with Christoph Huber, one of the world's leading scientists in cancer immunotherapy. Different from other companies, BioNTech specializes in individualized medication for cancer patients. As experts in cancer and immunology, they transfer their knowledge to virology and develop the vaccine 'Comirnaty' in the common project 'Lightspeed'. By the end of 2020, the company BioNTech applied for approval of the vaccine together with Pfizer for the European and the US markets. In 2020, the company employed 1,800 people in Germany and the UK. The US-company Pfizer as well as the Chinese company Fosun hold shares in the company, and Şahin cultivates a close friendship with the Greek chief executive officer of Pfizer. Although the couple has become wealthy, they show care for people independently of their cultural and social background.

These facts show that the couple integrates several cultures which make them creative, innovative and successful: they combine the Turkish and the German national cultures speaking several languages, they are scientists and (migrant) entrepreneurs, stemming from cancer research and immunology but transferring their knowledge to virology, and they have been working internationally with laboratories (Pfizer and Fosun). With their knowledge and background, the couple aims to make the world a better place.

Sources: Gelles (2020); Halliday (2020).

BOX 2.9   MOHED ALTRAD, A FRENCH BUSINESSMAN OF BEDOUIN DESCENT NOMINATED 'WORLD ENTREPRENEUR OF THE YEAR'

Born as a nomadic Bedouin in the Syrian desert, Mohed Altrad spent his childhood in Raqqa (Syria), where he was forbidden to attend primary school and therefore learned to read on his own. He was expected to become a shepherd, but he persisted and obtained the baccalaureate with high scores. He could then receive a scholarship from the Syrian government to study in Montpellier (France), where he obtained a PhD in computer science.

After his work experience at Abu Dhabi National Oil Company and the foundation of a company producing portable computers, he decided to buy a nearly bankrupt scaffolding company in Montpellier, which became the precursor of Altrad Group. Mohed Altrad made the company profitable again and developed their activities both in France and abroad, mainly through acquisitions. Today, Altrad Group is a leading company in the construction industry, specialized in cement mixers, scaffolding and wheelbarrows. In 2020, the company employed 42 000 people in more than 50 countries.

Due to his own history, Mohed Altrad placed the individual at the centre of his company. He was a thoughtful leader and declared: 'you can ask why I am doing this. It has never been for money. I am trying to develop a humanistic venture to make the people who work for me happy. If they are happy, they are more efficient, better performers, they have a better life.'

He thus advocates multiculturalism and respect for diversity. Altrad Group acquired more than a hundred companies who could keep their names and their identities. Mohed Altrad explained: 'a company is an identity, a piece of history; its products and clients. The general tendency of big groups like us is to reshape [the companies they buy] and make them more or less standard. This is absolutely against my concept [...]. It's a human venture.' He introduced a charter of shared values for all subsidiaries of the group, which new employees are asked to read and follow or to improve.

Mohed Altrad sleeps very little and also writes books, for example his partly autobiographical novel entitled 'Badawi'. His motivation is to keep the spirit of his mother alive, who died the day he was born, at the age of 12 or 13. His story has resonance in French schools, but also in Europe where immigration has become a major issue.

In 2015, Mohed Altrad was nominated 'World Entrepreneur of the Year' by Ernst & Young after having received the 'French Entrepreneur of the Year' award in 2014.

Source: Day (2015).

As shown by the two examples, intercultural managers are able to solve ethical dilemmas in companies by 'dual citizenship' (Hrenyk et al., 2016) and thus contribute to *constructive interculturality* in organizations. Intercultural CEOs (Chief Executive Officers) often have 'global identities' and act as bridges across cultural frontiers. They are faster in considering multiple perspectives and tend to pursue a contextualized approach to strategies and processes. In mergers and acquisitions, they have the ability to evaluate the cultural fit of different organizations and can take the role of 'integration managers' (Fitzsimmons et al., 2011).

3.3   Boundary Spanners

Boundary spanning individuals take on a vital function in organizations (Mäkelä et al., 2019). They have been described as individuals 'who are perceived by other members of both their own in-group and/or relevant out-groups to engage in and facilitate significant interactions between the two groups' (Barner-Rasmussen et al., 2014, p. 887). Although the intercultural boundary spanner takes on a pivotal role in *constructive intercultural management*, these individuals may also bridge boundaries between departments or functions. In general, they demonstrate good cultural and linguistic skills, which help them to execute several functions (Table 2.7): (1) they are able to exchange information through personal engagement in multiple networks, (2) they link social networks through their intermediary position, (3) they facilitate relationship-building and knowledge exchange across boundaries and (4) they are able to intervene in inter- and intra-organizational interactions, for example, by resolving misunderstandings, managing conflicts and contributing to building trust. Through their skills and functions, along with their insights and experience in multiple (cultural) systems, they are able to contribute to constructive communication and positive outcomes of interculturality (Barmeyer et al., 2020).

Table 2.7   Functions and skills of boundary spanners within and across organizations

Functions	Exchanging	Personal engagement in the exchange of information, knowledge and other resources with actors across units and organizations
	Linking	Utilization of personal networks to enable other, previously unconnected actors to connect across unit and organizational boundaries
	Facilitating	Personal engagement in facilitating and assisting others' cross-boundary transactions
	Intervening	Personal active intervention in inter-unit and inter-organizational interactions to create positive outcomes
Skills	Cultural skills	Extent to which individuals have internalized both tacit and explicit aspects of domain-specific knowledge, values, norms and beliefs
	Language skills	Extent to which individuals are able to interfere in and to master the linguistic and semantic signals that together constitute a particular language and to transfer meaning in that language

Source: Based on Barner-Rasmussen et al. (2014, p. 893).

An example of a boundary spanner is provided by Indra Nooyi, a US business woman of Indian descent and former CEO of PepsiCo (Box 2.10).

BOX 2.10 INDRA NOOYI AS BOUNDARY SPANNER AT PEPSICO

Born in Chennai, India, in 1955, Indra Nooyi was the CEO of PepsiCo from 2006 to 2018. Although she stems from a middle-class family, she already learnt in her early childhood about the shortages of water supply, as water was not an unlimited good in Chennai by then. After studying at the Indian Institute of Management in Calcutta, she moved to the United States and graduated from Yale School of Management. After her management experience in several US companies like Johnson & Johnson, Boston Consulting Group and Motorola, she was nominated CEO of PepsiCo in 2006.

> Although I'm a daughter of India, I'm an American businesswoman. ... Graduates, as you aggressively compete on the international business stage, understand that the five major continents and their people – the five fingers of your hand – each have their own strengths and their own contributions to make. Just as each of your fingers must coexist to create a critically important tool, each of the five major continents must also coexist to create a world in balance. You, as an American businessperson, will either contribute to or take away from, this balance. (BusinessWeek May 2005, extract from Fitzsimmons et al. 2011, p. 200)

In 2003, PepsiCo was accused of exploiting scarce water resources and confronted with the incident of pesticides in soft drinks in India. In the following years, the company had to deal with an immense image crisis in the country and sales numbers ceased drastically. Thanks to her bicultural profile, Indra Nooyi was able to span the boundaries between the Indian government and the US-American company and to manage this challenging crisis. Her language and intercultural communication skills enabled her to negotiate with the Indian media and government. Being raised in a developing country where water is a precious good also made her aware of the possible consequences of the *water crisis*. Her diplomacy helped PepsiCo to re-establish its reputation and sales figures in India.

Under the management of Indra Nooyi, PepsiCo merged successfully with several companies, for example with Tropicana and Quaker Oats Company. Moreover, based on her own bicultural origin, she fostered diversity management and innovation within PepsiCo, and the employees started to appreciate the richness of a diverse workforce, not just in terms of national culture, but also in terms of gender diversity. She thus acts as boundary spanner *par excellence* between national cultures (India, USA), companies (PepsiCo, Tropicana, Quaker Oats Company) and intraorganizational subcultures (gender, race, age).

Sources: Fitzsimmons et al. (2011); LinkedIn Profile of Indra Nooyi (2020).

A special type of boundary spanners can be third-country nationals (Barmeyer et al., 2020). Third-country nationals are individuals who belong neither to the culture of the parent company, nor to the culture of the host company, but to a third culture. An example is a person from India who works for a Chinese company in Senegal. Through their 'neutral' position they can take on an intermediary function between parent and host companies, they can arbitrate in inconsistencies and power struggles, and act as an intra- and inter-unit boundary spanner in and across organizations, departments and teams.

SUMMARY

In this chapter, we have shown that intercultural management is embedded in internationalization and globalization processes, which have profoundly changed over the past few decades. It is necessary to consider the underlying characteristics of the macro-, meso- and micro-contexts. The macro-context is primarily shaped by global investment flows, digitalization and the VUCA world as well as international migration and mobility. The meso-context mainly concerns the internationalization of companies, which can choose different market entry strategies, international orientations and organizational structures to develop in foreign countries. The micro-context refers to the cultural identities of individuals, and we can notice the increasing importance of intercultural individuals and boundary spanners who can play a key role in *constructive intercultural management*.

DISCUSSION QUESTIONS

1. What are the major trends associated with globalization, digitalization and migration? Which role do they play in (international) organizations?
2. What are the market entry strategies, international orientations and organizational structures that companies can choose to develop in foreign countries?
3. How are cultural identities shaped, and what role can intercultural individuals and boundary spanners play in organizations and in society?
4. Find examples of intercultural leaders. How do they use their intercultural profile to solve problems or to succeed in an intercultural world?

3
Culture(s) and cultural dimensions

This chapter focuses on the multi-layered concept of culture. We will first present the different definitions and concepts of culture as a value, meaning and solution system. We will then explain that the concept should not be reduced to national cultures and that it is necessary to extend it to subcultures, such as organizational, functional and professional cultures. We will also present cultural dimensions, namely those identified in the empirical investigations conducted by Edward T. Hall, Geert Hofstede, and Fons Trompenaars and Charles Hampden-Turner. Finally, we will propose a constructive approach for dealing with cultural dimensions.

CHAPTER LEARNING OBJECTIVES

1. Understand the concepts of culture as a value, meaning and solution system.
2. Know about the multiple layers of culture, their dynamics and interaction.
3. Identify the classical dimensions of cultural value orientations.
4. Learn how to deal with cultural dimensions constructively.

---

1. CONCEPTS OF CULTURE

Intercultural management deals with the influence of culture on actors and organizational practices, and more specifically on strategies, structures and processes within and across organizations. *Constructive intercultural management* thus focuses on understanding the logics and functioning of culture and its *positive* impact on organizational development.

The conception of culture has changed over time, namely with globalization, migration and diversity. The hermetic concept of culture, which regards social systems as closed, has been replaced by a pluralistic concept of culture that explicitly examines multiple cultures and identities (Adler & Aycan, 2018; Nathan, 2015). We can differentiate three ways of dealing with culture and interculturality, with different impacts on management and organizations:

(1) *Negation of culture*: the influence of culture on organizations is not perceived or is underestimated. An ethnocentric attitude can often be found among actors in higher positions, that is, who operate in economically developed countries, for example, or in large organizations.

(2)   *Acceptance of culture*: culture and interculturality enjoy a paramount and central role. Actors recognize the importance of culture and believe that culture is shaping societies and organizations.

(3)   *Deconstruction of culture*: this position emerged as a reaction to the overestimation of (national) cultural influences and interculturality. Actors attribute lower value to culture in comparison to other contextual, personal or situational factors.

In this book, we adopt the perspective of the *acceptance of culture* and consider that both culture and interculturality influence work behaviour, management and organizations. The main objective of this textbook is to understand and to raise awareness about the influence of culture in order to *constructively* manage the manifold complex intercultural work situations in organizations.

1.1   What is Culture?

Numerous definitions of culture have emerged in various disciplines (Kroeber & Kluckhohn, 1954), and scholars do not agree on a uniform concept of culture. This is because the concept of culture is difficult to grasp. It can have a different meaning according to the discipline and is used differently in practice and research. In accordance with the *constructive* orientation of this book, we perceive the often diverging concepts as complementary. Box 3.1 presents the definition of culture we adopted for this book.

BOX 3.1   DEFINITION OF CULTURE

Culture can be defined as a learned orientation and reference system of values and practices that is collectively lived, transmitted and changed by members of a particular group or society. Cultures enable their members to shape common and individual actions and behaviours. At the same time, culture is produced by individuals in interaction. Culture is therefore both a frame of reference and a product of human interaction.

In this sense, culture is not limited to national contexts and communities but embraces all forms of *social systems*. It therefore includes regional, organizational, industry, professional, generation, gender and Internet cultures. Culture thus functions as a construct that allows the reduction of complexity to achieve *constructive* outputs in intercultural interaction.

Sources: Barmeyer (2011a); d'Iribarne (1994, p. 92).

Like two sides of a coin, culture influences *and* enables human action, and emerges in specific socialization contexts (Parsons, 1952). Rather than reducing culture to a nation or ethnic group, it is about grasping a certain *space of experience* in which people are shaped by *socialization* and *enculturation* during their life. These life experiences are related to space and time, the conditions in which values and norms are conveyed and received, and the meanings and behavioural practices which people observe and learn. Moreover, these life experiences constitute an emotional and cognitive system that is unconsciously stored such as attitudes, rules of life and values (Kluckhohn & Strodtbeck, 1961).

Socialization then influences ideas about trust, freedom, equality, subordination or the 'correct' behaviour in work situations (Parsons, 1952). Socialization takes place in family and personal institutions, for example with parents, grandparents or friends, and in educational institutions, for example kindergarten, school or university. These institutions show relative continuity and stability. In most societies, the educational system has a significant impact on socialization: kindergarten, schools and universities are central places where children and students acquire knowledge and learn about social norms and behaviours. Within this temporally and spatially limited educational space, communication and interaction take place between different actors. Communication, in turn, conditions the ways of thinking and behaving, for example, in regard to authorities or problem-solving strategies.

Culture is created and developed in socialization contexts and thus embraces multiple cultures and identities. Intercultural individuals, for example, have internalized different cultural orientation systems, because their socialization contexts have changed through migration or because their parents and the social environments in which they have grown up are culturally different (Brannen & Thomas, 2010). In terms of cultural affiliation, we can differentiate three types of individuals (Box 3.2).

BOX 3.2   THREE TYPES OF INDIVIDUALS

- *Culturally normal individuals* largely represent the dominant cultural values within a society, for example, Germans who are punctual.
- *Marginally normal individuals* are people who adhere to the prevailing norms and values to a minor extent, for example, Germans who are not punctual.
- *Hypernormal individuals* are people who adhere to the values and norms extremely strictly, that is people who represent the prevailing values almost exaggeratedly, for example, Germans who are overpunctual.

These three types are ideal types, and the transitions between the categories can be fluid depending on the individual and the situation. In terms of frequencies, we can note that most people are considered 'culturally' normal.

Source: Brannen (1992).

1.2   Three Complementary Concepts of Culture

In the perspective of *constructive intercultural management*, we can consider three complementary concepts of culture (Table 3.1): culture as a value system, culture as a meaning system, and culture as a solution system.

Table 3.1   Three complementary concepts of culture

Culture as a …	Orientation
(1) … *value system* that influences thinking, feeling and acting	*Normative*: what is considered good and evil, right and wrong, desirable and undesirable?
(2) … *meaning system* that enables meaningful interpretations of reality	*Interpretive*: what is the meaning of practices and artefacts and what interpretations are attributed to them?
(3) … *solution system* that favours and integrates certain solutions	*Action-oriented*: how are challenges tackled, problems solved and goals achieved?

1.2.1   Culture as a value system

Values play a particularly important role in intercultural management because they influence human behaviour, working styles and organizational practices. Samovar and Porter (1991, p. 15) define values as 'a set of organized rules for making choices, reducing uncertainty, and reducing conflicts within a given society. Cultural values also specify which behaviours are important and which should be avoided within a culture.' Values are learned, culture-embedded, desirable guiding principles of action and decision-making rules that control behaviour (Parsons, 1952). Values are often ethical, religious or humanistic orientations of a society, such as security, diligence, order or the fulfilment of duties (Weber, 1963). Values influence and organize behaviour and preferences, and they become visible in social interactions and in the expression of ideas about *right* or *desirable* forms of living together.

However, values should not be understood as behavioural constraints, but rather as a repertoire of suggestions for solutions and behaviours that have been proved in the past (Inglehart, 2018). Values change more slowly than institutions or structures and show a high degree of continuity. In turn, they also influence institutions and structures.

The *World Values Survey*, a global study conducted every five years, empirically investigates value orientations, beliefs and norms across societies and how these change over time. The study examines cultural, political, economic and religious values of people, with the goal to assess the impact of values stability or change on the development of countries and societies (Inglehart, 2018).

The last survey was conducted between 2017 and 2020 in 77 countries, with 129 000 respondents. The questionnaire covered the following themes: social values attitudes and stereotypes; societal well-being; social capital, trust and organizational membership; economic values; corruption; migration; post-materialism; science and technology; religious values; security; ethical values and norms; political interest and political participation; political culture and political regimes; demography. Table 3.2 indicates the results for several dimensions and their values in 20 countries.

Table 3.2 Values of selected countries of the World Values Survey, 7th survey wave 2017–2020

Country	Importance of work in life[1]	Importance of leisure time in life[1]	Importance of religion in life[1]	Importance of politics in life[1]
Australia	80.3%	91%	28.8%	49.1%
Bangladesh	97.7%	69.8%	99%	27.6%
Brazil	96.2%	85.3%	84.6%	44.2%
China	88.4%	70.6%	13%	53.6%
Egypt	86.9%	54.6%	100%	30.2%
France	93.7%	86.5%	37.1%	38.9%
Germany	87.3%	91.9%	35.7%	65.8%
Indonesia	98.6%	77.5%	99.9%	44.2%
Iran	96.1%	91.5%	92.5%	58.2%
Italy	96.1%	90.7%	65.3%	46.1%
Japan	80.1%	90.3%	14.5%	64.3%
Mexico	92.2%	85.2%	74.5%	33.3%
Nigeria	96.4%	93.2%	98.6%	58%
Poland	92.8%	94.2%	78.1%	43.9%
Russia	74%	81.5%	50.6%	37.7%
Spain	95.6%	91.2%	38.1%	40.1%
South Korea	86.4%	91.6%	35.9%	60.1%
Turkey	83.7%	92.5%	88.4%	56.2%
United Kingdom	79.2%	91.7%	37%	53.7%
United States	78.1%	86.8%	59.6%	55%

Note: [1] Aggregated values of 'very important' and 'rather important'.
Source: World Values Survey (2020).

The successive waves of the *World Values Survey* show that cultural dynamics have led to shifts in values in many societies. We can thus observe a shift from materialistic to post-materialistic values when societies reach a certain standard of living. Material values refer to maintaining order or economic growth, while post-material values express themselves in participation in politics and labour or protection of freedom of expression. When survival problems no longer determine everyday life, people turn to self-realization (Inglehart, 2018).

The *World Values Survey* also observes a change in values from traditional values to secular and rational values. As a consequence, for instance, modernizing societies reveal more tolerance towards marginalized groups and more awareness of subjective well-being, thus promoting political stability.

Values and their differences do not only refer to national cultures, but also to organizations, generations or lifestyles. An example is provided by LOHAS (Lifestyle of Health and Sustainability) (Box 3.3).

BOX 3.3   LOHAS (LIFESTYLE OF HEALTH AND SUSTAINABILITY)

LOHAS is an acronym for Lifestyle of Health and Sustainability and describes consumers who strive for a healthier and more sustainable lifestyle, in line with their values regarding personal, family and community health, environmental sustainability and social justice.

They purchase products and services that are in line with their values, for example, renewable energy, solar hot water, organic foods, recycled and sustainable homewares, domestic rainwater tanks, sustainable timbers, natural cleaning products, alternative medicine, yoga and eco-tourism. This lifestyle has developed worldwide, given the importance of sustainable development and corporate social responsibility.

Source: LOHAS (2020); Ray and Anderson (2000).

1.2.2   Culture as a meaning system

Despite their uniqueness and individuality, people from one culture reveal a certain repertoire of similarities in communication. As advocated by Max Weber (1949[2017], pp. 80-81), this is due to the meaningful interaction and exchange of meanings through signs.

> The conclusion [...] is that an 'objective' analysis of cultural events, which proceeds according to the thesis that the ideal of science is the reduction of empirical reality of 'laws', is meaningless. It is not meaningless, as is often maintained, because cultural or psychic events for instance are 'objectively' less governed by laws. It is meaningless for a number of other reasons. Firstly, because the knowledge of social laws is not knowledge of social reality but is rather one of the various aids used by our minds for attaining this end; secondly, because knowledge of cultural events is inconceivable except on a basis of the significance which the concrete constellations of reality have for us in certain individual concrete situations. In which sense and in which situations this is the case is not revealed to us by any law; it is decided according to the value-ideas in the light of which we view 'culture' in each individual case. 'Culture' is a finite segment of the meaningless infinity of the world process, a segment on which human beings confer meaning and significance.

Culture consists of shared knowledge, basic assumptions and expectations that create unambiguity within a group. These learned and shared ideas, symbols and meanings enable members of a culture to communicate and cooperate in a meaningful and goal-oriented way (Geertz, 1973). Social groups do not necessarily have to share the same knowledge or system of meaning; rather, they create a largely shared understanding of social reality through a common frame of reference (Berger & Luckmann, 1966). During their socialization process, individuals acquire this system of meaning, which serves for the appropriate interpretation of communicative actions: 'All cultures [...] provide interpretative systems that provide meaning to the problems of existence, presenting them as elements in a given order that have therefore to be endured, or as the result of a disturbance of that order, that have consequently to be corrected' (d'Iribarne, 1994, p. 92).

According to Geertz (1973), signs and symbols play a key role in turning culture into a 'web of significance' and a 'semantic inventory'. Within the webs of significance, the common and the individual, the shared and the particular, the unambiguous and the ambivalent are confronted with each other. It is necessary to highlight that culture as a meaning system cannot be equated with a certain society on a national level. Meanings within countries are not stable and can vary according to the multiple cultures that prevail within them (d'Iribarne et al., 2020).

Meaning systems are different across cultures, which can have important consequences on human interaction in organizations. For example, concepts such as quality and customer relationships can show divergent meanings (Boxes 3.4 and 3.5).

BOX 3.4 DIFFERENCES IN UNDERLYING (HIDDEN) CONCEPTIONS OF QUALITY IN GERMANY AND BRAZIL

In Germany, quality plays a central role and companies often face difficulties when transferring their conception of German quality ('*deutsche Qualität*') to foreign subsidiaries. This was the case for a German multinational which produces construction machines and which transfers its quality processes to Brazil. For the German headquarters, quality means functionality, appearance and perfection, which is also manifested in the appearance of products. The underlying cultural values are '*Liebe zum Detail*' ('love of detail') and strict rule orientations. In contrast, the Brazilian subsidiary attached more importance to functionality, practicability, customer orientation and competitive pricing. The underlying cultural values are personal orientation towards customers and '*orgulho brasileiro*' ('Brazilian pride'). The two different conceptions led to misunderstandings and conflicts, and it was necessary to find solutions in order to meet the German quality standards.

Source: Bausch et al. (2020).

BOX 3.5 DIVERGENT CONCEPTIONS OF CUSTOMER RELATIONSHIPS IN FRANCE AND CHINA

The Chinese market is characterized by the existence of a vast number of customers due to the large size and strong economic growth. Customer relationships thus take a different form from Western countries where companies often operate in saturated markets and need to dedicate important resources to customer relationship management. For example, Mixel Agitators, a French small and medium-sized enterprise (SME) specialized in industrial mixers, decided to establish a production and sales subsidiary in Beijing (China) to serve their customers such as the French multinational Veolia. The objective was to strengthen the business relationships with existing customers and to become their main supplier in Asian markets. From the perspective of the Chinese subsidiary manager of

Mixel Agitators: 'the French are afraid to lose their clients but in China, there are so many potential customers that it is possible to just select 1 or 2% of the demands [...]. Why should I work with multinationals who put pressure on prices? [...] If you want to earn respect in China, you should show your muscles and that is something that the head office finds hard to understand.' The diverging conceptions of customer relationships – building customer loyalty for the French headquarters and selecting new customers for the Chinese subsidiary – created tension because the French SME feared losing historical customers in the case of deteriorated business relationships in China. The French Chief Executive Officer (CEO) had to explain the importance of certain customers to the Chinese subsidiary manager and follow-up business relationships with historical clients both in France and in China.

Source: Dominguez and Mayrhofer (2018b).

Meaning systems become interculturally relevant when interaction partners do not understand certain symbols or rules for interpretation. Outsiders of such systems find themselves confronted with a 'multiplicity of complex conceptual structures, many of them superimposed upon or knotted into one another, which are at once strange, irregular and inexplicit, and which [they] must contrive somehow first to grasp and then to render' (Geertz, 1973, p. 10). When confronting these complex conceptual structures, something ambiguous, vague and novel emerges in intercultural situations, which can be perceived as either threatening or stimulating.

1.2.3 Culture as a solution system

According to Kluckhohn and Strodtbeck (1961), culture functions as a system for solution finding. In other words, in social systems, actors find specific forms and ways of achieving objectives. Despite the existence of multiple possible solutions, individuals prefer certain proven, 'dominant' solutions for the optimal regulation of interpersonal activity and for the survival and continued existence of the system they belong to (Parsons, 1952). Social systems are based on (often unconscious) values, experiences and expectations. Rules, methods or institutions can offer possible solutions for problems. When communities share relatively similar value orientations which have proven successful, they are likely to develop certain solution patterns with frequency and specific characteristics. In this respect, Kluckhohn and Strodtbeck (1961) formulate three assumptions:

First it is assumed that there is a limited number of common human problems for which all peoples at all times must find some solution. This is the universal aspect of value orientations because the common human problems to be treated arise inevitably out of the human situation. The second assumption is that while there is variability in solutions of all the problems, it is neither limitless nor random but is definitely variable within a range of possible solutions. The third assumption [...] is that all alternatives of all solutions are present in all societies at all times but are differentially preferred. Every society has, in addition to its dominant profile of value orientations, numerous variants or substitute profiles. Moreover, it is postulated that in both the dominant and the variant profiles there is almost always a rank ordering of the preferences of the value-orientation alternatives. (Kluckhohn & Strodtbeck, 1961, p. 10)

Consequently, societies develop a certain value system which influences their behaviour and actions in the sense of problem-solving (Kluckhohn, 1953). Kluckhohn and Strodtbeck (1961) elaborated five general human problems. Each problem has a specific orientation, with a possible range of variations as 'solutions'. The so-called 'Value Orientation Method' proposes five categories that allow the comparison of cultures (Table 3.3).

Table 3.3 About general human problems

Orientation	General human problem	Range of variations
Nature of people	What is the character of innate human nature?	• Evil • Neutral (mixture of good-and-evil) • Good
Relationship to nature	What is the relation of man to nature (and supernature)?	• Subjugation-to-nature • Harmony-with-nature • Mastery-over-nature
Time orientation	What is the temporal focus of human life?	• Past • Present • Future
Activity orientation	What is the modality of human activity?	• Being • Being-in-becoming • Doing
Relationships among people	What is the modality of man's relationship to other men?	• Linearity • Collaterality • Individualism

Source: Based on Kluckhohn and Strodtbeck (1961, p. 12).

The cultural approach, the value variations and the methodology developed by Kluckhohn and Strodtbeck (1961) have shaped intercultural management for decades, and the adopted model can also be transposed to organizations. In business practice, it is often difficult to elaborate a common solution to general problems, since the acceptance and implementation may vary across cultural contexts (Box 3.6). In the perspective of *constructive intercultural management*, organizations should attempt to develop solutions that satisfy the different parties involved or even lead to added value for the company through complementarity.

BOX 3.6   THE 360° FEEDBACK

An example of a general problem in organizations deals with how to give feedback and advice to colleagues. The 'Western' instrument of 360° feedback provides a possible solution to that problem. However, the implementation of a 360° feedback is highly culture-dependent and is subject to the risk of cultural misinterpretation. In some countries, it is assumed to be an objective, honest evaluation, whereas in other countries it is seen as a critique of colleagues and bosses which is feared and avoided. In countries with flat and informal hierarchical relationships, for example in Scandinavian, German-speaking and English-speaking countries, an instrument such as the 360° feedback can be used more successfully than in countries where formal hierarchical relationships are important, for example in Latin, Arab and East Asian countries.

Changes and developments in cultural systems happen when individuals discover that certain solution patterns are no longer suitable for mastering existing challenges. In search of effective new solutions, people question self-evident facts and thus gain more awareness of their problem-related solutions. The emergence of new structures and processes can thus contribute to the development of cultural systems:

> The values of any living culture had helped it survive in the environment where it found itself. Borrowing from evolutionary theory, it has become common to ask how well these cultural values fit the environment so that the culture survives. These survival values are passed down the generations. There are therefore as many sets of different cultural values as there are environments across the globe. These are not good or bad, high or low, civilized or primitive. They are to be judged, if at all, by their evolutionary fit. (Hampden-Turner & Trompenaars, 2006, p. 57)

The more values are opposed to each other, the more conflicting is their influence on the social system. The more they are harmonized, the more they have a stabilizing effect on the social system. In terms of balanced and effective interculturality, it is therefore necessary to allow opposites and differences in values, which may interact positively as mutual forces (Hampden-Turner & Trompenaars, 2020). In this sense, *constructive intercultural management* is about the complementary and synergetic solutions found in intercultural teams and organizations.

Table 3.4 presents the characteristics and functions of the three complementary concepts of culture.

Table 3.4   Characteristics of three complementary concepts of culture and their impact on management

Culture as a ...	Explanation	Function	Impact on management
(1) ... value system	*Mental software*: specific patterns of thought, feeling and action acquired through socialization that constitute an emotional and cognitive system.	Orientation and 'self-evident facts', which influence decisions and enable optimal regulation of interpersonal action.	Alignment and ethical orientation: which goals are declared as desirable? How are decisions and behaviour justified?
(2) ... meaning system	*Semantic inventory*: shared knowledge, symbols and meanings lead to common assumptions, expectations ideas and interpretations.	Unambiguity, clarity, meaning, goal-oriented and adequate interpretation of communicative action.	Communicative action and language: what sense do symbols and behaviours make? How are they understood and interpreted?
(3) ...solution system	*Problem-solving*: specific coping with basic, universal challenges and problems.	Proven patterns of problem-solving are reproduced and consolidate. Despite the variety of possible solutions, societies show certain solution patterns with particular frequency and characteristics.	Working and organizational practices: how are challenges dealt with? How are goals achieved? How is work organized, controlled, designed?

1.3   Constructive Use of the Concepts of Culture

In line with *constructive interculturality*, the three concepts of culture show that culture has an identity-forming and sense-giving function, along with giving orientation and providing order. Culture enables individuals to find their way within a social system and to live permanently together in a group or society without major contradictions. However, we raise the question of development and change with regard to the three cultural concepts, because with the development of societies, cultural concepts are also subject to change. The shift from a static to a dynamic concept of culture allows us to view culture as 'a loose network of multiple and sometimes conflicting knowledge and values […] that can be activated (or suppressed) depending on the demands of the situation' (Adler & Aycan, 2018, p. 311). Rather than distinguishing culture into 'either-or' dichotomy, *constructive intercultural management* sees culture from a 'both-and' perspective, integrating differences, opposites and contradictions. For example, due to the increasing multiculturalism of societies through immigration, we can observe the development of pluriculturalism, with intercultural individuals who can facilitate the management of cultural diversity in organizations (Pollock et al., 2003) (Chapters 2 and 13).

It is also interesting to examine how actors influence culture and interculturality according to the three concepts of culture. Although the *value system* is difficult and slow in development, actors can actively change it through their behaviour. *Meaning systems* can be extended by cultural knowledge, especially by language, and progressively changed. *Solution systems* can be influenced by finding new possibilities of action and the creation of alternative solutions that fit constructively the environment and the purpose. It is therefore necessary to recognize the complementarity of the three concepts to use them constructively.

2.   MULTIPLE CULTURES AND CULTURAL DYNAMICS

Scholars on intercultural management criticize that the concept of culture is often reduced to national culture (Adler & Aycan, 2018; McSweeney, 2009). The primary criticism is that cultural concepts are often referred to as rather homogeneous societies and regarded as 'autonomous islands', which are marginally affected by external influences. Metaphorically speaking, many cultural concepts represent 'corsets', which are blasted by the diversity of modern cultural systems. For this reason, intercultural research and practice has been considered to be too homogeneous. For example, d'Iribarne et al. (2020) emphasize that national culture does not 'only' serve to emphasize its specifics, but rather to analyse and understand how the encounter of people from different societies leads to a specific culture, that is a common way of doing things. They further highlight the importance of the multiple meaning systems associated with different cultures or subcultures, reflecting their collective memory, history and language:

> This attention given to the constructed character of universes of meaning and to the many ways of giving meaning within the same society suggests that it is only legitimate to speak of culture at a much smaller level than a country: a workshop, a sports club, or at most

a company. Indeed, it can be assumed that while one is on this level, at any given time, one finds sorts of shared meanings, associated with a set of shared values and behaviours. These meanings remain local and transitional. However, the value of these arguments should not be overestimated. In fact, the unquestionable existence of differing interpretations does not mean that the specific ways of interpreting of the various actors belonging to the same society do not have anything in common. (d'Iribarne et al., 2020, p. 56)

2.1   Multiple Cultures

Intercultural management therefore questions to what extent culture affects the thinking, feeling and acting of individuals, and to what extent they are 'typical' representatives of their culture. It is necessary to consider the context in which interculturality takes place, but also the cultural characteristics of individuals. Therefore, the national concept of culture is considered too deterministic. Individuals in intercultural organizations are shaped by various cultural influences and identities, which are far more diverse than just one national culture. As a consequence, intercultural management is increasingly dealing with subcultures such as organizational, functional, professional and industrial cultures. In organizations, they also concern gender, age, social classes and hierarchical positions. Three subcultures appear to be particularly relevant to intercultural management: organizational, functional and professional cultures (Table 3.5).

Table 3.5   Organizational, functional and professional cultures

Organizational culture	*Organizational culture* represents the common identity of organizational members, providing a frame for orientation and decision-making and thus shapes the actions of employees. As a mechanism for coordination, integration and motivation, it can facilitate the reduction of costs and the development of synergies and improve employee satisfaction. In this respect, organizational culture is a central element of *constructive intercultural management* (Schein, 1986 [2016]).
Functional culture	*Functional culture* concerns basic collective assumptions, that is, values, practices and artefacts, within the functional departments of an organization. Functional departments can have specific objectives, behaviours and languages. Functional culture can have an identity-creating effect on the collective by othering: '*we* in marketing against *those* in development'. In *constructive intercultural management*, functional cultures can generate positive impulses and enriching interactions (Chevrier, 2013).
Professional culture	*Professional culture* is associated with self-image and reflects the common understanding of roles, knowledge, competences, experience and practices, shared by people of the same profession. They often have a common expertise and language, with a similar conception of the work environment. Professional culture evolves through socialization, reflects the profession's values and ideas over time and has identity-forming functions, which can facilitate *constructive intercultural management* (Zander & Romani, 2004).

It is important to highlight that the different subcultures are intertwined. For example, professional socialization is shaped by national influences and thus reflects the respective values and practices. It appears that professional cultures with a scientific and technical focus (for example engineers) show more similarity than other professional cultures. People who share the same professional culture can communicate implicitly and collaborate more effectively due to a common professional basis. Professional cultures are not bound to single nations, industries, organizations or individuals and can therefore represent a unifying element of communication across cultural borders. For example, in international teams, professional cultures can facilitate cross-border cooperation, with their members sharing similar attitudes, interests, ways of thinking and competences (Chevrier, 2013).

Nations are heterogeneous social systems that are exposed to manifold cultural influences and therefore unite many cultures, identities and collectives: 'the multiple cultures perspective acknowledges that individuals may identify with and hold simultaneous membership in several cultural groups' (Sackmann & Phillips, 2004, p. 378). For example, a person can be female, young and athletic, belong to the upper class of society, work as an engineer in a research department of a large French company in the chemical industry, lead a team as a manager and hold an Italian passport. So, this person performs many different roles and belongs to several cultural groups.

The different subcultures can play various roles. In certain situations, the membership of national or regional cultures can be more important, whilst in others it can be gender, organizational, functional or professional culture (Schneider et al., 2014). Depending on the type of task, previous experience, interaction situation and context, certain characteristics can come to the forefront, with certain differences being paramount. Some differences might then be more important than others. With regard to the dimensions of diversity, this may imply that patterns of thought and behaviour based on national cultural affiliation play a more important role than the members' gender or age. In other groupings, the career or degree may play a greater role than task-related knowledge and the ability to solve a particular problem. Examples from practice are provided in Boxes 3.7 and 3.8.

BOX 3.7 MULTIPLE CULTURES AT THE GERMAN MULTINATIONAL INFINEON

In 2014, the German semiconductor manufacturer Infineon acquired the US multinational International Rectifier, including its foreign subsidiaries. One of them is located in southern France and managed by a French engineer. For almost 20 years, the subsidiary had mainly employed French engineers and computer scientists from Paris and northern France, who had been socialized by US management methods, integrating them into their work practices. With the acquisition by Infineon, new methods and processes were introduced, namely those of the German headquarters, which replaced or overlaid existing ones. At the same time, new engineers and computer scientists were hired who had just graduated and belong to the younger generation of *digital natives*. The French subsidiary thus subsumed different national cultures (France, USA, Germany), regional cultures (northern and southern France), corporate cultures (International Rectifier and Infineon) and generational cultures (young and older generations), which represented important challenges for the integration within Infineon.

BOX 3.8　MULTIPLE CULTURES AT TOYOTA PEUGEOT CITROËN AUTOMOBILE (TPCA) IN THE CZECH REPUBLIC

Toyota Peugeot Citroën Automobile (TPCA) was established in the Czech Republic as a joint venture between Toyota Motor Corporation and PSA Peugeot Citroën. The Japanese and French car manufacturers decided to cooperate for the development and production of small city cars, designed primarily for the European markets. One of the main motivations for the joint venture was cost efficiency. The Czech Republic is an attractive territory for the automotive industry, characterized by relatively cheap labour costs, skilled workforce and well-developed infrastructure. The country has a strong automotive tradition and is highly integrated into the European value chains. The TPCA plant was established in Kolín, 60 km from Prague. The creation of the joint venture was marked by the coexistence of three national cultures (Czech Republic, France, Japan) and two organizational cultures (Toyota Motor Corporation and PSA Peugeot Citroën), but the strong industry culture of the two partner companies and the automotive tradition of the Czech Republic helped them to integrate cultural differences in a constructive way. The shared values inherent to the automotive culture facilitated communication, the harmonization of work practices as well as day-to-day operations. The alliance partners organized regular meetings between the management teams, which took place alternatively in France, Japan and the Czech Republic. Moreover, they were able to build trust relationships with the Czech employees, who were guaranteed employment stability. To demonstrate his long-term commitment and attachment to the city of Kolín, the Japanese president of TPCA changed his civil status to add the term Kolín to his surname. In 2018, Toyota announced to take financial ownership of TPCA, but the plant will continue to produce the three car models (Peugeot 108, Citroën C1 and Toyota Aygo).

Source: Machkova and Mayrhofer (2018).

Multiple cultures allow a substantially differentiated image of cultural realities. The diversity of cultures might be a strength if the specific characteristics of individuals are taken into account and if diversity is accepted within the community. *Constructive intercultural management* addresses the complexity of multiple cultures in a strategic and coordinating way, for example, by emphasizing commonalities such as the professional or organizational culture. However, the overemphasis on singularities (Reckwitz, 2020), and the pluralization and differentiation of culture(s) in organizations and societies can also be problematic: instead of bringing together and combining cultures and their characteristics, there is also a risk of segregation and fragmentation.

Countries present significant differences concerning their cultural diversity (Marcus et al., 2019). Some countries are relatively homogeneous, for example Portugal and Sweden, whilst others reveal a strong heterogeneity with the existence of multiple cultures, for example, South Africa, Brazil, Indonesia, India and Turkey. Reasons are migration, colonialism and political intervention as well as economic and climatic differences between regions. Moreover, people may have different interpretations of their 'national culture', as a symbol of identity. For example, Taiwanese self-initiated expatriates show conflicting interpretations of their national culture and thus use different social resources when doing business in London (Moore, 2020). India is characterized by a strong cultural heterogeneity, shaped by the pressure of global, national and regional institutional forces. There are nine distinct subcultural regions, which can explain the coexistence of contradictory values within the Indian society (Dheer et al., 2015).

The ethno-linguistic fractionalization (ELF) framework, proposed by Luiz (2015), allows for assessment of ethnic, linguistic and religious heterogeneity and cultural dynamics. The purpose of the framework is to unravel the complexity of multiple cultural identities in ethnically diverse countries. Table 3.6 presents the scores for selected countries. Measuring the three dimensions over time reveals that culture is undergoing changes and that 'there is no such thing as a homogenous culture' (p. 1088) in many countries. The empirical study shows that measures of culture and cultural distance based on national dimensions do not capture the real complexity of culture.

Table 3.6 Measuring multiple cultural identities in selected countries

Country	Ethnicity	Language	Religion
Brazil	0.5408	0.0468	0.6054
India	0.4182	0.8069	0.3260
Indonesia	0.7351	0.7680	0.2340
Morocco	0.4841	0.4683	0.0035
Portugal	0.0468	0.0198	0.1438
South Africa	0.7517	0.8652	0.8603
Sweden	0.0600	0.1968	0.2342

Note: Measure: the value of 0 corresponds to a perfectly homogeneous population; the maximum value of 1 corresponds to a population divided into infinite groups of one member.
Source: Extract from Luiz (2015, pp. 1096-1097).

2.2 Stability and Dynamics of Cultures

Intercultural management has long been dominated by the functionalist paradigm that ordered culture into separable cultural dimensions (Fang, 2006; Lowe et al., 2019). However, describing national cultures through the functionalist lens has provoked criticism (McSweeney, 2009) since the investigation of bipolar dimensions requires a certain stability of values. Assuming that national identity is contextual and dynamic implies that the cultural frame of reference anchored in national identity can be modified and adapted in new intercultural contexts. Meanings, practices and norms can thus be recombined and changed over time in interactions and negotiations (Brannen & Salk, 2000, p. 458). Consequently, deterministic cultural dimensions do not allow the in-depth understanding of intercultural processes.

The metaphor of the 'cultural onion', proposed by Hofstede et al. (2010), regards cultures as isolated, multi-layered constructs (rituals, heroes, symbols and practices) with a stable core composed by values. Conversely, the metaphor of the 'ocean' developed by Fang (2006) illustrates behaviours and values in a certain context and at a certain time. The latter helps to understand culture as flowing and transcending values and behaviours. As culture is full of contradictions, contents and processes of culture are never fully visible at any time, because, as symbolized by the ocean metaphor, it hides beneath the surface and constantly promotes new developments. Intercultural interaction can thus lead to changes in behaviour and values. The two metaphors are in line with the two concepts 'culture as code' and 'culture in context' (Bjerregaard et al., 2009). Whereas 'culture as code' corresponds to the onion and a stable and functionalist cultural approach, 'culture in context' refers to the ocean and a dynamic and interpretative cultural approach. Table 3.7 summarizes the two perspectives.

Table 3.7   Are cultures stable or dynamic?

Characteristics	Culture as stable	Culture as dynamic
Management and organization	Stability through historical traditions and national institutions such as education systems and laws	Dynamism through intensification of interactions between actors with different cultural backgrounds
Assumptions	Homogeneity through stable value and meaning systems	Heterogeneity through internationalization processes and multiculturality
Cultural approaches	Cross-border cultural comparison	Intercultural interaction and multiple cultures
Context	'Culture as code': decontextualized	'Culture as context': contextualized
Metaphor	Culture as an 'onion'	Culture as an 'ocean'
Perspective	Culture as a 'billiard ball'	Negotiated culture

Source: Adapted from Barmeyer et al. (2019b, p. 257).

3.   CULTURAL DIMENSIONS

Cultural dimensions are categories or variables that describe social phenomena and serve for their analysis. They are often used to characterize and compare social systems such as societies, organizations and groups. Cultural dimensions contribute to a better understanding of perceptions, ways of thinking, emotions and behaviours of people from other cultures. They often refer to the dealing with time, information or space and value orientations such as individualism, power distance or particularism.

3.1   Well Established Cultural Dimensions

In the following, we will present the cultural dimensions developed by Edward T. Hall, Geert Hofstede, and Fons Trompenaars and Charles Hampden-Turner.

3.1.1 Cultural dimensions of E.T. Hall

The anthropologist Edward T. Hall is regarded as the founder of intercultural communication. He adopted a qualitative approach to develop a profound understanding of human coexistence and behaviour. The three identified dimensions refer to the density of information (high context and low context communication), spatial behaviour (proxemics) and the dealing with time (monochronic and polychronic time) (Hall & Hall, 1990) (Table 3.8).

Table 3.8 Cultural dimensions according to Hall and Hall (1990)

Information: Context	
High context cultures	**Low context cultures**
Indirect, playful and ambiguous transmission of information	Direct, detailed and clear transmission of information
Implicit communication is faster. Only participants who already have prior knowledge (context) understand information correctly.	Explicit communication is slower. All participants have a similar level of knowledge.
Space: Proxemics	
Refers to the physical distance (proximity and distance) between people. Distribution, order and use of space in private life (apartment, house), in public life (infrastructure) and in organizations (size, arrangement and design of buildings and offices according to affiliation, functions, hierarchies, etc.). Human and culture-specific communication system whose basic units (posture or body touch) are transmitted through various communication channels.	
Time	
Polychronic cultures	**Monochronic cultures**
Doing several tasks at the same time: unforeseen interruptions and improvisation are normal.	Doing one task after the other: time is divided into small, independent units.
Individuals attach less importance to punctuality than in monochronic societies.	Risks are reduced or eliminated through planning and formalization.
Interpersonal relationships have a higher priority than work-related tasks.	Working rhythm is constant and stress situations are therefore rare.
	Uncertainty is perceived as disturbing, confuses the process and can cause disorientation.

Source: Hall and Hall (1990).

3.1.2 Cultural dimensions of G. Hofstede

Geert Hofstede was one of the first scholars to conduct a quantitative study based on questionnaires to examine cultural differences. His work relies on the assumption of Kluckhohn and Strodtbeck (1961) that cultures are facing universal problems, for which they find different solutions based on their value orientation. The first survey concerned work-related value orientations and attitudes of 116 000 IBM employees in 72 countries. The six cultural dimensions identified are intended to provide comparable criteria for describing and analysing different societies. They exhibit relative differences and are ranked by country on the basis of indices (Hofstede et al., 2010) (Table 3.9).

Table 3.9   Cultural dimensions according to Hofstede et al. (2010)

High power distance – Low power distance	
Extent to which the less powerful members of organizations expect and accept that power is distributed unequally.	
Centralization is popular.	Decentralization is popular.
Subordinates expect to be told what to do.	Subordinates expect to be consulted.
The ideal boss is a benevolent autocrat, or 'good father'.	The ideal boss is a resourceful democrat.
Collectivism – Individualism	
Degree to which members of organizations are integrated into groups.	
People are born into extended families or other in-groups that continue protecting them in exchange for loyalty.	One grows up to look after oneself and one's immediate (nuclear) family.
The employer–employee relationship is basically moral, like a family link.	The employer–employee relationship is a contract between parties in the labour market.
Management is management of groups.	Management is management of individuals.
Relationship prevails over task.	Task prevails over relationship.
Masculinity – Femininity	
Masculinity as a preference for achievement, heroism, assertiveness and material rewards for success. Femininity as a preference for cooperation, modesty, caring for the weak and quality of life.	
Challenge, earnings, recognition and advancement are important.	Relationships and quality of life are important.
People live in order to work.	People work in order to live.
Rewards are based on equity.	Rewards are based on equality.
Conflict resolution by letting the strongest win.	Conflict resolution by compromise and negotiation.
Weak uncertainty avoidance – Strong uncertainty avoidance	
Extent to which the members of a culture feel threatened by ambiguous or unknown situations.	
Time is a framework for orientation.	Time is money.
Work hard only when needed.	There is an emotional need to be busy and an inner urge to work hard.
Tolerance for ambiguity and chaos.	Need for precision and formalization.
Motivation by achievement and esteem or belonging.	Motivation by security and esteem or belonging.
Short-term orientation – Long-term orientation	
Extent to which the members of a culture are oriented toward the future, past and present.	
Fostering of virtues oriented toward future rewards, in particular, perseverance and thrift.	Fostering of virtues related to the past and present, in particular, respect for tradition, perseverance of 'face' and fulfilling social obligations.
Main work values include learning, honesty, adaptiveness, accountability and self-discipline.	Main work values include freedom, rights, achievement and independent thinking.
Disagreement does not hurt.	There is a need for cognitive consistency.
Respect for circumstances.	Respect for traditions.
Perseverance, sustained efforts toward slow results.	Efforts should produce quick results.
Indulgence – Restraint	
Extent to which members of a culture tend to enjoy life and have fun.	
Free gratification of basic and natural human desires related to enjoying life and having fun.	Conviction that such gratification needs to be curbed and regulated by strict social norms.
Less moral discipline.	Moral discipline.
A perception of personal life control.	A perception of helplessness: what happens to me is not my own doing.
Higher importance of leisure.	Lower importance of leisure.

Source: Hofstede et al. (2010).

3.1.3 Cultural dimensions of F. Trompenaars and C. Hampden-Turner

Similar to Geert Hofstede, Fons Trompenaars and Charles Hampden-Turner (2020) also adopt the assumption of Kluckhohn and Strodtbeck (1961) that cultures face universal problems and find different solutions. The authors conducted quantitative surveys with 80 000 question-naires collected in companies in about 50 countries (Hampden-Turner & Trompenaars, 2020) (Table 3.10).

3.2 Constructive Handling of Cultural Dimensions

Despite all criticism, cultural dimensions serve for orientation in intercultural contexts if they are dealt with in a reflected way (Barmeyer & Franklin, 2016). It is necessary to consider that they do not determine behaviours and that they rather reflect typical solutions and behaviours of actors, which have been proven effective. Cultural dimensions should not be understood in absolute but in relative terms, that is they point out particularities and are always integrated into specific contexts. Similar to culture, they are only *constructs* that can help to understand social phenomena:

> CULTURE DOESN'T EXIST. In the same way values don't exist [...]. They are constructs, which have to prove their usefulness by their ability to explain and predict behaviour. The moment they stop doing that we should be prepared to drop them, or trade them for something better. I never claim that culture is the only thing we should pay attention to. In many practical cases it is redundant, and economic, political or institutional factors provide better explanations. But sometimes they don't, and then we need the construct of culture. (Hofstede, 2002, p. 1359)

These constructs can be understood as 'intercultural maps'. Therefore, the principle of con-structivism applies: people construct their reality through previous experiences, selective perception and reflection (Berger & Luckmann, 1966). Thus, the map is a simplified rep-resentation and an interpretation of reality. While it reflects some elements, it ignores others. So, the map helps people for orientation and organization. Difficulties arise when the respec-tive map is considered to be reality.

In the sense of *constructive intercultural management*, cultural dimensions serve as an orientation guide that can help in intercultural interaction (Barmeyer & Franklin, 2016). They can be understood as meta-knowledge, or 'control programmes' which allow to become aware of one's own culture, to better understand a foreign culture and thus to act *constructively* and appropriately in intercultural situations. Table 3.11 summarizes the risks and opportunities associated with the use of cultural dimensions.

Constructive intercultural management therefore views and uses cultural dimensions dynamically and circularly according to a postmodern fluid and flexible understanding of culture (Fang, 2006; Barmeyer et al., 2019b). The basic idea is to dissolve rigid bipolarity by dynamic circularity. Thus, opposites are not located as poles on a straight line, but are opposite elements of a circle (Hampden-Turner, 1992), such as in systemic thinking and cybernetics.

Table 3.10 Cultural dimensions according to Hampden-Turner and Trompenaars (2020)

Universalism – Particularism
Degree of importance a culture attaches to either law or personal relationships.

Universalism searches for similarity and tries to impose to all members of a society or an organization the laws of their commonality.	Particularism searches for differences and attaches more importance to particular obligations concerning certain members than general norms and rules.

Individualism – Communitarianism
Degree to which people are more likely to see themselves as individuals or as belonging to a community.

Individuals are more important than the community. This means that individual happiness, fulfilment and well-being dominate, that people show self-initiative and care for themselves.	The community is more important than individuals. It is the responsibility of people to act in the interest of society. Individual interests are thus automatically considered.

Specificity – Diffuseness
Degree to which responsibility is specifically assigned or diffusely accepted.

Individuals first analyse the elements individually and then put them together. The whole is the sum of its parts. People's lives are divided accordingly and only one component can be addressed at a time. Interactions between people are clearly defined. Individuals focus on facts, standards and contracts.	A diffusely oriented culture begins with the whole and sees individual elements from the perspective of the whole. All elements are linked together. Relationships between elements are more important than individual elements.

Neutrality – Affectivity
Degree to which individuals show their emotions.

People are taught not to display their feelings openly. The degree to which feelings manifest themselves is therefore minimal. Emotions are controlled when they occur.	In an affective culture, people show their emotions, and it is not considered necessary to hide feelings.

Achieved status – Ascribed status
Degree to which individuals must prove themselves to obtain a certain status, as opposed to a status that is simply attributed.

Individuals derive their status from what they have achieved themselves. Achieved status must be verified again and again.	Individuals derive their status from birth, age, gender or wealth. Status is not based on performance, but on the nature of individuals.

Sequential time – Synchronous time
Degree to which individuals do things one after the other, as opposed to several things at the same time.

In a sequential time culture, people structure time sequentially and do things one after the other.	In a synchronous time culture, people do several things simultaneously because they believe that time is flexible and immaterial.

Inner direction – Outer direction
Degree which locates the origin of virtue.

Inner direction conceives virtue as inside each of us – in our souls, wills, convictions, principles and core beliefs – in the triumph of conscious purpose.	Outer direction conceives virtue as outside each of us in natural rhythms, in the beauties and power of nature, in aesthetic environments and relationships.

Attitudes to nature
The degree to which individuals believe that nature can be controlled instead of believing that the environment controls them.

Individuals have a mechanistic view of nature; nature is complex but can be controlled with the right expertise. Individuals believe that they can control nature.	Individuals have an organic view of nature. Individuals are regarded as one of the forces of nature and should live in harmony with the environment. Individuals adapt to external conditions.

Source: Hampden-Turner and Trompenaars (2020).

Table 3.11 Risks and opportunities

Cultural dimensions *could* be:	Cultural dimensions *should* be:
Categorization and classification of cultural differences	Orientation frameworks and explanatory *approaches to* cultural differences
Used separately	Be combined
Static, rigid	Oscillating, swinging
Black and white	Light grey to dark grey
'Either-or'	'Both-and'

Source: Adapted from Barmeyer (2000, p. 129).

Cybernetics describes the structure, functions and laws (such as self-regulation, linear and non-linear back coupling) of systems (Wiener, 1948):

> Think of collectivism as water and individualism as molecules of ice. As the temperature changes, the ice crystals expand. At all times you have some water and some ice. Thus cultures have both collectivist and individualist elements all the time and are changing all the time. At any one point of time, we take a picture of the culture when we really should be taking a movie of constantly changing elements. In this metaphor, the earth is entering a new ice age! (Triandis, 1995, pp. 173-174)

Similar approaches of cultural dynamics concern cultural paradoxes (Osland & Bird, 2000). They reveal that cultures cannot be positioned on a certain point on a continuum between dichotomies, as indicated by classical cultural approaches (for example Hofstede et al., 2010; Hampden-Turner & Trompenaars, 2020), but rather represent both sides of the continuum. This is the case when people within a certain culture behave differently than suggested by cultural studies. For example, a person from a collectivist culture can adopt individualist behaviour; and a person from an individualist culture can take on collectivist behaviour. This 'culture as paradox' perspective thus views culture as 'two sides of a coin' (Lowe et al., 2019). It assumes that every culture integrates both collectivist *and* individual, monochronic *and* polychronic characteristics, universalism *and* particularism or high power *and* low power distances. However, depending on the situation, one side can be more pronounced than the other. To solve cultural paradoxes, these approaches call for an integration of differences and for considering 'cultural dualities' (Lowe et al., 2019).

SUMMARY

In this chapter, we have explained the concept of culture and highlighted its multiple layers. It is important to remember that culture can be conceived as a value, meaning and solution system. The concept should not be reduced to national cultures, but organizations should also consider subcultures, such as organizational, functional and professional cultures, which are intertwined. Several studies have identified cultural dimensions that allow differentiating national cultures. The empirical investigations conducted by Hall, Hofstede, and Trompenaars and Hampden-Turner have become major references in the field of intercultural management. They provide insightful findings about cross-national cultural differences and can be handled in a constructive way. We have also pointed out that cultural values and dimensions are not fixed, but that they underlie dynamics and constant change. Every culture integrates various, sometimes contradictory values which can be used in a complementary way.

DISCUSSION QUESTIONS

1. How can culture be defined and what are the different concepts of culture?
2. What are the possible interactions between subcultures in organizations? Find examples.
3. What are the major cultural dimensions identified by Hall, Hofstede, and Trompenaars and Hampden-Turner? How do they manifest in your culture? Find examples from your culture and compare them to others. Regarding the Hofstede dimensions, you can visit https://www.hofstede-insights.com/country-comparison/ for comparing country scores.
4. How can cultural dimensions be handled in a constructive way?

4
Models of intercultural analysis

This chapter discusses three models for intercultural analysis, which contribute to the analytical classification and comprehension of *constructive intercultural management*. They provide guidance for the constructive design of interculturality in organizations. We will first present the three-level model, which allows analysing the relationships between micro, meso and macro levels. We will then focus on the three-step model, which helps to generate intercultural sensitivity and to facilitate the practical design of interculturality. Finally, we will present the three-factor model, which facilitates the classification of intercultural situation practices and the evaluation of influencing factors.

CHAPTER LEARNING OBJECTIVES

1. Be familiar with models for constructive intercultural analysis.
2. Know how to use the three-level model for analysing the relations between micro, meso and macro levels.
3. Understand how the three-step model can help to analyse interculturality.
4. Be able to apply the three-factor model for studying intercultural situations.
5. Be aware that these models can facilitate the constructive design of interculturality.

1.   THE THREE-LEVEL MODEL

Constructive interculturality takes place in and between social systems, which can be presented as three interrelated levels (Barmeyer, 2013). The three-level model explains the relationship between three levels of aggregation (Figure 4.1). The micro level focuses on *actors* and their interactions, the meso level concerns *organizations* and the macro level refers to *societies* in which organizations are embedded. The model indicates at which level interculturality takes place and to what extent intercultural actions can be developed.

The basic assumption of this model is that actors and their actions are embedded in a complex social system. Although this system does not determine their actions, actors cannot completely detach themselves from it. The macro level of society, in which actors have been socialized, shapes and influences the meso level of the organization and the micro level of individuals. At the same time, cultures and cultural identities can have a pluralistic effect on behaviour at work. Individuals can reveal several identity affiliations, among others, to the region, profession or generation. So, the micro level of actors, the meso level of organizations and the macro level of societies influence each other. They are systemically interrelated and interconnected. The three-level model helps to specify the level of analysis when examining culture and highlights the interdependence of actors, organizations and societies. Moreover, it attempts to consider intercultural interactions at the three levels.

Source: Adapted from Barmeyer (2010, p. 43).

Figure 4.1   The three-level model

1.1   Three Levels of Analysis

Micro level

During their socialization, actors internalize specific cultural reference and interpretation systems. In their interactions, they display certain behavioural patterns, which manifest themselves in organizations in work, leadership and management styles. Examples are the definition of objectives, decision-making, the exercise of authority, and the design and control of processes. The interaction partners act in specific *contexts*, which are often characterized by constraints, constellations of interests and power as well as by individual ideas, goals and strategies. In intercultural management, diverging ideas about organizations, strategies, roles and behaviours are of particular interest, for example, for leadership and teamwork. The quality and success of interaction between individuals largely depend on the correct interpretation of behaviours of actors from other cultures.

Meso level

Organizations are formed by actors, who are interdependent through functional descriptions and hierarchies. Intercultural communication and cooperation takes place *within* organizations, but also *between* organizations. For example, *within* organizations, intercultural communication arises through the combination of the actors' resources (knowledge, skills and experience), for example in intercultural teams. Actors, teams and organizations bring in their experience and use specific structures and processes to achieve certain goals. They are subject to organizational as well as financial objectives and constraints. Organizations also develop specific organizational cultures with values, norms, rituals and routines which create identity and can influence cooperation *between* organizations in a positive or negative way.

Macro level

Actors and organizations are embedded in *social* and *economic systems*. Within a social system, such as a national state, there are specific social, political, economic and cultural institutions. They represent a system of orientation and reference and thus influence the meaning and interpretation of individuals. Intercultural management should take into account institutional factors such as educational systems and laws *and* cultural factors such as values, norms and practices when analysing interactions and organizations, because actions are neither acontextual nor ahistorical.

1.2 New Dynamics of Multiple Cultures

As a result of societal changes, each level becomes increasingly pluralistic. Intercultural and multicultural influences lead to the emergence and coexistence of multiple cultures that affect inner- and interpersonal processes. At the *micro level*, there are increasingly more people with intercultural backgrounds. At the *meso level*, teams and organizations become more heterogenous and multicultural, and are thus characterized by cultural diversity. At the *macro level*, societies are confronted with cultural transfer and transformation processes through migra-

Table 4.1 Extended three-level model involving multiple cultures and constructive interculturality

Level	Concerned areas	Forms of multiple cultures	Constructive interculturality
Micro level: actors	• Communication and cooperation • Leadership and management • Identity • Language	• Intercultural identities, multiple cultural affiliations	• Personal development, satisfaction and fulfilment • Appreciation of interculturality • *Boundary spanning* and cultural mediation for constructive communication and exchange
Meso level: organizations	• Organizational structures and cultures	• Intercultural teams • Organizational diversity • Born globals and multinational companies • Functional cultures	• Achievement of objectives, performance and value creation • Community and identity building with professional fulfilment • Creation of bicultural (leadership) dyads and cross-functional, intercultural teams
Macro level: societies	• Social, political, economic and cultural institutions	• Multicultural societies	• Harmonious peaceful coexistence and mastering social challenges through institutional stability and cultural complementarity

tion, globalization and digitalization. Table 4.1 presents the extended three-level model, with the consideration of multiple cultures and *constructive interculturality*.

Interculturality can be problematic at each of the three levels. Bi-, multi- or interculturality (on a micro level) often goes along with identity crises, intercultural teams (on a meso level) often have difficulty achieving their goals, and multicultural societies (on a macro-level) may face political or economic conflicts. Therefore, multiple cultures do not automatically lead to intercultural complementarity and synergy. The ambition of this book is therefore to show how *constructive interculturality* can be achieved through specific actions.

2.   THE THREE-STEP MODEL

The three-step model helps to differentiate the specifics of cultural systems (step 1), to conduct cultural comparison (step 2) and to develop interculturality (step 3) (Barmeyer, 2012a, p. 46) (Figure 4.2). The three-step model is an *integrative* development model for individuals and organizations, whose successive application can uncover 'blind spots' and minimize ethnocentrism. Steps 1 and 2 help to overcome ethnocentrism and thus enable intercultural learning processes in step 3, which is essential for the *constructive* design of interculturality in organizations.

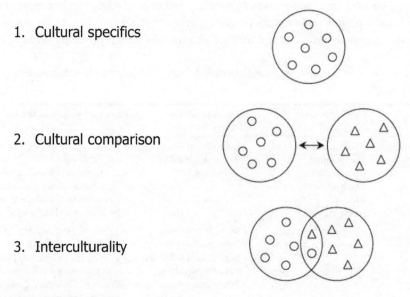

1. Cultural specifics

2. Cultural comparison

3. Interculturality

Figure 4.2   The three-step model

Cultural specifics generally provide insights into cultural and institutional characteristics and provide a description of a cultural system. *Cultural comparison* comprises the search for similarities and differences between cultural systems. It can lead to the relativization of one's own cultural points of view and assumptions, and thus an appreciation of elements of other systems. Understanding *interculturality* can lead to reciprocal intercultural development and learning processes that allow for a combination of different cultural elements and possibly the formation of a new hybrid culture. It is necessary to differentiate 'emic' and 'etic' approaches for conducting intercultural analyses (Box 4.1).

BOX 4.1   ETIC AND EMIC APPROACHES FOR INTERCULTURAL ANALYSIS

When describing cultural systems, intercultural management differentiates between 'emic' (culturally adapted) and 'etic' (cross-cultural) approaches. Originating from linguistics (Pike, 1954), the two terms present an analogy to the sound structure of phonetics and phonemics. While *phonetics* describes the sound of languages in general, phonemics is concerned with signifying units, that is phonemes, of a particular language. A phoneme is the smallest unit of sound that distinguishes one word from another in a language. The emic approach is therefore culture-specific.

Accordingly, the *emic* approach assumes that certain attitudes and behaviours are unique to a certain culture, depend on the respective social context and do not allow for cross-cultural comparison. The goal of *emic* approaches is thus to describe inherent cultural characteristics of only one or few specific cultures.

Contrariwise, the *etic* approach assumes that cultures are comparable along universal, culture-independent categories, for example through cultural dimensions which apply to all societies or social groups. The goal of *etic* approaches is thus to develop objective standards for cultural comparisons.

Sources: Based on Bhawuk and Triandis (1996); Headland et al. (1990).

The three steps allow understanding the processes and outcomes of intercultural interactions, which can be either problematic or enriching. After the description and analysis of cultural characteristics of a system (step 1), specific characteristics are contrasted (step 2) before *constructive* intercultural interaction processes can be developed (step 3). Table 4.2 presents the three steps with their objectives and their relevance for organizations.

In the following, the three-step model is illustrated by exemplary studies which aim to contribute to a better understanding of cultural specifics, differences and interactions, and thus a more accurate interpretation of behaviours.

2.1   Culture-Specific Studies

There are numerous studies that attempt to describe cultural characteristics, mostly in the form of national country studies. In line with an emic approach, they emphasize peculiarities that show certain continuity and can be explained by history and social institutions. The existence of *cultural specifics* suggests that people as carriers of culture are integrated into historical and institutional contexts with specific structures and processes. In such social systems, values

Table 4.2   The three-step model

Step	Objectives	Relevance for organizations
Step 1: Cultural specifics *Contextual:* Description, analysis and interpretation of characteristics of one or few particular contexts, for example institutions, values and cultural practices	Identifying and explaining cultural characteristics in depth	*Awareness*: Cultural elements have emerged in a specific context, based on assumptions about processes, structures and relationships between actors
Step 2: Cultural comparison *Static and contrastive:* Comparison of characteristics shows relative differences	Contrasting a limited number of cultural characteristics and putting one's own cultural system into perspective Searching for similarities and differences	*Knowledge*: Comparison leads to the questioning and relativization of a universal/universalistic thinking
Step 3: Interculturality *Processual and interactive:* Analysis of values and cultural practices (in intercultural processes) and symbolic actions due to divergent meanings and interpretations	Analysing irritations and misunderstandings in intercultural interactions Understanding processes and forms of complementary or synergetic hybrid culture that arises through social negotiation	*Action*: Development of intercultural interactions and transfer processes in and between organizations through *awareness* and *knowledge* about cultural specifics and cultural differences

and practices develop and shape ways of thinking and acting, which do not necessarily occur in other systems. The aim is therefore to understand the characteristics of cultural systems, their institutions and their history (Box 4.2).

BOX 4.2   CULTURAL IDEAL TYPES

Culture specifics can be described with Max Weber's *ideal types*. According to the German sociologist, an ideal type is a rational, empirical and logical construction,

> which helps us to answer the question as to what a behaviour pattern or thought pattern (for example a philosophical system) would be like if it possessed completely rational, empirical and logical *correctness* and *consistency*. [...] The construction of such a rationally *correct utopia* or *ideal* is, however, only one of the various possible forms of the *ideal type*. (Weber, 1949[2017], p. 42)

The ideal type represents optimal logical rationality and 'its function is the comparison with empirical reality in order to establish its divergences or similarities, to describe them with the most unambiguously intelligible concepts, and to understand and explain them causally' (Weber, 1949[2017], p. 43). It is a construct that highlights certain aspects of social reality, especially those considered as essential.

Source: Based on Weber (1949[2017]).

In the sense of ideal types, culture can be illustrated by metaphors, that is, symbolic or pictorial representations that are associated with certain countries often linked to national history, education and politics. These *emic* metaphors consider the uniqueness of societies rather than universally comparable – *etic* – dimensions. They rely on characteristics of specific phenomena in societies and thus address their dynamics and contradictions. However, metaphors are not to be conceived as stereotypes. Table 4.3 presents metaphors associated with selected countries (Gannon & Pillai, 2016).

Table 4.3 Cultural metaphors

Metaphor	Explanation
Brazilian Samba	• Small-step circularity of the dance represents economic advancement. • Physical proximity during the dance represents its importance in society. • Mixing business and social life. • Samba rhythm expresses cultural complexity.
Estonian Singing	• Estonia claims to have 133 000 recorded folk songs. • Lyrics convey Estonian history and have preserved Estonian language. • Occupation by Swedes, Danes, Germans and Russians. • Singing as tool of political struggle: 'The Singing Revolution'. • Global audience: Estonia as pioneer for digital technology (e-Estonia).
Finnish Sauna	• Living in harmony with nature. • Equality: everyone is equal in a sauna, there are no symbols of social status, which indicates flat managerial hierarchies. • Active silence: respecting the privacy of others. • Sauna as a symbol of cleanliness: clarity of individual moral and physical responsibilities.
German Symphony	• Importance of discipline, (written) rules and order. • Collective interaction is coordinated by the conductor as a leader, importance of consensus. • Preference for precision and synchronicity. • Positional arrangement of musicians: security and home as 'safe haven'. • Communication style: Germans do not interrupt, each instrument is heard until the end.
Indian Dance of Shiva	• Dancing as the most important of the ancient arts (tradition orientation). • The dance symbolizes the cycle of construction, existence, destruction and re-incarnation as the main driving forces of Indian society (harmony and chaos).
Nigerian Market Place	• Market place as a place of diversity (ethnicities) where every commodity seems available. • Importance of the community in Nigerian culture. • Represents social dynamism: energy, vigour and adaptability. • Market place balancing tradition and modernity. • Status differences reflected by product diversity.
American Football	• Pregame party: taking place in parking lots at the stadium, everyone is friendly, although they do not know one another personally. • Individualized achievement: everyone has a specialized role to play. • As in business, there is both cooperation and competition. • Huddling: coming together of the team to strategize and motivate.

Source: Based on Gannon and Pillai (2016).

The French social scientist Philippe d'Iribarne (2012) used a qualitative approach to analyse the influence of national cultures on organizations, management and work behaviour. He believes that, in every society, there exist relatively uniform emotional elements to avoid the occurrence of fear. Cultural worldviews are rooted in the opposition between a 'fundamental concern' shared by the members of a society and the means that enable them to avoid this associated fear. The existence of a basic concern does not mean that there are no other concerns, but these do not necessarily affect the functioning of organizations (Chevrier, 2016, p. 233). Box 4.3 presents one of his emblematic case studies.

BOX 4.3   IDEAL-TYPICAL CHARACTERISTICS OF FRANCE, THE NETHERLANDS AND THE UNITED STATES

In one of his case studies, d'Iribarne analyses the functioning of a French multinational company in France, the Netherlands and the United States. The production plants examined in the three countries use identical machines and are similarly productive, but each organization is characterized by its own management style embedded in the national context. D'Iribarne explains the observed differences by ideal-typical characteristics:

In France, relationships are governed by the 'logic of honour'. Each individual has a specific rank with certain privileges (rights) and obligations, and performs tasks attributed by this social position. In organizations, social status is largely determined by the profession and it is necessary to value the professional honour of employees.

In the Netherlands, relationships are based on the constant search for consensus and the respectful and tolerant way of cooperation ('logic of consensus'). In organizations, it is important to listen, discuss and explain situations to employees.

In the United States, the virtuous and equal conduct of employees in their relationships is determined by contracts, which must not be violated ('logic of contract'). In organizations, employees should be treated in accordance with political values of equality.

Source: d'Iribarne (2012).

In certain contexts, there are social practices that reflect the links between national culture, organizations and working practices. Examples are provided by *Ubuntu* in Africa, *Jeitinho* in Brazil, *Guanxi* in China, *Wasta* in Egypt, *Système D* in France and *Jante's law* in Scandinavia. Their impact on societies and management are summarized in Table 4.4. Box 4.4 highlights the role of gatekeeping in Chinese *Guanxi* networks, and Box 4.5 explains how Chinese *Guanxi* and African *Ubuntu* practices can influence human resource management of Chinese companies investing in Africa.

Table 4.4 Culture-specific social practices in national and regional contexts

Concept/ Cultural context	Definition and origin	Impact on management
African *Ubuntu* (Lutz, 2009)	Recognition of the mutual relevance of individuals for one's own success and responsibility for the community	Respectful and appreciative cooperation and the emphasis on one's own dependence on the organization lead to trust-worthy cooperation.
Brazilian *Jeitinho* (Duarte, 2006)	Informal approach based on social capital and networks to solve difficult (bureaucratic) problems by circumventing or breaking rules	Questions of favours, compliance and adherence to rules in business should be interpreted and handled in a flexible way.
Chinese *Guanxi* (Milliot, 2016)	System of personal relationships and dependencies to reduce uncertainty and opportunistic behaviour *Mianzi* ('face'), the respect of the social status of an individual, is a key component of *Guanxi*	Building and developing *Guanxi* is necessary to compete with local companies. Access to key decision-makers is difficult for foreign managers.
French *Système D* (Barmeyer, 2000)	Achieving goals and solving problems through imaginative and creative use of resources. Flexible and targeted reaction to unpredictable situations using common sense	Reduction of the originally required amount of work and time to achieve a 'good' result. Making the impossible possible and overcoming bureaucratic structures.
Maghreb/Middle East *Wasta* (Mohamed & Mohamad, 2011)	Network building to ensure loyalty and trust in key positions and hierarchies Despite its widespread use, it is considered immoral by Islam faith	Foreign companies need to be aware of and sensitized to the concept to build up a network of people with influential positions.
Scandinavian *Jante's law* (Smith et al., 2003)	Canonical self-limitation and self-suppression to promote individual modesty as a success factor for the collective	Reserved and collegial behaviour should not be seen as a weakness or a lack of assertiveness, but rather as a personal 'sacrifice' for team success.

BOX 4.4 GATEKEEPING IN CHINESE *GUANXI* NETWORKS

The access to Chinese *Guanxi* networks represents a challenging task for foreign companies. Therefore, they often work with relational gatekeepers who can facilitate the development of relationships between in-group and out-group members of *Guanxi* networks in an intercultural context. Relational gatekeepers accomplish (1) reciprocal, (2) adaptive and (3) symbolic roles. First, they can facilitate the establishment of trust, commitment and reciprocal arrangements, assuring *Guanxi* insiders that the support of outsiders will be reciprocated in the future. This is why Guanxi insiders accept to work with outsiders through their facilitation. Second, gatekeepers are able to adapt the responses from outsiders to the expectations of insiders, which is particularly important when the rules and norms of both parties appear to be contradictory. They have the ability to develop creative 'translations' of conflicting norms and rules so that the involved individuals feel comfortable with the proposed solutions. Third, gatekeepers can understand implicit and emotional signals from insiders and respond to them in a symbolic way. Chinese people avoid expressing their thoughts and feelings, and 'losing face'. They expect a symbolic response to their emotional signals to build trust relationships. *Guanxi* gatekeepers can therefore facilitate intercultural interactions and help foreign outsiders to reach decision-makers in local business networks.

Source: Gao et al. (2014).

BOX 4.5   WHEN CHINESE *GUANXI* MEETS AFRICAN *UBUNTU* PRACTICES

When Chinese companies invest in Africa, they need to deal with a diverse cultural, economic and institutional environment, which strongly affects their human resource management (HRM) practices. Some companies have succeeded in adopting crossvergence HRM practices, mixing divergent contextual factors and convergent cultural factors. They rely on the cultural proximity between African *Ubuntu*, based on relationship, community and loyalty, and Chinese *Guanxi* and Confucianism, based on harmony, benevolence and family values. This cultural proximity can strengthen the consideration of local employee benefits by Chinese managers and promote the sense of belonging of local employees to the Chinese parent company. Chinese managers need to adapt to the local environment before levering cultural influences to improve local employee commitment and work efficiency. Developing crossvergence HRM practices requires time and patience. Intercultural training and mutual learning between Chinese managers and African employees can facilitate this challenging process. It is necessary that Chinese multinationals consider indigenous cultural factors seriously when designing and implementing HRM practices in their African subsidiaries. Governmental agencies, business consultants and educational institutions can support the intercultural understanding and thus contribute to the performance of Chinese investments in Africa.

Source: Based on Xing et al. (2016).

2.2   Comparative Studies

Cultural specifics often become clear through contrast, when cultures are compared with each other. In the sense of *constructive intercultural management*, the aim of cultural contrast is to relativize culture-specific points of view and to broaden one's own horizon by opening up and recognizing differences. By doing so, individuals might develop an ethnorelativist attitude.

Comparative studies of culture do exist with etic and emic approaches. Examples of etic approaches are Hofstede's study on cultural dimensions (Chapter 3) and the GLOBE study

(Chapter 6). Such studies attempt to map cultures along established cultural dimensions and classify value orientation using scales and measures. Emic approaches primarily refer to qualitative studies, which compare only a few countries or cultural contexts highlighting their respective peculiarities. An example is provided by Usunier's (2019) studies on the dealing with time (Table 4.5).

Table 4.5 Cultural comparison of time

Cultural orientation	Examples
(1) *Economicity of time: is time money?*	United States, most European countries
• Time as a scarce resource	
• Waiting is perceived as a waste of time	
(2) *Monochronic vs. polychronic time*	Northern Europe, United States
• Monochronic time: one task at one time	China, Japan, Latin America
• Polychronic time: multiple tasks at the same time	
(3) *Linear, cyclical or procedural time*	
Linearity:	Europe, Anglo-Saxon countries
• Time is perceived as an arrow	
• As a scarce resource, time can be measured and scheduled	
• Manifests in language: time can be saved, spent or wasted	
Cyclicity:	Asia
• Time is perceived as a circle	
• Oriented towards nature (recurrence of natural seasons)	
• Reincarnation in religions	
Procedurality:	Africa
• Emphasis on the process of doing things rather than on results	
(4) *Past, present or future orientation*	
Past orientation:	Europe
• Emphasizing the role of the past for the present	
• Restoration of buildings	
• Teaching of history	
Present orientation:	Arab cultures
• Favour the 'here and now'	
• Humans do not decide about the future, rather God	
Future orientation:	Anglo-Saxon countries
• Assumption that nature can be mastered and future predicted or influenced	
Special case: *Makimono* time	Japan
• Combines different types of time, with the past flowing into the present and the present flowing into the future (continuity and simultaneous existence of past, present and future)	

Source: Based on Usunier (2019).

Time is a central concept in intercultural management. The perception of time has a significant impact on business negotiations, marketing and strategic action. We can identify four dimensions of cross-cultural differences dealing with time: (1) economicity of time, (2) monochronic vs. polychronic use of time, (3) linearity, cyclicity or procedurality and (4) time orientation towards the past, present or future (Usunier, 2019).

Another example of cultural comparison is Davoine and Ravasi's study (2013) on national career paths in top management. Based on the findings on career paths by Evans et al. (1989), the study shows the characteristics of profiles for elite career development in four countries: France, Germany, Great Britain and Switzerland (Table 4.6). There is a relative stability in the legitimacy-creating educational prerequisites and career models embedded in national institutional contexts. These include, for example, the high status of doctoral degrees in Germany, the prestige of *Grandes Ecoles* (elite higher education institutions) in France and the importance of Masters of Business Administration in Great Britain. At the same time, internationalization is slowly changing classical career paths.

Table 4.6 Comparing profiles of top executives

France	• Role of *Grandes Ecoles* • Senior civil service • Importance of networks
Germany	• Importance of titles, such as the doctoral degree (knowledge) • Limited inter-company mobility • Step-by-step career before reaching top management positions • 'Mountain climber careers'
Great Britain	• Smaller percentage of university graduates • Education in public schools and professional institutes • Importance of Master of Business Administration (MBA)
Switzerland	• Hybrid national model of top management careers • Highly international profiles • Laboratory for the new global managerial elite

Source: Based on Davoine and Ravasi (2013).

2.3　Intercultural Studies

Intercultural studies consider the dynamics, processes and outcomes of intercultural interaction. *Constructive intercultural management* is particularly interested in the positive results of interculturality, such as creativity, innovation or the development of a hybrid culture. The three-step model, which is based on the knowledge of cultural specifics (step 1) and the awareness of contrasts through cultural comparison (step 2), pays particular attention to the level of interculturality (step 3). The aim is to consciously design interculturality in a *constructive* way, for example by changing and adapting behaviour through learning about cultural specifics, similarities and differences.

An example is provided by the study on a French non-governmental organization (NGO) that attempts to provide sustainable, innovative responses to the challenges of poverty and inequalities (Chevrier, 2011). One project concerns the development of farming through microfinancing in Vietnam. The empirical investigation is based on the understanding of culture developed by d'Iribarne (2009, p. 318) who considers that culture concerns the interactive (re-) production of meaning and interpretation patterns shared by a particular group of individuals. The study follows three steps:

In the first step, systems of meaning and interpretation of both cultures are analysed. It appears that the position of French employees is largely determined by role and status, and that they have strong convictions that they defend. There is a tendency to separate private and professional life. Task descriptions serve more for orientation and leave room for interpretation, which encourages individual creativity and initiative. For the French, employees act competently when they achieve goals by resorting to different solutions. In contrast, for Vietnamese employees, family relationships and membership of certain groups are essential. Relationships represent obligations, and they are prioritized over labour relations with 'strangers'. Employees do not express their opinion directly, and superiors are not openly contradicted. Vietnamese employees expect managers to provide detailed instructions and approaches to solutions for achieving the objectives. Competent employees have the know-how to solve a task and further develop their skills.

In the second step, the two cultures are compared by identifying differences between their systems of meaning that emerge in intercultural interactions, especially with regard to individual autonomy, authority and work ethics (Table 4.7).

Table 4.7   Systems of meaning in France and Vietnam

Characteristics	French perspective	Vietnamese perspective
Individual autonomy	Changes of opinion as a sign of inconsistency	Social system is more important than professional obligations
Authority	Strict supervision as a sign of limited trust	Perceived distance through limited support and exchange of information
Work ethics	The focus is on the achievement of objectives	The focus is on processes with detailed instructions.

Source: Based on Chevrier (2011).

In the third step, learning processes are put in place to *constructively* combine cultural elements and favour the formation of a new hybrid culture within the organization.

Another study is a case on Chinese–Tanzanian interculturality, which was developed with a private Chinese information technology company operating in Tanzania. The objective was to explore (step 1) and compare (step 2) the perceptions of interculturality on both sides. The findings show that challenges emerge in different fields, for example in decision-making, management styles, working conditions and knowledge-sharing. They also indicate how both sides can contribute to improve intercultural interaction (step 3) (Mayer et al., 2017, 2019) (Table 4.8).

Table 4.8   Interculturality in a Chinese company in Tanzania

Chinese perception of Tanzanians	Tanzanian perception of Chinese
• Lack of time management • Lack of experts and skills • Influenced by Western management, disobedient • Corruption and bankruptcy • Lack of work ethic • Low effectivity and work-output	• Arrogance and superiority • Disrespectful, 'bossy', result-oriented • Missing social responsibility • Limited interpersonal interaction, no integration in society, show no interest in the local culture • Do not believe in God • Unwilling to learn the local language: Kiswahili
Indications for improvement	
Tanzanians should	**Chinese should…**
• Understand Chinese culture, language and history • Respect principles of Chinese culture: fast, hard-working (16 hours a day) and important use of high technology • Accept that Chinese do not believe in God • Strive for sound planning, goal achievement and efficiency • Keep to deadlines • Follow the truth and be honest	• Use English and Swahili language to make friends • Collect information about Tanzanian history over the last 100 years • Know Tanzanian lifestyle, tribal culture, dressing and food habits • Respect Tanzanians • Recognize that most Tanzanians believe in God • Take care of nature

Source: Based on Mayer et al. (2017, 2019).

3.   THE THREE-FACTOR MODEL

The *three-factor model* differentiates three types of factors that are likely to influence intercultural interaction situations: (1) actors, (2) cultures and (3) institutions (Figure 4.3).

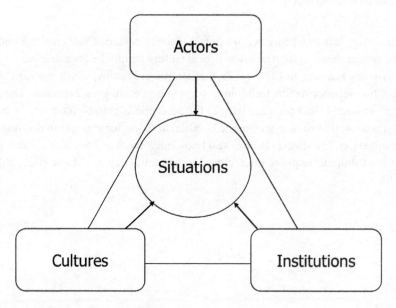

Figure 4.3   The three-factor model

The model shows the interaction of the three factors and relativizes the influence of national culture. For example, the behaviour of actors from other cultures can cause surprise, irritation or even annoyance. The question arises to what extent such reactions are due to the personality or cultural affiliation of the interaction partner, or due to institutional influences. The three-factor model emphasizes the necessity to analyse interculturality from different perspectives. Indeed, culture is only *one* influencing and explanatory factor. When analysing intercultural situations, two other factors should therefore be considered: actors and institutions (Barmeyer & Haupt, 2016).

3.1 Actors, Cultures and Institutions

Actors

Actors play an important role for designing organizations and intercultural encounters: they participate in the creation and development of relationships, and thus influence and shape interculturality within and between organizations (Box 4.6). Actor-centred perspectives are becoming more popular in intercultural management, especially with the ambition to manage interculturality *constructively*.

BOX 4.6 MICROPOLITICS OF ACTORS

The two sociologists Michel Crozier and Erhard Friedberg (1979) have examined the micropolitics of actors within organizations. The focus is on the acquisition, development and use of freedom and power through 'playing'. Playing is understood as 'a concrete mechanism by means of which people structure and regulate their power relationships and yet allow themselves freedom' (Crozier & Friedberg, 1979, p. 68). Culture – and an implicit determinacy of thought and behaviour as well as an assumed non-strategic attitude of the actors – plays only a limited role in the 'strategies of actors'.

Source: Based on Crozier and Friedberg (1979).

Cultures

Intercultural management assumes that difficulties in cross-border interactions are due to culture and/or cultural differences. This assumption must certainly be critically questioned. Some intercultural consultants and trainers almost missionarily practise 'intercultural educational work' in organizations and point out to managers the unconsidered 'blind spot' culture (Romani & Szkudlarek, 2014). Culture does sometimes explain situations, but sometimes it does not, and then actors and institutions come into play.

Institutions

Institutions form the framework that organizes, enables and limits social action. They can be understood as regulative and normative elements, shaping economic and social life (Scott, 2014). Institutions manifest themselves in concrete, legally sanctionable rules and laws as well as in binding, moral norms and societal expectations. They also shape fundamental ideas and assumptions that are taken for granted and whose violation can result in irritation and misunderstandings (Rose et al., 2021).

3.2　The Three-Factor Model and Constructive Interculturality

The three factors interact with each other and influence intercultural situations. The application of the model allows understanding to which extent culture plays a role, or other influencing factors, namely actors and institutions. Table 4.9 shows attributes associated with the three influencing factors.

For the *constructive* design of interculturality in organizations, it is important to analyse how actors, cultures and institutions complement and interact with each other. Actors play a central role in the sense that they can influence and control culture, institutions and situations. Culture and institutions are only partially controllable.

In conflictual situations, knowledge about culture and interculturality helps to relativize misunderstandings and supposed 'personal attacks'. It is also necessary to take into account the personality and personal ambitions of actors as well as their cultural socialization and institutional constraints, which are likely to influence behaviour. Being aware of these factors allows maintaining a more 'relaxed' attitude and to adopt a more objectivist perspective on intercultural (conflictual) situations. It is even possible to develop a positive attitude towards the foreign culture, which can lead to the willingness to appreciate other cultural elements and integrate them into one's own behaviour and culture.

Table 4.9　Allocation of elements in the three-factor model

Influencing factors	Attributes
Actors: shaping and influencing	• Personality • Interests and 'hidden agendas' • Experience • Training and education • Characteristics and attitudes • Position and function • Competences (technical, intercultural, communicative, foreign language, leadership)
Culture: partially controllable	• Expectations and perceptions • Patterns of perception and stereotypes • Meaning and sense (symbols), interpretations • Communication and language • Practices • Values and norms (cultural dimensions) • Organizational culture • Professional culture
Institutions: partially controllable	• Socio-economic environment: market, politics, competitive situation • History • Vocational training system and education • Laws, rules and standards

Source: Based on Barmeyer and Haupt (2016).

SUMMARY

In this chapter, we have presented three models for intercultural analysis, which can facilitate the constructive design of interculturality in organizations. The three-level model allows distinguishing different levels of intercultural interactions as well as analysing the interrelations between micro, meso and macro levels. The three-step model helps to differentiate the specifics of cultural systems before conducting cultural comparisons and developing interculturality. The three-factor model highlights three types of factors – actors, cultures and institutions – that are likely to influence intercultural situations. Applying the three models can enable organizations to analyse and design interculturality in a constructive way.

DISCUSSION QUESTIONS

1. How can the three-level model be used for analysing intercultural situations? Provide your own examples of interculturality on the three levels.
2. How can the three-step model help organizations to develop interculturality? Find examples of the three steps either from your own culture or other cultures.
3. How can the three-factor model be applied for understanding intercultural situations?
4. Why can the three models contribute to constructive interculturality?

5
Negotiated interculturality

This chapter focuses on the constructive negotiation of interculturality. First, we will specify the concept of interculturality, which can be understood as a social negotiation process, and the impact of critical incidents. Second, we will present several forms and concepts of negotiated interculturality, namely the construction of a third culture, dilemma theory and negotiated culture. Third, we will consider negotiated interculturality as a dynamic interaction process in which actors are likely to change their cultural practices while pursuing their interests and objectives.

CHAPTER LEARNING OBJECTIVES

1. Understand the concept of interculturality and the possible impact of critical incidents.
2. Analyse the role of contextualization and actors in cultural negotiation.
3. Be aware of different forms of negotiated interculturality.
4. Perceive interculturality as a constructive negotiation process.

1.   INTERCULTURALITY AND INTERCULTURAL INTERACTIONS

In intercultural management situations, there exists a constant – conscious or unconscious – negotiation of different positions, options and decisions: which objectives will be pursued? Which strategies and tactics are applied? Which ideas, decisions or solutions appear reasonable, feasible and acceptable? Which organizational practices are implemented? Who will participate in their implementation?

Due to different cultural imprints, professional socialization and experience, individuals have their own ideas about the *good* and *right* solution. If these ideas are not sufficiently communicated, unspoken divergences of ideas might complicate successful intercultural cooperation.

1.1   What is Interculturality?

The central premise for the constructive approach is to understand interculturality as a dialectical process that moves between differences and that serves the development of individuals and groups. Interculturality can be defined as a reciprocal and dialogical, if possible symmetrical, process of negotiation, communication and cooperation between actors in which adaptation, learning and development take place. It includes processes of exchange, interaction, understanding, interpretation and construction, but also of surprise and irritation, which can lead to transformation and change in social systems. It is necessary to differentiate the concepts of interculturality, multiculturality and transculturality (Box 5.1 and Figure 5.1).

BOX 5.1   INTERCULTURALITY, MULTICULTURALITY AND TRANSCULTURALITY

Interculturality: negotiation of (new) rules of communication and behaviour which, as a result of mutual interpretation and adaptation processes, may differ from those in the respective cultures of the involved individuals.

Multiculturality: the coexistence of members from different cultures within *one* social system, for example in a country, *with limited interaction*.

Transculturality: blurring of cultural boundaries through networking and interconnectedness of many elements which belong to multiple cultures. Emergence of communities carrying pluralistic cultural identities.

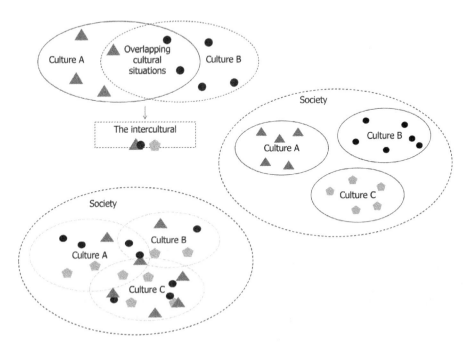

Figure 5.1   Interculturality, multiculturality and transculturality

Interculturality becomes relevant when people from different cultures meet in organizations or teams and when individuals reveal multiple cultural value orientations, meaning systems or knowledge. *Inter*, to be translated as 'between', 'mutual' or 'mediating', suggests that intercultural situations might result in the emergence of something new. Interculturality is thus created when one's own and foreign elements become significant in interaction and when there are mutual relationships between individuals. In intercultural situations, individuals might perceive the ambiguous, vague and novel either as something threatening or stimulating, depending on the context and the situation.

1.2   Critical Incidents

Interculturality can take various forms, which in their extreme are either 'positive' and constructive or 'negative' and destructive. The aim of this book is to develop complementary and synergetic facets of interculturality. Nevertheless, it is also necessary to attach particular importance to problematic intercultural situations, so-called critical incidents (Box 5.2).

BOX 5.2   DEFINITION OF CRITICAL INCIDENTS

A critical incident, also called 'critical interaction situation' (Flanagan, 1954), is an event in which misunderstandings arise between interaction partners in intercultural encounters. These misunderstandings are significant to the interaction partners and triggered by cultural differences such as diverging norms, interpretation or value systems. Interaction partners perceive the other cultural partners' behaviour as strange, irritating or even infringing, and the different behaviour causes emotional reactions in one or both partners (Batchelder, 1993).

Intercultural misunderstandings and conflicts mostly arise unintentionally and for initially inexplicable reasons. Intercultural conflicts therefore significantly differ from *intracultural* conflicts (for example conflicts of goals, power or interests). In principle, actors show a will and interest for successful communication and cooperation. Critical incidents can be explored by 'thick description' (Geertz, 1973), based on 'situational frames' (Hall, 1981) that represent parts of the complex cultural reality, at a certain time and in a certain context.

The situational frame is the smallest viable unit of culture that can be analysed, taught, transmitted, and handed down as a complete entity. Frames contain linguistic, kinesic, proxemic, temporal, social, material, personality, and other components. The framing concept is important not just because it provides the basis for identifying analytic units that are manageable when put in the hands of the expert, but framing can be useful when learning a new culture. [...] Frames represent the materials and contexts in which action occurs – the modules on which all planning should be based. [...] In other words, a situation is a complete entity, just as a sentence is a complete entity. Situational frames are the building blocks of both individual lives and institutions and are the meeting point of: the individual and his psychic makeup, institutions ranging from marriage to large bureaucracies, and culture, which gives meaning to the other two. (Hall, 1981, pp. 129 and 140)

An example of a critical incident, observed in the Brazilian subsidiary of a German multinational, is provided in Box 5.3.

BOX 5.3 CRITICAL INCIDENT 'YELLOW IS NOT YELLOW'

The critical incident happened in a German family owned multinational producing construction machinery. The Brazilian plant of the company imports the parts manufactured in Germany and installs them on site to assemble the entire machine. The corporate design specifies that the machines must be painted with the yellow varnish of the parent company to ensure global corporate identity. Due to import barriers and cost issues, the Brazilian subsidiary decided, against the company's internal regulations, to buy the varnish from a local supplier. The colour appeared to be the same (both are yellow). The Brazilian plant used the varnish of the local supplier for manufactured parts whereas the parts coming from Germany were painted by the German supplier. The parts were assembled into complete machines, which were delivered to local customers.

During a visit to Brazil, the German managers noticed that the Brazilian machines had two yellow tones: one was the yellow of the Brazilian supplier, the other was the yellow established by the parent company. The German managers raised the issue with the local production manager who was not concerned by the 'two-tone' look: 'The machine works! What is the problem?' For the German managers, the situation was clear: the machines must no longer be delivered! The quality image of the brand could suffer serious damage if customers complained. And there was the important company value 'Highest quality in everything we do'. In Brazil, however, the issue was not taken seriously by the local team.

Source: Based on Bausch et al. (2020).

Critical incidents often focus on conflictual elements in intercultural interactions. Although the term 'critical' has a negative connotation, such incidents can also be positive or neutral. Therefore, the term is occasionally replaced by terms such as 'cultural analyses' or 'awareness episodes' (Batchelder, 1993, p. 102). Critical incidents can be considered as a starting point for personal development and intercultural learning.

1.3   Interculturality as a Negotiation Process

To understand and design interculturality in organizations, it is necessary to take into account the cultural contexts and involved actors.

1.3.1   The role of contextualization in cultural negotiation

Contextualization concerns the consideration of meaningful elements in the social and organizational environment, which influence human action and which contribute to its development. Contextual elements include a variety of factors, for example, the cultural background of interaction partners, language, the historical, institutional, legal and educational environment, structures and processes as well as the actors' strategies and tactics. Contexts are therefore highly differentiated, with numerous constellations of actors and relationships.

Intercultural relationships are often shaped by the distribution of power within and between organizations. Power asymmetry, that is constellations of super- and subordination, can lead to pressure for adaptation, for example from the minority to the majority or from the employee to the manager. In a similar way, headquarters often hold a predominant position and thus determine the strategy and processes, whereas subsidiaries are considered as executing sites. The same holds true for acquiring companies in cross-border acquisitions. Legal and financial resources then legitimize the decision-making power of headquarters and acquirers (Mayrhofer, 2013).

There are also contexts where power is distributed more equally, for example in temporary project teams, in network organizations or in joint ventures in which both parties collaborate on an equal basis. Even in such situations, certain actors tend to assert their interests and force the interaction partners to make 'tacit' adjustments. In this case, the 'weaker' actor is more affected by possible (financial or emotional) costs of interculturality.

1.3.2   The role of actors in cultural negotiation

To assess the dynamics of intercultural interaction, we need to remember that, besides the context, it is also the actors themselves who bring in their cultural imprints and perceptions.

As suggested by comparative management studies (for example Hofstede et al., 2010), bipolar continua, such as cultural dimensions (Chapter 3), can be used to describe individual behaviours in organizations, assuming relatively homogeneous and stable national cultures. This 'national culture model' considers that cultures collide as distinct entities like 'billiard balls' and, to stay with the metaphor, even repel each other: 'by endowing nations, societies, or cultures with the qualities of internally homogeneous and externally distinctive and bounded objects, we create a model of the world as a global pool hall in which the entities spin off each other like so many hard and round billiard balls' (Wolf, 1982, p. 6).

Opposites can fulfil different functions of interculturality: they contribute to balance and adjustment, to the relativization of perspectives and self-evident facts, they create awareness and enable the adoption of meta-levels. However, the prevailing dichotomies of cultural characteristics consider neither contextual factors nor individual cultural imprints, which are essential for the development of hybrid, that is culturally diverse, organizations (Brannen & Salk, 2000). Indeed, cultural identities and behaviours of individuals are redefined in intercultural situations. They overlap and develop.

For example, intercultural individuals possess a core identity and peripheral identities. The main identity is always present and serves as an anchor, while the peripheral identities are 'switched on or off', depending on the situations and the contexts. These individuals integrate different ways of thinking, and they can therefore switch between cultural frames and accordingly adapt to their communication partners or to task-related issues. This concept, called 'cultural frame switching', refers to the ability to shift between multiple cultural contexts and their respective interpretation systems.

Cultural frames are developed through individual sense-making activities in an iterative process (Su, 2015):

(1)   *Enactment* concerns the cultural knowledge of individuals, which can be leveraged during social interactions to interpret and respond to other people, who belong to the same or other organizations. The repertoire of cultural knowledge is based on the cultural background, training and experience of individuals.

(2)   *Alignment* means that individuals can align their enacted cultural frames to different degrees with the cultural frames of others. Discrepancy between cultural knowledge structures can lead to misalignment, but repeated interactions enable individuals to incorporate or delete certain cultural elements. Individuals thus have the possibility to transform (change key elements or generate new ones), amplify (strengthen key elements), extend (integrate new elements) or even bridge (link unconnected frames) their cultural frames.

(3)   *Retention* means that individuals select certain cultural frames through repeated realignment. Certain cultural frames can gain increasing significance and then be enacted during subsequent interactions with other individuals from the same culture.

Box 5.4 presents the example of cultural frame switching by employees of a Chinese IT service supplier.

BOX 5.4   CULTURAL FRAME SWITCHING BY EMPLOYEES OF A CHINESE IT SERVICE SUPPLIER

In IT outsourcing relationships, employees of offshore service suppliers need to interact effectively with customers in culturally diverse environments. This is the case for the members of a Chinese IT service supplier who is serving customers located in Japan, the United States and China. The Chinese employees have to switch between cultural frames to collaborate with their customers. They have adopted different mindsets and behaviours to understand their expectations and construct appropriate responses. In the context of IT outsourcing, three dimensions of cultural knowledge are particularly important: coordination, communication and bonding, which is the development of reciprocal trust relationships.

1.   Cultural frame for interaction with Japanese customers: accepting a passive role with the objective to achieve high quality; exchanging detailed and precise information; adhering to rigorous processes while paying attention to social relationships.

2.   Cultural frame for interactions with US customers: playing an active role and engaging clients in joint problem-solving; seeking specific information through frequent interactions; following standardized processes while allowing some flexibility in execution.

3.   Cultural frame for interactions with Chinese customers: assuming an active role for managing the relationship; accepting abstract and often ambiguous information; focusing on interpersonal relationships with key stakeholders (*Guanxi*).

Source: Su (2015).

Due to the increasing number of intercultural individuals and the complexity of working environments, national categories are losing their relevance. They are considered to be too static and decontextualized, and it is necessary to consider individuals and their identity construction. Often, people with intercultural profiles feel their belonging to multiple cultures, so that they must 'choose' and 'negotiate' their own identity in intercultural situations. This process is called 'cultural identity negotiation'. When used constructively – that means, when identity and cultural frame fit within an intercultural situation – intercultural individuals can play a mediating role when cultural issues need to be negotiated within and between organizations (Yagi & Kleinberg, 2011).

Consequently, static concepts of culture cannot explain processes of adaptation, learning and development. The analysis of complex and dynamic cultures requires a conscious and action-oriented understanding of cultural differences to create constructive interculturality.

2. FORMS OF NEGOTIATED INTERCULTURALITY

There exist several approaches to study negotiated interculturality. In the following, we will present (1) the concept of a third culture, (2) dilemma theory and (3) negotiated culture.

2.1 Third Culture

With a dynamic understanding of interculturality, it is possible to promote the development of new processes and to construct a *third culture*. This development is based on cultural interactions marked by mutual respect as well as common values and communication. The third culture thus integrates new, effective and mutually acceptable ways to benefit from intercultural encounters (Casmir, 1993, 1999):

> Using the concept of a third-culture, that is, the construction of a mutually beneficial interactive environment in which individuals from two different cultures can function in a way beneficial to all involved, represents my attempt to evolve a communication-centred paradigm. The focus of my third-culture building is not on short-term interactions, but instead it was developed to assist us in a better understanding of the long-term building processes which are at the root of any cultural construction. (Casmir, 1999, p. 92)

The approach distinguishes four interactive and related phases, which represent a communication process (Casmir, 1999, pp. 109-111):

(1) *Need:* the first phase concerns the first contact of a person with a different culture. This contact can refer to an object, an event or a person from another culture. It is possible that the contact might cease due to fear, lack of competence or lack of time. The third culture development process then ends.

(2) *Interaction:* the second phase begins when the contact is perceived as interesting, necessary or satisfying. Here again, the process can end if the actors are not prepared to accept the values, norms and rules of others. It is also possible that contacts are extended and deepened, which leads to the change and adaptation of processes.

(3) *Dependence:* in the third phase, the actors rely on each other to achieve certain goals. Within their communicative interactions, they develop jointly accepted rules and behaviours, which lead to the creation of a third culture.

(4) *Interdependence:* the fourth phase represents a further development and the continuity of the third culture, in which the involved actors facilitate mutual learning and confidence-building through dialogical communication. The formation of the third culture is a fluid process, which requires time, understanding, dialogue and creativity.

2.2 Dilemma Theory

Dilemma theory, developed by Hampden-Turner (1990), allows dealing constructively with interculturality to solve problems and to achieve goals. When two possible forms of solutions are opposed to each other and contribute in opposite ways to goal attainment, they are in a tense relationship to each other and form a dilemma. A dilemma (originating from Greek: 'double proposition') is a situation characterized by a predicament in which a decision has to be made between two possible alternatives. This means that there are two proposed solutions with regard to a goal or a conflict. There is no clear wrong or right solution. Like the principles of Taoism, a Chinese philosophy, interculturality can be considered a dialectical concept (Box 5.5).

BOX 5.5 TAOISM AND INTERCULTURAL MANAGEMENT

Taoism addresses the existence and balance of opposites and thus also the relativity of multiple viewpoints and perspectives, which can find rapprochement and connection in processes. Dao (Tao) means 'way' or 'method' and is described as the unification of opposites, whose transformations, movements and interactions lead to the emergence of the world. Opposites as two contrary but complementary forces are Yin (shadow, black) and Yang (light, white). According to Taoism, the union of Yin and Yang leads to harmony and balance. Taoism can thus also be understood as an attitude: mutability and spontaneity as well as serenity and non-interference, balance and relativization of values. The dualistic, balancing and therefore ethnorelative principles are central characteristics of intercultural competence and *constructive interculturality*.

Source: Fang (2012).

In organizations, it is the task of individuals to deal with these tensions and, if possible, to solve them. Typical dilemmas in organizations concern, for example:

- Standardization versus differentiation
- Centralization versus decentralization
- Continuity versus change
- Cooperation versus competition
- Autonomy versus dependence
- Shareholder value versus stakeholder value.

The more dilemmas exist, the more conflictual is their influence on a social system; the more they are reconciled, the more harmonious the social system appears. For a balanced and effective interculturality, it is essential to allow opposites and differences in values to positively influence each other as mutual forces.

> Every culture more or less reconciles its own contrasting values. In other words, prepon-derantly communitarian cultures succeed to the extent that they nurture the individuality of their members, whereas preponderantly individualist cultures may vindicate their indi-viduality by contributing in a major way to their community and society. In all probability, some bias remains. Americans are perhaps too individualistic, whereas the Chinese are too shaped by their communities. What we are claiming is that cultural intelligence, or trans-cultural competence, is a measure of the extent to which contrasting values are synergized. We call this the synergy hypothesis. (Hampden-Turner & Trompenaars, 2006, p. 8)

For the context of organizations, dilemma theory suggests that (Hampden-Turner & Trompenaars, 2000, p. 348):

- Shared values make the organization more efficient
- Unresolved conflicts reduce the efficiency of individuals and groups
- The combination of values leads to better products and services
- The need to reconcile value differences can be ceaseless
- Intercultural competence helps to transform contradictory values into complementary values.

To solve a dilemma, it is necessary to consciously integrate differences and to balance and reconcile diverging values.

> Culture is a pattern by which a group habitually mediates between value differences, such as rules and exceptions, technology and people, conflict and consensus, etc. Cultures can learn to reconcile such values at ever-higher levels of attainment, so that better rules are created from the study of numerous exceptions. From such reconciliation come health, wealth, and wisdom. But cultures in which one value polarity dominates and militates against another will be stressful and stagnate. (Trompenaars & Hampden-Turner, 2004, pp. 22-23)

Compensation is a circular process between opposite poles, which has neither a beginning nor an end (Hampden-Turner, 1992). This can be illustrated with the example of the value orientations of particularism vs. universalism (Chapter 3) (Figure 5.2). Universalism is found in organizations with strong centralism, which aims at transparency and equality through structures and rules. Following the rules serves to solve problems. If the following of rules is exaggerated, then processes slow down due to bureaucracy. For this reason, the value of particularism appears as a counterbalance and creates flexibility through autonomy. Changing and interpreting rules to respond to current circumstances serves, in turn, to solve problems. However, too much autonomy might lead to anarchy. So, the value of universalism balances the value of particularism. In many situations, the balancing of opposites occurs unconsciously as a circular process.

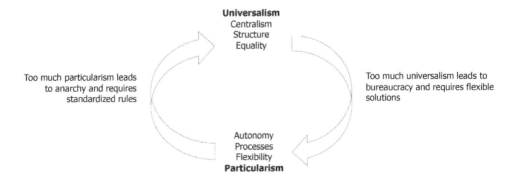

Universalism
Centralism
Structure
Equality

Too much particularism leads to anarchy and requires standardized rules

Too much universalism leads to bureaucracy and requires flexible solutions

Autonomy
Processes
Flexibility
Particularism

Figure 5.2   Balancing values in organizations: the example of universalism and particularism

Dilemmas as mutual forces can display a 'vital tension' and thus constructively interact and reinforce each other. They enable a positive development when values are united and combined, thus forming the 'virtuous circle' (Hampden-Turner, 1992). In contrast, in a 'vicious circle', forces act negatively against each other. In the virtuous circle, values can be brought into a harmonious relationship. Social systems develop specific values to control their environment. Consequently, intercultural encounters can provoke tensions between complementary and synergetic combination on the one side, and oppositional confrontation and crises on the other side (Hampden-Turner & Trompenaars, 2000, p. 348). Box 5.6 provides an example for dilemmas faced by Airbus, the European leader in the aerospace sector.

BOX 5.6   NATIONAL CENTRALIZATION VERSUS MULTINATIONAL DECENTRALIZATION AT AIRBUS

The European Airbus group resulted from the merger of three companies: the French Aérospatiale-Matra (merger of public company Aérospatiale and private company Matra), the German DASA (Deutsche Aerospace Aktiengesellschaft) and the Spanish CASA (Construcciones Aeronáuticas Sociedad Anónima). After the merger, Airbus faced several dilemmas, namely the legal form (public enterprise versus private company), the strategy (civil versus military aerospace technology) and the organizational structure (centralization versus decentralization). National centralization requires *one* responsible entity for strategic decisions, whereas multinational decentralization requires several local responsibilities for the business units. Airbus solved this dilemma by choosing different locations: aircraft are located in Hamburg (Germany) and Toulouse (France), helicopters in Marignane (south of France) and satellites in Bremen (Germany).

	National centralization	Multinational decentralization
Assumption	The interests of private and public shareholders and stakeholders must be subordinated to a controlling and determining central power.	The interests of private and public shareholders and stakeholders of local subsidiaries are considered and defended.
Advantage	The central authority can make decisions faster and act more effectively.	The consideration of local interests contributes to the appreciation, commitment and motivation of actors.
Disadvantage	The interests and local problems of actors are not sufficiently considered, which can have a negative impact on the motivation and performance of the organization.	Diverging interests increase the complexity of the organization and can lead to confusion and waste of resources.

Source: Barmeyer and Mayrhofer (2008, 2014).

Trompenaars and Hampden-Turner (2011) propose several steps to use dilemmas for *constructive* interculturality in organizations:

(1) *Awareness* of cultural differences: describing the situation and the problem. Existing cultural specifics and differences can be perceived and presented with the help of critical incidents in a 'value-free' manner. Cultural specifics and differences are therefore not ignored or minimized, but consciously addressed, appreciated and considered as legitimate alternatives.

(2) *Recognition and respect* of cultural dilemmas: identifying and analysing cultural dilemmas. Applying and integrating cultural dimensions or value orientations, for example universalism versus particularism, in a circular way favours the identification of dilemmas as well as the appreciated integration of differences.

(3) *Reconciliation* of cultural dilemmas: solving intercultural dilemmas by combining different potentials, that is the respective strengths of actually opposing views and value orientations. In this way, one-sided intercultural adaptation processes and asymmetrical super- and subordination are avoided, thereby increasing the authenticity and satisfaction of the actors. This favours organizational synergies and reduces potentially costly tensions and conflicts at an early stage.

In the sense of *constructive intercultural management*, dilemma theory does not consider values as static and bipolar, but as dynamic and circular. By integrating differences, it contributes to the dynamics and the development of culture and interculturality. Dilemma theory highlights the possibility of making interculturality appropriate and – if possible – profitable for all interaction partners.

2.3   Negotiated Culture

The *negotiated culture* perspective, developed by Brannen (1998), is another approach that helps to understand and develop *constructive interculturality* in organizations. Negotiated culture is based on the concept of *negotiated social order* proposed by the sociologist Anselm Strauss:

> Negotiation [...] is one of the possible means of 'getting things accomplished'. It is used to get done the things that an actor (person, group, organization, nation, and so on) wishes to get done. [...] Necessarily other actors are involved in such enterprises. Indeed, I would draw a crucial distinction between agreement and negotiation (which always implies some tension between parties, else they would not be negotiating). (Strauss, 1978, p. 11)

According to Strauss (1982), social order is negotiated in the sense that social processes and systems (for example identity formation, cooperation and conflict) arise through interactions between individuals, that is the interplay of action, reaction and adaptation. This contributes to the creation of meaning (sense-making) for actors, thus leading to the construction of realities (Berger & Luckmann, 1966). To fulfil roles and tasks in social systems, actors must continuously negotiate the creation, stability and change of social structures. The concept of *negotiated social order* thus allows understanding processes that influence structural change and stability as well as social structures and pre-conditions that shape such processes (Strauss, 1982). The negotiated culture perspective is based on the anthropological concept of culture (Geertz, 1973). Culture is seen as dynamic and emerges through the interactive (re-)production of patterns of meaning and interpretation, which are created, shared and changed by specific groups of individuals.

Negotiated culture implies to examine processes of meaning creation between individuals in an organizational context. In organizations, meaning is generated through verbal information exchange and various patterns of social interaction. For example, d'Iribarne (2009, p. 310) emphasizes that the culture of a collective is deeply anchored in history. Culture is thus the result of socially shared meanings, connotations and interpretations. The negotiated culture perspective assumes that, when people from different cultures interact with each other, a new 'negotiated' culture can emerge through the recombination and modification of cultural characteristics (Brannen & Salk, 2000). Meaning is not simply transferred, but rather generated, depending on the communication context (Figure 5.3):

> Negotiate is used as a verb to encourage us to think of organizational phenomena as individual actors navigating through their work experience and orienting themselves to their work settings. Focusing on culture as a negotiation includes examining the cognitions and actions of organizational members particularly in situations of conflict, because it is in such situations that assumptions get inspected. 'Negotiation' is identified in the construction and reconstruction of divergent meanings and actions by individual organizational actors. (Brannen, 1998, p. 12)

The formation of negotiated culture is illustrated with a German-Japanese joint venture operating in the paper industry and located in Germany. This binational structure is marked by a relatively equal distribution of power. Several factors contributed to an emergent negotiated culture (Brannen & Salk, 2000, p. 458): the history of the organization; the number and training of involved individuals; the balance of power and influence of individuals; the balance of power and influence of national cultural groups; the nature and complexity of issues arising during cooperation; prior knowledge of the other's culture; international orientation of individuals and organizational cultures.

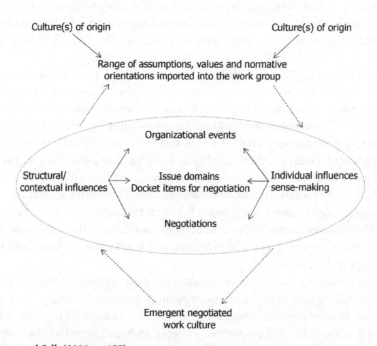

Source: Brannen and Salk (2000, p. 457).

Figure 5.3   Model of negotiated culture

The case study shows that the creation of a new working culture can take four forms, which can evolve over time in the sense of dynamic interculturality (Brannen & Salk, 2000, p. 478) (Table 5.1):

(1) *Division of labour:* the different cultural groups (departmental, professional or national cultures) act independently. There is little interaction between them, thus avoiding confrontation and negotiation. The division of labour in a culturally diverse organization can be driven by pragmatic and institutional factors.

(2) *Compromise by one group:* one cultural group adapts to the other and thereby modifies its own work practices. This is often due to the fact that the group with more resources (influence, financial resources, knowledge, etc.) can assert itself earlier or better.

(3) *Meeting in the middle:* both groups negotiate mutual processes of adaptation and integration that affect cultural working practices. Each group integrates new practices of the other group. This is often the case when there is a balance of power.

(4) *Innovating something new:* both cultural groups accept cultural differences in intercultural processes. The negotiation considers different positions, competences and resources, which can have an enriching and complementary effect on work processes and results. This type of negotiated culture is particularly relevant for *constructive intercultural management.*

Table 5.1 Forms and examples of negotiated culture

Forms	Example
Division of labour	Division of management tasks: German managers are responsible for production and administration; Japanese managers are responsible for marketing and sales, technology and quality management.
Compromise by one group	Japanese managers no longer expect their free time to be spent together with German colleagues.
Meeting in the middle	Meetings become less frequent and shorter than Japanese managers are used to, but more frequent and longer than German managers are used to.
Innovating something new	English as a working language is abandoned during certain phases in joint meetings (monolingual splitting).

Source: Adapted from Brannen and Salk (2000, p. 478).

The concept of negotiated culture has been applied in different cultural contexts. Box 5.7 gives the example of the Franco-German joint venture Alleo.

BOX 5.7   ALLEO, A FRANCO-GERMAN JOINT VENTURE

Alleo is a joint venture between the German train company Deutsche Bahn (DB) and the French train company Société Nationale de Chemins de fer Français (SNCF). Alleo jointly operates cross-border high-speed trains in France and Germany: ICE (Intercity-Express) and TGV (*Train à Grande Vitesse*). The company operates in two national systems, with different railway systems and work practices that are integrated in a complementary way and put in practice in management. On-board services are provided by Franco-German teams on all the trains and during the entire journey. This required a certain degree of harmonization and standardization through mutual negotiation, learning and adaptation processes. Alleo is a central interface with several forms of negotiated culture: (1) compromise by one group, (2) meeting in the middle and (3) innovating for something new.

1. *Compromise by one group*: a compromise was found for working clothes so that train conductors look similar for passengers. In France, train conductors are used to wearing a cap with their (formerly grey) uniform during their working hours, whereas German train conductors do not wear a cap, especially when they are on the train. Initially, German train conductors refused to wear a cap, but they compromised to

wear the cap during their presence on the platform (they are allowed to take it off in the train). The French train conductors agreed to replace their grey uniform by a dark blue uniform, which is similar to the German one.

2. *Meeting in the middle*: one of the divergences concerned Metro ticket sales and taxi reservation in Paris, a service that should be proposed by train conductors to first class passengers. Initially, there was resistance on the French side to sell Metro tickets; finally, they agreed that German train conductors would sell the Metro tickets and that French train conductors would make the taxi reservations.

3. *Innovating something new*: the company was able to develop several innovations. For example, in German trains, drinks and food are served by the on-board staff, including train attendants, in the first class. There was resistance from French train conductors, as this was also the case in Germany when the service was introduced. The new solution was to assign this task to the staff of the restaurant car. Another innovation was to offer trilingual service (German, French and English) on cross-border trains.

Source: Barmeyer and Davoine (2019).

The presented analysis shows that interculturality is a dynamic process leading to the emergence and development of something new. When actors present different – and sometimes contradictory – characteristics, they can still influence, complement and even enrich each other (Hampden-Turner & Trompenaars, 2020). The central question is not to negate or minimize cultural specifics and differences, but rather to accept and to combine and integrate them in a dynamic way.

3.   NEGOTIATED CULTURE FOR CONSTRUCTIVE INTERCULTURAL MANAGEMENT

Dynamically negotiated culture considers context and ambiguities rather than bipolar, essentialist categories. Outcomes and consequences of intercultural interactions cannot be predicted or determined a priori, but they emerge as a new and hybrid culture in ongoing communication, reciprocal learning and knowledge acquisition (Brannen & Salk, 2000). Negotiated culture is not the result of a 'one plus one' logic and cannot be placed on a continuum between the original cultures.

A central contribution of the negotiated culture perspective is to introduce sensitiveness to local workplace social processes in shaping the possible emergence of shared cultural meanings, and how possible cultural tensions play out over time. How culture become [sic!] salient during social interactions cannot, according to this literature, properly be understood without understanding the local context of interaction, which may serve to produce both cultural tensions and convergence. (Bjerregaard et al., 2009, p. 212)

Negotiated culture suggests that interculturality is a social interaction process in which actors modify their cultural practices in different ways while pursuing their interests and goals. Figure 5.4 depicts this iterative process: Actors (A, B and C) bring in their cultures, interests and identities, and constantly negotiate and renegotiate their positions within the context. It is likely that during this process culture, interests and identities change, which are then brought in again in the next negotiation phase.

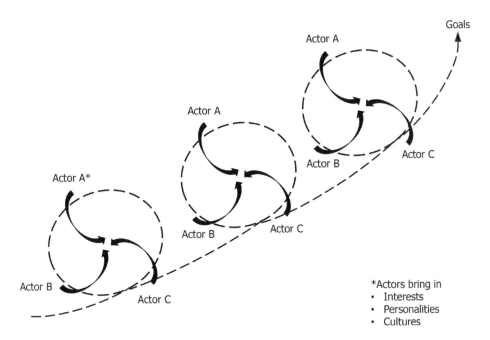

Figure 5.4   Negotiated interculturality as a dynamic process

The approach refers primarily to organizational cultures and working practices that can be adapted, combined and developed in dialogical interaction processes. It also takes into account *multiple* cultural affiliations and identities. National culture is recognized, but as one element among others. However, other cultural elements such as basic assumptions and values (Kluckhohn & Strodtbeck, 1961) are masked, because they are less or not at all negotiable.

Negotiated culture shows a proximity to concepts such as third culture (Casmir, 1999), *reconciliation* in dilemma theory (Hampden-Turner, 1990) and *hybrid* culture. Negotiated culture focuses on particular contextual factors such as history and power relationships, prior cultural knowledge and the complexity of relationships. Likewise, the term 'negotiated' indicates activity and reciprocity. Negotiated culture can thus be understood as a preliminary stage and form of intercultural complementarity and synergy (Chapter 10). It represents a form of rapprochement, overlapping and mixing of different cultural practices through intercultural interaction, which enable the constructive and complementary use of differences and contrasts inherent to interculturality.

SUMMARY

In this chapter, we have explained how interculturality can be negotiated in a constructive way. We have defined the concept of interculturality as a dynamic interpretation and adaptation process that can lead to new rules and behaviours. We have examined the possible impact of critical incidents as well as the role of contextualization and actors in intercultural negotiation. We presented three approaches to negotiated interculturality: the construction of a third culture, dilemma theory and negotiated culture. Negotiated interculturality should be considered as a dynamic process where actors interact to change their organizational and work practices while pursuing their interests and goals.

DISCUSSION QUESTIONS

1. How would you define the concept of interculturality?
2. Which role do critical incidents, contextualization and actors play in intercultural negotiation?
3. Provide examples of forms of negotiated interculturality, either from practice or from personal experience.
4. How can negotiated culture contribute to *constructive intercultural management*?

PART II
EXPERIENCING CONSTRUCTIVE INTERCULTURAL MANAGEMENT

6
Intercultural leadership

This chapter is dedicated to intercultural leadership, which plays a key role in organizations who internationalize their activities. This type of leadership is strongly influenced by the cultural differences between managers and employees. Following the intercultural three-step model (Chapter 4), we will first present the cultural specifics of leadership in the global context. We will then focus on comparative leadership, based on the GLOBE study, to highlight the diversity of leadership styles in different cultures. Finally, we will discuss the constructive implementation of intercultural leadership.

CHAPTER LEARNING OBJECTIVES

1. Understand the cultural specifics of leadership in the global context.
2. Be able to compare leadership styles and their cultural foundations.
3. Be aware of major findings of the GLOBE study.
4. Know how to implement intercultural leadership constructively.

1. CULTURAL SPECIFICS OF LEADERSHIP

Leadership in organizations that operate internationally is strongly influenced by cultural characteristics (Gehrke & Claes, 2014). Leading in an international context requires intercultural competence and cultural experience to achieve the goals of the organization (Northouse, 2018).

Leadership refers to the ability of a person to guide and influence the behaviour of other individuals to meet organizational goals. The objectives are to motivate and involve employees to reach the targeted performance and to design, develop and manage organizations so that they can implement their strategies (Mendenhall et al., 2018). Leadership is mostly situational, which means that managers must adapt their tasks, measures and methods to the organizational context. Box 6.1 presents examples of leadership tasks.

BOX 6.1 EXAMPLES OF LEADERSHIP TASKS

- Definition of work content, decision-making and delegation of responsibilities to employees
- Definition of objectives, which determine the targeted results

- Allocation of resources such as budgets (financial resources) and staff (human resources)
- Motivational activities such as appreciation, support and rewards
- Performance evaluation through assessment interviews
- Joint planning for the long-term training, development and careers of employees
- Assistance with the integration of employees in teams and in the organization

Ideally, leaders need to be aware of the various interests within the organization: does the leader prioritize the interests of the organization or the interests of employees? Does the leader strive for a balance of interests? The leader can thus be more oriented towards the organization or towards the employees.

However, this consideration must be clearly distinguished from individual leadership styles: whatever the choice of interests, managers can display an authoritarian leadership style by expecting employees to follow instructions or adopt a more participative leadership style by involving employees in decision-making processes.

Intercultural leadership is also situational and dependent on individual leadership styles. When leaders and collaborators from different cultures come together, they are subject to intercultural dynamics, which may provoke misunderstandings and challenges. At the same time, there are opportunities to create added value from diversity. *Constructive intercultural management* enables to develop common added value for individuals involved in intercultural leadership situations.

Multiple societal influences are likely to affect organizational behaviour and thus leadership, namely through values, norms and practices (Delmestri & Walgenbach, 2005), which are shaped by socio-historical developments (d'Iribarne et al., 2020), and educational and economic systems (Redding, 2005; Whitley, 1999). Therefore, leaders and leadership – including mutual role expectations of managers and employees – are embedded in cultural and institutional contexts.

1.1 Transformational and Agile Leadership in Response to the VUCA World

Globalization and digitalization show that organizations and leadership are subject to continuous change, as advocated by the VUCA world (Volatility, Uncertainty, Complexity and Ambiguity) (Chapter 2). Leaders are confronted with major challenges: sustainability (ecological, social and economic sustainability), ethical and moral issues (for example, with artificial intelligence), citizenship (responsibility for social and environmental justice and protection) and diversity (reflected in multiple interests and contradictory behaviours). They are thus facing paradoxes and dilemmas they have to solve to advance and develop organizations (Ehnert & Claes, 2014). Leaders must be increasingly agile and adaptive to respond to increasing complexity and external pressure for change (Joiner, 2019).

'Transformational leadership' (Burns, 1978) can help leaders to face these challenges. This type of leadership advocates that managers attempt to inspire, stimulate, empower and motivate employees to propose new ideas with the objective to better adapt to the fast-changing environment (Bass & Riggio, 2006). Transformational leaders are proactive and view challenges as opportunities that can help employees and the organization to develop. Moreover, they foster collaboration instead of competition among employees and 'believe in the intrinsic values of their people' (Gehrke, 2014, p. 134).

In addition to being adaptive to the external environment, leaders also need to be 'agile' towards intercultural dynamics within organizations. Agile leaders are able to react quickly and efficiently to external changes and crises (such as the COVID-19 pandemic), and they can find synergistic solutions. As indicated in Box 6.2, agile managers can fulfil various roles within organizations (Morrison et al., 2019). An example is provided by Bernard Arnault, Chief Executive Officer (CEO) of the French LVMH (Louis Vuitton Moët Hennessy) group, the world leader in the luxury industry. At the beginning of the COVID-19 crisis in March 2020, Bernard Arnault announced that LVMH would use their perfume and cosmetics factories to manufacture hydroalcoholic gel for French health authorities and hospitals, thus responding to the French government's call for hand sanitizers within 72 hours (Newburger, 2020).

BOX 6.2　TEN ROLES OF AGILE MANAGERS IN ORGANIZATIONS

- *Conversation guides*: understanding employees, establishing and fostering communication within the organization
- *Questioners:* questioning the state-of-the-art of practices and routines
- *Inventory takers:* identifying skills and strenghts of employees
- *Experimenters*: being open for the implementation of new ideas
- *Connectors:* linking ideas and resources to build something new
- *Prioritizers:* being able to make decisions and to determine future paths
- *Dreamcatchers:* setting into practice the 'unthinkable'
- *Deal-closers*: taking into consideration multiple interests, for example by 'shared leadership'
- *Conveners:* fostering individual and organizational learning and new habits
- *'Chief doing officers':* nudging, connecting and promoting new habits

Source: Adapted from Morrison et al. (2019).

An intercultural, globalized and digitalized world calls for global leaders who are engaged in sustainable change, develop personal relationships with their employees and have the necessary intercultural sensitivity to lead through challenges and crises. Especially in collectivist cultures, for example Asian, African or Latin American cultures, it is necessary to establish emotional connections between managers and employees to foster engagement and involvement (Gehrke, 2014). In such cultures, the leader's emotional intelligence strongly influences subordinate task performance and organizational citizenship behaviour, that is discretionary behaviour, which promotes the effective functioning of organizations without being explicitly recognized by formal reward systems (Miao et al., 2018). Agile organizations often adopt democratic leadership styles, thus offering the opportunity to employees to participate actively in decision-making processes. In some technology companies, managers are even elected by employees, which guarantees stronger support for managerial decisions.

1.2 Career Paths of Leaders in Different Countries

Professional socialization largely determines the way actors become managers, and how they understand their role and legitimize their actions and behaviours in regard to other members of the organization. This socialization usually takes place in early adulthood at schools, universities and other educational institutions, and integrates individuals into the norms and values of specific professional cultures.

Professionalization and career paths of leaders reveal significant differences between countries, and are often rooted in educational systems. In fact, career and leadership potentials are not identified and developed in the same way across cultures, and it is thus possible to differentiate national career path models. Table 6.1 indicates major characteristics of four career path models: (1) the Anglo-Saxon and Dutch model, (2) the Germanic career model, (3) the Latin career model and (4) the Japanese career model.

Table 6.1 National career path models

Anglo-Saxon and Dutch career model	Managed development: Egalitarian recruitment policies, based on technical and functional competences Matching the performance and potential of managers Human resource development strategies for high-potential managers
Germanic career model	Functional development: Broad professional socialization through vocational education and trainee programmes, followed by specialization in a defined functional area Promotion and legitimacy are gained through professional expertise ('specialists') and social capital 'Mountaineer' with 'chimney career' development (life-long promotion within *one* profession or function)
Latin career model	Elitist political approach: Recruitment from elitist higher education institutions (termed *Grandes Ecoles* in France) Advancement through successful change between functional departments Building of social capital through informal relationships Generalist transversal approach without particular specialization
Japanese career model	Elitist cohort development: Elite pool or cohort recruitment to identify future managers Long-term career in the same organization with job rotation and intensive training Strong competitiveness with equal opportunities and multifunctional mobility

Sources: Evans et al. (1989); Walther (2014).

Educational systems play an important role for career paths of top managers. It is possible to identify national educational prerequisites which create legitimacy and favour careers. A comparative study of 916 European top managers shows that educational prerequisites and career path models are relatively stable over time, even if globalization is likely to change 'traditional' career paths. For example, the study confirms the status of three top *Grandes Ecoles* (elite higher education institutions) – Ecole Polytechnique, HEC Paris (*Ecole des Hautes Etudes Commerciales de Paris*) and ENA (*Ecole Nationale d'Administration*) – in France and the high value attributed to the doctoral degree in Germany (Davoine & Ravasi, 2013) (Table 6.2).

Table 6.2   Divergent educational prerequisites of European managers

Educational prerequisites	France	Germany	Switzerland	United Kingdom
Three top higher education institutions	38%	14%	18%	14%
Doctoral degree	6%	45%	25%	7%
Mountain climber	52%	61%	59%	57%
University educated	95%	90%	86%	72%
International experience	56%	56%	74%	62%
MBA (Master of Business Administration) or similar programme	10%	12%	29%	20%
Audit/consulting firm	9%	15%	14%	14%

Source: Based on Davoine and Ravasi (2013, p. 158).

1.3   Culture and Leadership

Leadership takes distinct forms in different cultures, since employees have diverging expectations of how leaders should behave. For example, US leadership is considered to be individualistic, performance- and competition-oriented. Leaders are often stylized as 'heroes' with a strong vision. The heroic charisma includes visionary and unconventional behaviour. Leaders seize opportunities and build harmonious interpersonal relationships without changing directions too quickly. Moreover, leaders are expected to inspire employees and to empower with enthusiasm (Hoppe & Bhagat, 2007). However, the notion of 'empowerment' can have different meanings in other cultural contexts.

It is therefore evident that Western leadership styles cannot be easily transferred to emerging or developing countries. It is necessary to consider leadership situations and to adapt leadership practices to achieve effectiveness. In the following, we will explain cultural characteristics of leadership styles in several geographic areas. It is important to bear in mind that variations exist within countries and regions.

In *China*, leadership is characterized by the interplay of authoritarian leadership (centralized power structures), Confucianism (morality principles and justice) and reciprocal care (paternalistic leadership) (Su, 2015). A leader is expected to exercise justice and power to maintain the social order. *Guanxi* and *Celestial bureaucracy* help to understand Chinese leadership:

- *Guanxi* refers to established and closely interwoven social interdependencies between leaders and employees, which result in family like relationship structures. An employee is considered a family member, who owes the organization a performance commitment and the leader's obedience (Chen et al., 2009).
- *Celestial bureaucracy*: The task of a strong leader is to maintain the public order, carried out by a large administration acting on behalf of the 'Son of Heaven'. The idea is linked

to the religious belief that heaven (as a metaphor to Earth) is ruled by king Jade who maintains the social order by bureaucracy, leading his servants to keep the books, issue decrees and take care of the correspondence (d'Iribarne, 2010).

In *East Asia*, striving for harmony, a strong seniority and a reserved attitude are part of leadership behaviour. Nevertheless, leadership is hierarchical, often paternalistic, which at the same time emphasizes the importance of group membership and a humane relationship orientation. Collectivism meets with a high long-term orientation (Blunt & Jones, 1997). For example, in Thailand, humanistic leadership relates to guiding, bridging, emotionally supporting, socializing and indirectly communicating, which are consistent with Asian holistic thinking (Vora & Kainzbauer, 2020).

In *Latin America*, leadership refers to reciprocity and personal orientation, but also to paternalism and autocracy. In *Mexico*, paternalistic leadership style is marked by the Spanish colonial *hacienda system* which advocates strong dependencies between the servants and the *hacendero*, the landowner. These *patrones* ('fathers') are considered benefactors who financially support employees, organizations and villages. Often, they are consulted by employees in case of difficulties and problems (Maletzky, 2010). The authoritarian but paternalistic leadership style is linked to the image of the *caudillo*, a term that emerged in the nineteenth century after the Latin American independence wars from Spain. A *caudillo* describes an autocratic, but charismatic strongman who rules a certain territory or executes power on regions and people.

In *Central and South Africa*, paternalistic leadership prevails along with rigid bureaucratic control. Traditional values, communalism, teamwork, mythology and religion play a major role in leadership (Nkomo, 2011). The relation to nature is emphasized by *Ubuntu*, a traditional philosophy which advocates an extreme form of collectivism. *Ubuntu* highlights the importance of community, respect, esteem and humanism, and is expressed by sharing resources and generosity, solidarity and compassion. The term stems from the saying '*umuntu ngumuntu ngabantu*' which means 'a person is a person because of other persons' (Bekker, 2008, p. 19).

In *North Africa*, leadership reflects the feelings of belonging to the group, called *asabiya*. Coined by the philosopher Ibn Kaldhun, the term dates back 800 years, but it is still reflected in today's organizations. *Asabiya* considers leadership relationships as family ties and social networks which are oriented towards religious values such as humanism (Sidani, 2008).

2. COMPARATIVE LEADERSHIP

The cultural comparison of leadership highlights the diversity of role perceptions and expectations of leaders in different cultures and contributes to a better understanding of how leadership works in foreign cultures. This is of particular importance when managers are required to take leadership positions in other cultural contexts, for example in the case of expatriation in multinational companies, in cross-border joint ventures, merger and acquisitions or within a multicultural workforce.

Comparative leadership explores leadership styles in different cultural contexts, and helps to analyse and design intercultural leadership situations. *Constructive intercultural leadership is based on the recognition of differences in leadership selection, development and perception.* The comparison between leadership action and performance allows seizing the effectiveness of leadership styles in different cultural settings. In intercultural situations, it is necessary to provide particular importance to perceptions of leadership, that is the 'beliefs held about how leaders behave in general and what is expected of them' (Herd & Lowe, 2020, p. 358).

The term 'leadership' has diverging meanings across cultures and is often historically and politically connoted (Dickson et al., 2012). Table 6.3 presents the terms used for the word 'leader' in different languages and the associated meanings.

Table 6.3   Meanings associated with the term 'leader' across languages

Language	Term	Associated meanings
English	'Leader'	Empowers and motivates Egalitarian concept: participative decision-making, open discussions and teamwork
Chinese	'Lingdao'	Authorative power Making decisions and taking responsibility Maintaining superior status with possible abuse of power
French	'Cadre'	Defining 'frames' for tasks, responsibilities and budgets Providing support and care for employees Employees act rather autonomously, but without exceeding the 'frame'
German	'Führungskraft' 'Vorgesetzter'	Authority is based on technical competence and functional autonomy Refers to horizontal relationships
Russian	'Rukovoditel' 'Načal'nik'	Someone who leads something or someone is a mentor Official person having staff and power
Spanish	'Líder', 'Patrón'	Directive and authoritarian with delegation of work Directive decision-making, high assertiveness and less teamwork

Sources: Based on Barmeyer and Davoine (2006); Dickson et al. (2012); Hoppe (2004).

2.1   The GLOBE Study

The GLOBE (Global Leadership and Organizational Behavior Effectiveness) study is among the largest comparative studies on leadership. The study highlights the influence of culture on leadership expectations and the necessity to match leadership behaviour with expectations to achieve effectiveness. For the first study in 2004, data was collected from 17 000 mid-level managers in 62 countries (House et al., 2004). The second study in 2014 concerns over a hundred CEOs and 5 000 senior executives in 24 countries (House et al., 2014). In 2020, a new data collection wave started, concerning more than 120 countries (GLOBE, 2020). The investigations are conducted by an international research team and include data from surveys, interviews, focus groups and discussions with leaders.

Table 6.4 Leadership styles in regional clusters

Regional cluster	Charismatic and value-based leadership	Team-oriented leadership	Participative leadership	Human-oriented leadership	Autonomous leadership	Self-protective leadership
Latin America	High	High	Medium	Medium	Low	Medium/high
Anglo-America	High	Medium	High	High	Medium	Low
Sub-Saharan Africa	Medium	Medium	Medium	High	Low	Medium
Latin Europe	Medium/high	Medium	Medium	Low	Low	Medium
Eastern Europe	Medium	Medium	Low	Medium	High/high	High
Germanic Europe	High	Medium/low	High	Medium	High/high	Low
Nordic Europe	High	Medium	High	Low	Medium	Low
Confucian Asia	Medium	Medium/high	Low	Medium/high	Medium	High
South Asia	High	Medium/high	Low	High	Medium	High/high

Source: House et al. (2004, p. 684).

The findings of the studies show the existence of six global leadership styles (GLOBE, 2020):

- *Charismatic and value-based leadership*: managers achieve employee performance through inspiration and motivation, with basic values being respected and followed.
- *Team-oriented leadership*: managers set common goals for teamwork and subordinate themselves and their leadership behaviour to this goal.
- *Participative leadership*: managers involve employees in decision-making processes.
- *Human-oriented leadership*: managers support employees and treat them with generosity and care.
- *Autonomous leadership*: the independence and individuality of managers are in the foreground.
- *Self-protective leadership*: managers seek the preservation of their own and the group's face, and act status-oriented, self-centred and conflict-oriented.

The six leadership styles manifest themselves in different cultures, but there are important divergences across geographic regions. Moreover, certain leadership styles such as charismatic and value-based leadership are adopted in several regional clusters, whereas others such as self-protective leadership are used in only a few regions. Table 6.4 indicates the importance of leadership styles in different geographic regions.

According to the GLOBE study, challenges in intercultural interaction arise in the cooperation of people who belong to different clusters. For example, relationship-oriented employees may find a task-oriented superior uninspiring and inaccessible, and feel that they are not being taken seriously, which can have a demotivating effect. In the same way, leaders who are accustomed to a participative leadership style can become frustrated when they lead employees who are used to an authoritarian leadership style and do not express their opinions or get intrinsically involved in tasks and processes. Consequently, there may be erroneous attributions such as incompetence or lack of reliability. From a constructive lens on interculturality, it is necessary to recognize and understand differences to be able to adapt leadership behaviours accordingly.

2.2   Comparative Leadership Studies

Several studies rely on a qualitative approach to analyse leadership styles across countries. For example, a study on British, German and Italian middle and senior managers shows major characteristics of leadership styles in the three countries. There are several commonalities between the three cultures, namely the social dimension of leadership. Interviewed managers emphasize the importance of developing a positive atmosphere and human relationships to achieve effective leadership results. However, the study highlights differences concerning the tasks and skills of middle managers. In Great Britain, managers are often generalists, with social and managerial competences, who tend to delegate technical work. In contrast, in Germany and Italy, managers are rather expected to be specialists, with social and technical skills, who supervise and solve technical issues. The results can be explained by institutional factors, and more specifically by educational systems and predominant career paths (Delmestri & Walgenbach, 2005) (Table 6.5).

Table 6.5 Tasks and competencies of middle managers in Great Britain, Germany and Italy

Country	Tasks	Competences
Great Britain	Brokering specialized knowledge Team and conflict management	More generalist: social, managerial and tolerance of uncertainty in technical issues
Germany	Supervising and performing technical problem-solving Managing people	More specialist: social, technical and partly managerial
Italy	Supervising and performing technical problem-solving Managing people	More specialist: social, technical and partly managerial with tolerance for ambiguity in role definition Proactive attitude for skill development

Source: Adapted from Delmestri and Walgenbach (2005, p. 215).

Another qualitative study compares leadership styles at Toyota Motor Company (Japan) and Hyundai Motor Group (South Korea). The two companies reveal divergences concerning strategic leadership and organizational cultures, even if they operate in the same industry. The Japanese and Korean cultures are both marked by neo-Confucian values with 'high degrees of collectivism, group harmony, respect for nature, and mutually beneficial human relationships [...] filial piety, strict seniority, saving face, and absolute loyalty to the family or organization' (Shim & Steers, 2012, p. 583). However, they differ in certain value orientations: Japanese culture is characterized by future orientation, gender egalitarianism, human orientation and uncertainty avoidance, whereas Korean culture is more oriented towards assertiveness, in-group collectivism and power distance.

The case study reveals that Toyota Motor Company relies on stability through planning and work systems to mitigate external turbulence, with the 'symbolic leadership' of the CEO. Company performance is based on 'a steady step-by-step progression and a passion for quality', and the CEO is seen as the 'father' of the company, thus representing 'a symbol of security and stability in a sea of change' (Shim & Steers, 2012, p. 585). In contrast, Hyundai Motor Group demonstrates more flexibility to deal with external uncertainty and associated risks. Managers are therefore more involved in daily operations. The CEO is seen as an active decision-maker and less as a formal authority. The study shows how national cultures can shape leadership and employee behaviours. Major findings of the study are summarized in Table 6.6.

Table 6.6   Leadership styles at Toyota and Hyundai

Leadership patterns	Toyota Motor Company	Hyundai Motor Group
Cultural roots	Japanese	Korean
Focus	*Steady state leadership* Focusing on stability, predictability, planning and risk minimization Developing system-wide solutions that anticipate and mitigate potential problems Encouraging routine compliance with organizational plans and policies	*Entrepreneurial leadership* Focusing on creative problem-solving and reasoned risk-taking Developing flexible operating policies Anticipating and responding to environmental changes rapidly to capitalize on opportunities and manage problems
Leader's role	Chief strategist and symbolic leader	Chief strategist and 'hands-on' manager
Approach to business environment	Working to stabilize the environment Reducing uncertainty through deliberate planning	Working to capitalize on unstable environment through operational flexibility Accepting risk
Management systems	Globalized systems Creating standardized procedures and control systems	Optimizing systems Creating tailored policies according to local situations

Source: Adapted from Shim and Steers (2012, p. 586).

3.   CONSTRUCTIVE INTERCULTURAL LEADERSHIP

Intercultural leadership concerns the communication and leadership interactions between leaders and employees from different cultural backgrounds who may have diverging expectations, perceptions and values towards the leadership behaviour. The focus of intercultural leadership is on dynamic interaction relationships. Leadership challenges and conflicts can arise from divergent expectations with regard to objectives, roles, authority, participation, delegation and freedom of action. This is the case for leaders of multicultural teams, expatriates who take on management positions in foreign countries or when leadership tools are transferred to other countries (Chevrier, 2009) (Box 6.3). These challenges can be mitigated or solved by cultural awareness and the anticipation of possible challenges. It is therefore necessary to carefully design and manage interactions with employees from other cultural contexts.

BOX 6.3   DELEGATION IN FRENCH–MALAGASY LEADERSHIP SITUATIONS

A case study conducted at the non-governmental organization (NGO) GRET (governed by French law) in Madagascar explains how delegation is addressed in intercultural leadership situations. The study shows that French managers and Malagasy employees have different expectations in regard to (1) the formalization of roles and structures, (2) skill development, (3) implementation of collective work and (4) clarification of decision-making processes. For example, for French managers, decision-making means that employees take personal responsibilities in line with their 'métier' (profession), whereas for Malagasy employees, decision-making responsibilities lie clearly in the managers' scope of tasks.

Malagasy employees only feel comfortable to perform decision-making procedures if managers explicitly formalize delegation-making procedures. Moreover, they tend to prefer collective decision-making to limit the risks decisions might bring for themselves and for the group.

Source: Based on Chevrier and Viegas-Pires (2013).

3.1 Multiple Cultures and Leadership

With globalization and digitalization, organizations and leadership situations are becoming increasingly diverse. It is evident that cultural differences influence leadership expectations and behaviour which makes 'effective leadership' more complicated than previously assumed. Moreover, managers and employees are gaining international experience and are thus likely to be influenced by multiple cultures (Sackmann & Phillips, 2004) (Chapter 3). It is therefore necessary to take into account several levels of cultures, including gender, generational, departmental and professional cultures. Consequently, the 'one-size-fits-it-all' approach to leadership is not always effective, even in a culturally homogeneous group.

- *Gender cultures* are influenced by gender equality and initiatives to promote women in management positions. Female managers often show more empathy and collective interest, and they are more inclined to develop open, egalitarian and cooperative relationships (Adler & Osland, 2016). For example, Spain has a more recent history of gender equality than other Western countries, which explains stronger differences in the assessment of leadership behaviour and career opportunities than in more gender-experienced countries (Hernandez Bark et al., 2014). Vietnam has a long tradition of gender equality, with men and women being equally responsible for bringing up children, which is likely to explain leadership specifics (Hang, 2008).
- *Generational cultures* demonstrate significant differences, for example between generations of baby boomers, generations X, Y and Z, and digital natives which manifest themselves across national cultures. Whereas baby boomers tend to follow and expect more hierarchical leadership styles, the X generations and digital natives are more oriented towards decentralized, flexible and egalitarian styles of leadership (Yu & Miller, 2005; Rudolph et al., 2018). These different assumptions on leadership might lead to challenges in leadership situations. Their mutual relationships are likely to be influenced by country-specific socialization, economic development and education.
- *Departmental and professional cultures* can also have an impact on intercultural leadership relationships. So, for example, leaders who have a different professional background might not be considered sufficiently competent by employees, if they do not have the necessary expertise. This is especially important in countries such as Germany and Italy (Delmestri & Walgenbach, 2005). Moreover, employees in more 'modern' professions such as IT (information technology) specialists are more likely to expect decentralized and flat leadership than professionals from more 'traditional' areas such as accounting and production. The belonging to different professional groups can then lead to tensions, but divergent competences between leaders and employees can also contribute to complementary effects, for example in the case of cross-functional teams.

In contrast to intercultural leadership, which focuses on the dynamics and outcomes of inter-cultural leadership situations, global leadership captures the increasing complexity faced by managers, namely diversity, interdependence, interconnectedness and volatility: 'global lead-ership is the process and actions through which an individual influences a range of internal and external constituents from multiple national cultures and jurisdictions in a context char-acterized by significant levels of task and relationship complexity' (Mendenhall, 2018, p. 23). Global leadership goes beyond the 'national cultures and jurisdictions', and embraces multiple cultures and power dynamics in social interactions within and between organizations, but also between individuals (Bird & Mendenhall, 2016).

3.2   Leadership in Intercultural Contexts

When leadership styles and behaviours are incompatible in specific intercultural settings, leaders and collaborators need to negotiate the forms of interaction. It is possible to differenti-ate four constellations of intercultural leadership behaviour (Festing & Maletzky, 2011):

- Leader adjustment: the manager adapts to the employees.
- Follower adjustment: the employees adapt to the manager.
- Integration: both sides move towards each other and create something new.
- Separation: contact is avoided due to conflicts.

The type of adaptation taking place depends on the (positive or negative) perception on both sides, associated stereotypes and power relationships. In extreme situations, inappropriate behaviour may be sanctioned (Box 6.4).

BOX 6.4   WESTERN LEADERS IN RUSSIA

A qualitative study on 20 Western expatriates and 15 Russian employees reveals diverging leadership styles and expected behaviours. Ideal-typical Russian managers are described as paternalistic, whereas Western managers have a more participative management style. In contrast to Western assumptions, Russian employees expect authoritarian-paternalistic behaviour from their managers. At the same time, they also appreciate Western partic-ipatory leadership. However, the study shows that too much freedom can rapidly lead to a reduction in productivity. The interviewed managers and employees believe that a 'mixture' of both leadership styles might lead to synergies. Combining the two leadership styles, Western managers and Russian employees were able to negotiate a new, synerget-ic leadership culture. For example, a Russian employee described the ideal intercultural management style of his Western superior in the following way:

> I think that he has a good combination of different leadership styles. Sometimes, when he needs to be more pushing, he can be pushing. The other approach is that he always involves his employees in the decision-making process, and he always listens to what they say, and he really likes the details, I think. Sometimes, when his employees come to him with good analysis, he can change his mind, which is good.

Source: Kashubskaya-Kimpelainen et al. (2009).

Managers can thus adopt various behavioural strategies to handle intercultural leadership situations for achieving organizational goals in competitive environments. They can behave as (Scholz & Stein, 2013):

(1) *'Culture chameleons'*: managers adapt their leadership style to the behavioural norms of the target culture. They largely abandon their own cultural positions to avoid unpleasant reactions. Their goals are only achieved if they do not pose any problems for all people involved.
(2) *'Culture cowboys'*: managers transfer their ethnocentric leadership style to leadership situations in the target culture. This strategy can be perceived as provocative and may not fit certain cultures. It might prevent the successful achievement of goals, unless managers hold the necessary power.
(3) *'Culture equalizers'*: managers consider cultural differences to a limited extent and they believe that cultural differences should not disturb leadership relationships. This strategy may be challenged by diverging cultural realities. Often, intercultural conflicts are likely to arise.
(4) *'Culture positivists'*: managers behave according to their own culture, but without invading other's norms and expectations, which would make them unpopular. In this case, it is necessary to know behavioural norms in target cultures and their positive or negative impact on leadership situations. Managers can then profile themselves and act successfully.

In this perspective, *constructive intercultural leadership* means consciously avoiding conflict situations while pursuing one's own leadership goals. The creation of a 'win-not-lose' situation can evolve towards a synergetic 'win–win' situation when employees can benefit from the achieved success, for example by more job security or a better climate. In general, organizational goals are difficult to achieve without strategic and structural measures, and the lack of systematic reflection on intercultural leadership constellations can inhibit leadership effectiveness.

3.3   Designing Intercultural Leadership Constructively

What can organizations and individuals do to develop constructive intercultural leadership? Given the diversity of intercultural challenges, organizations can consider four dimensions that should allow them to generate added value through intercultural complementarity and synergy. These dimensions refer to (1) leadership personnel selection, (2) intercultural leadership development, (3) leadership structure and (4) organizational culture.

(1)   Selecting intercultural leaders

When selecting leadership personnel, organizations should ensure to hire the best fitting individuals to meet the requirements of an intercultural world. There are three recommendations when selecting intercultural leaders: they should be cosmopolitans, they should bridge boundaries, and they might – if necessary – be atypical leaders.

Intercultural leaders should be *global cosmopolitans*, that is individuals with a 'global mindset' who have the ability to look at the world from different angles, who bring in openness towards the new and unknown, and who are able to 'reconcile global versus local tensions' (Ehnert & Claes, 2014, p. 160). In complex global environments, effective intercultural leadership relies much on a leader's cognition and behaviour. Thus, intercultural leaders should reveal the following characteristics (Bird, 2018; Caligiuri, 2013; Javidan & Bowen, 2013):

- Personality traits: openness and extraversion, optimism and emotional stability
- Attitudes: result orientation, tolerance of ambiguity, cultural flexibility and low ethnocentrism
- Cognitive abilities: cognitive complexity and intellectual capital
- Motivations: motivation to learn and persistence
- Knowledge: technical skills and global business knowledge
- Behavioural skills: intercultural communication skills, language skills, social capital and boundary spanning abilities.

Companies can also choose to nominate intercultural leaders (intercultural individuals) (Fitzsimmons et al., 2013) or third country nationals (Barmeyer et al., 2020), who may act as *boundary spanners* between different cultural systems (Barner-Rasmussen et al., 2014). Due to their intercultural background, they can leverage synergies by integrating the positive elements of involved cultures and balance diverging expectations. They reveal a higher degree of intercultural sensitivity, cultural intelligence (Earley & Ang, 2003) and cultural agility (Caligiuri, 2012), and can thus more easily apply transformational leadership. Their higher attributional complexity and knowledge increase their intercultural competence. This helps them to make more accurate attributions, which are culturally less biased. The resulting managerial behaviours increase intercultural leadership effectiveness (Lakshman, 2013). Examples are Richard A. Gonzalez, Latino-American CEO of AbbVie, a biotechnology and pharma company, and Antonio Neri, Argentinian-American CEO of Hewlett Packard Enterprise.

With the increasing demand for diversity in leadership positions and executive boards, organizations can also rely on *atypical leaders* who are rarely associated with leadership positions because they '[originate] from non-privileged, non-dominant, under-represented, disadvantaged or unusual demographic backgrounds' (Samdanis & Özbilgin, 2020, p. 101). Atypical leaders can bring new and fresh ideas to the organization and thus become innovators. They can be female or people from the LGBT (lesbian, gay, bisexual and transgender) community. An example is Ursula Burns, former CEO of Xerox (until 2016) and first female CEO of a Fortune 500 company and currently member of the Board of Directors at Uber.

(2)   Developing intercultural leadership

Intercultural learning and development take place at the individual and organizational levels (Chapter 12). Organizations should establish a favourable context for intercultural learning, with the aim to create awareness of cultural differences related to leadership and to implement measures for finding a shared meaning system between managers and employees. In this way, it is possible to facilitate intercultural interaction, to reduce misunderstandings and to promote synergetic cooperation between leaders and employees.

A favourable context can be established by fostering exchange and collaboration, and by offering trainings on intercultural learning and development. This is, for example, the case for

Singapore Airlines which is regularly training managers and staff on intercultural issues. It is also important to highlight that international experience and expatriation do not lead *per se* to interculturally effective leadership. It is necessary that leaders collaborate *regularly* with people from other cultures, acquire knowledge, skills and intercultural competence, and receive feedback on their performance in an intercultural context.

In the dynamics of the VUCA world, globally 'effective' leaders further need to develop *agile* leadership competences. They must be able to adjust their leadership behaviour when addressing intercultural issues by choosing between cultural adaptation, minimization and integration (Caligiuri, 2013, p. 176):

- *Cultural adaptation* refers to the leaders' adaptation to cultural differences and adjustment to the expected norms in each culture.
- *Cultural minimization* implies that leaders attempt to control existing cultural differences to create consistency and limit variations across countries.
- *Cultural integration* means that leaders collaborate across cultures to create new practices and solutions which are acceptable to all cultures involved.

To achieve constructive interculturality in organizations, leaders must be able to choose the most appropriate solution.

In addition, *mindfulness* can help to develop intercultural leadership competences to create complementarity and synergy within organizations (Comfort & Franklin, 2014). Mindfulness means 'paying attention in a particular kind, benevolent and non-judgemental way to the present moment and to what thoughts, emotions or voluntary or involuntary physiological reactions are arising inside a person' (Ehnert & Claes, 2014, p. 163). Mindfulness can be achieved through meditation, which helps to raise awareness of inner feelings and thoughts. It can thus help to improve well-being, reduce stress, and solve paradoxes and tensions linked to a complex global environment. For example, the Indian manager Padmasree Warrior, former CTO (Chief Technology Officer) at the US Cisco group and CEO at the US subsidiary of the Chinese NIO group, meditates to distance herself from stress and excessive digital media use in everyday life. In 2019, she founded Fable, a company offering stories as 'social experiences' to promote well-being and reduce stress.

(3)   Creating bicultural leadership dyads

Organizations can draw on specific structures to support constructive interculturality in leadership. They can create *bicultural leadership dyads*, that is, the staffing of a leadership position with two leaders from diverse cultural backgrounds (Barmeyer & Davoine, 2019). Leadership dyads enable companies to integrate different perspectives and competences in one position and to use the respective networks for gathering information and decision-making (Chreim, 2015). Leadership dyads are more likely to consider the interests and decisions made by employees of the two (or more) cultures. Bicultural leadership dyads thus enable both sides (or groups) to get involved in decision-making processes and to develop symmetrical power relationships. Bicultural leadership dyads might pose a fruitful basis for the negotiation of a new hybrid culture (Chapter 5). This can be a suitable solution for international joint ventures, mergers and acquisitions. For example, the European Airbus group introduced bicultural leadership dyads after the merger, but they were replaced by national managers after the successful integration of the associated companies (Barmeyer & Mayrhofer, 2008, 2014).

(4)   Defining a supportive organizational culture

Lastly, constructive intercultural leadership can only unfold within an appropriate environment, constituted by a supportive organizational culture. This type of organizational culture might be established and maintained by a transnational corporate identity, which considers interests, values and practices from individuals of all countries and locations, as proposed by the geocentric orientation (Perlmutter, 1969). Moreover, intercultural leadership in an agile world requires an organizational culture which is open for diverse thinking and ideas, fosters collaboration across cultures and provides the necessary tools to facilitate intercultural work (Caligiuri, 2013), for example, flexibility in structures and processes, intercultural learning and training, and intercultural competence development (Chapter 11).

In summary, with internationalization and globalization, organizational leaders have to manage intercultural teams with increasing complexity. A positive approach to global leadership can help them to leverage their own strengths and those of their team members to more effectively meet the challenges linked to distance, cultural differences and intercultural barriers (Youssef & Luthans, 2012).

SUMMARY

In this chapter, we have focused on intercultural leadership, which has become essential for organizations that wish to perform in international contexts. According to the intercultural three-step model (Chapter 4), we have presented the cultural specifics of leadership before analysing comparative leadership and discussing the constructive implementation of intercultural leadership. Global leadership is strongly shaped by cultural characteristics and the transformations of the VUCA world. The GLOBE study compares leadership styles in different cultures and regional clusters, highlighting the influence of culture on leadership expectations and leadership behaviour. To implement intercultural leadership constructively, it is necessary to attach particular attention to personnel selection, intercultural leadership development, organizational structures and organizational culture.

DISCUSSION QUESTIONS

1. Which factors influence culture-specific leadership? Provide examples.
2. How do the transformations of the VUCA world influence intercultural leadership?
3. What are the main findings of the GLOBE study?
4. Which role do multiple cultures play in intercultural leadership situations?
5. How can organizations succeed in implementing intercultural leadership constructively?

7
Intercultural teams

With internationalization and globalization, an increasing number of organizations are working with intercultural teams. Team members often have to collaborate under cost and efficiency pressures, and they need to be agile to fit the VUCA (Volatility, Uncertainty, Complexity and Ambiguity) world (Chapter 2). We will first present major characteristics of intercultural teams and the skills required for leading them. The following section will be dedicated to the functioning of intercultural virtual teams. Finally, we will explain how organizations can develop intercultural teams, so that their members' intercultural competence, performance and satisfaction contribute to teamwork quality and efficiency.

CHAPTER LEARNING OBJECTIVES

1. Define the main characteristics of intercultural teams.
2. Know the required leadership skills for intercultural teams.
3. Be aware of the challenges linked to intercultural virtual teams.
4. Identify the appropriate mechanisms for intercultural team development.

1. INTERCULTURAL TEAMS

When people are working in teams, they need to collaborate and contribute different but complementary skills to achieve common goals (Bouncken et al., 2016). In contrast to *monocultural* teams, *intercultural* teams are composed of individuals with diverse cultural affiliations and experiences and thus diverging meaning systems. Intercultural teams can be used to disseminate information across locations, to achieve uniform socialization and identity formation, and to develop creative problem solutions. However, team members often have limited common knowledge and experiences, and different ideas about teamwork, which can influence processes, effectiveness and thus the goals to be achieved. Cultural diversity in teams can generate both benefits and risks which need to be addressed to constructively deal with intercultural teamwork (Table 7.1).

Business practice shows that intercultural teams are either highly effective or highly ineffective, depending on the task and their management (Adler & Gundersen, 2008). When creative work is required, multicultural teams often outperform monocultural teams due to the richness of perspectives, expertise and ideas. Conversely, for routine tasks, intercultural teams tend to be less effective, because of divergent thinking and possibly contradictory problem-solving styles (Paulus et al., 2016).

Table 7.1   Benefits and risks of intercultural teams

Benefits of intercultural teams	Risks of intercultural teams
Increasing creativity	Lack of team cohesion
Developing different views	Distrust and stereotyping
Producing numerous ideas	Communication difficulties due to several languages
Enabling participants to better understand the contribution of other team members	Stress and tensions due to different behaviours and communication styles
Improved problem identification as well as better solutions and decisions can lead to higher efficiency in the whole team.	Difficulties in overviewing ideas, lack of consensus and disagreements can lead to lower efficiency in the whole team.

Source: Adapted from Adler and Gundersen (2008, p. 135).

1.1   Characteristics of Intercultural Teams

Intercultural teams can take the form of (1) *bicultural teams* or (2) *multicultural teams.*

Bicultural teams are composed of members from two cultures. They often are used in the context of cross-border alliances, mergers and acquisitions. Bicultural teams can offer a great potential for synergies if both sides bring their respective strengths and perspectives to the group to improve processes. However, conflicts are likely to arise if the members of one culture are in a dominant position, which is usually the case for acquiring companies. The dominant partner is then likely to impose ideas, strategies, working styles and the language. It is possible that the other party attempts to establish a tactical balance of power rather than focusing on the objectives of the cooperation. Feelings of superiority or inferiority and distrust may take place in such constellations. Competition between team members can have stimulating and sometimes discouraging effects. Therefore, bicultural teams require clear rules that should be accepted by all team members along with strong managers with high intercultural sensitivity who can effectively lead them.

Multicultural teams are composed of members from at least three different cultures. They are becoming increasingly common within and between organizations due to cultural diversity. In contrast to bicultural teams, the issues of power imbalance and competition are less pronounced. Members can propose a variety of ideas, rules of conduct and working methods, and adapt more easily by finding solutions through consensus. It is easier for them to agree on a common working language – usually English as a lingua franca – and on team managers, who often belong to the organizational unit in charge of the project.

For *constructive intercultural management*, it is necessary to provide bi- and multicultural teams with appropriate resources. For example, the problem of power asymmetry in bicultural teams can be counterbalanced by strategic and structural measures, such as reducing the numerical dominance of one culture in the team or by using leadership dyads (Chapter 6). In the same way, it is necessary to consider the cultural composition of multicultural teams to avoid dysfunctions. Multicultural teams often result from contextual or organizational circumstances and it is recommended to develop a more strategic (which cultures are represented in a team?) and structural (which functions are performed by which members?) approach.

In intercultural teams, the characteristics of team members have a decisive influence on the team and the work processes. They can be more or less compatible in terms of values, norms, communication, language, leadership styles and professional groups (Canney-Davison & Ward, 2021). From a constructive perspective, the team manager should know the effects of such similarities and differences on group dynamics and use these factors to initiate cooperation within the team. Work-related and group dynamic processes within the team include trust building, dealing constructively with expectations and stereotypes, communication, motivation and conflict management. The team performance concerns the effective achievement of initial goals, but also the quality of joint processes.

The typical stages of team development can also be found in intercultural teams: (1) forming, (2) storming, (3) norming, (4) performing and (5) adjourning (Tuckman & Jensen, 1977) (Table 7.2). Team members often feel the need to improve communication, interaction and work processes to be efficient, but such changes require time. Teams can pass through

Table 7.2 Five development stages of intercultural teams

Phase		Monocultural teams	Intercultural teams
1.	Forming	Getting to know the team members, exchange of personal and task-related information Polite, impersonal, tense and careful (mutual relationships are still unclear)	This phase can be easily mastered by intercultural teams: team members begin to interact with curiosity and politeness, and the atmosphere is pleasant since cultural differences do not cause tensions yet.
2.	Storming	Emergence of tensions and disagreements about work processes, attitudes, behaviour, role allocation, tasks, working styles, meanings or team leadership Surprises, enthusiasm, but also conflicts, confrontation and clan building, with success being achieved with difficulty	When the project is progressing, team members become aware of their different expectations and perceptions about their tasks, working and management styles. Divergent opinions can either cause conflicts or produce original ideas and new approaches to problem-solving.
3.	Norming	If the team is able to control the differences through explicit norm setting or implicit negotiation, good relationships with mutual support can develop, with the distribution of roles and tasks. Development of new know-how and new behaviours, sense of belonging, feedback, clash of perspectives and conflict resolution	Intercultural moderation and team leadership should favour cohesion to develop team motivation and joint efforts to reach the goal: a clear allocation of roles and the establishment of functional rules can help to bring team members to agree with each other.
4.	Performing	Relationships and operational activities reach a mature stage: team members work actively together, solve problems and are productive. Inventiveness, flexibility, performance-enhancing openness and willingness to perform	Cultural diversity can be an asset: team members build on their complementary resources to create competences adding value to goal achievement.
5.	Adjourning	End of the work process: the goal has been achieved or it is impossible for the team to continue working together. Celebrating success, less interactions between team members and termination of project	Team members who have worked together with pleasure and enrichment in a culturally diverse working environment must return to their original contexts following the termination of the project.

Sources: Adapted from Tuckman and Jensen (1977); Barmeyer (2018).

the five stages in a different order and some stages may be avoided or passed through quickly, while others might possibly not be reached.

Intercultural teams need to adapt continuously to cultural differences while being constrained by their local environments, such as local institutions, norms and practices. This cultural adaptation is a dynamic process in which teams attempt to deal with divergences in communication styles, organizational control, authority relationships, work-related knowledge and problem-solving approaches. Intercultural team adaptation is driven by the local embeddedness of team members and the interdependence across sites, since actors attempt to resolve tensions within and across social structures. This requires discussion and learning, but also experimentation to understand underlying differences and to develop new solutions (Cramton & Hinds, 2014).

1.2   Leading Intercultural Teams

Leading intercultural teams requires actors with excellent skills in communication, cooperation and leadership, because of the culturally different ways of thinking and working of their members. If diversity is not managed in an appropriate way or even ignored, there may be a loss of efficiency and expectations might not be met (Adler & Gundersen, 2008).

Central disturbance factors are:

- Stereotypes: in emotionally charged situations of overstrain and crisis, members of intercultural teams may tend to reduce the complexity of the situation by simplifying it, which means that stereotypes may emerge. Particularly negative stereotypes concerning the performance of certain individuals can lead to a situation in which the proposals and professional skills of some team members are given special attention, while those of others are given less.
- Foreign languages: in intercultural communication, language has a decisive influence on the way discussions and work are organized (Chapter 9). Communication problems in multicultural teams are due to causes such as a lack of a lingua franca, foreign language dominance, linguistic inaccuracies, semantic differentials, divergent conversational styles and different non-verbal behaviour. These can lead to misinterpretations and thus to efficiency losses.
- Basic assumptions, value orientations and working styles: these basic cultural influences can have an impact on the way team members deal with time, leadership, personal responsibility, problem-solving strategies, criticism and team roles, among other things.

Intercultural team leadership should also deal with the potential impact of gender, age, profession and function. In a constructive approach, these forms of diversity can also contribute to complementarity and synergy effects.

Even if intercultural teamwork is often challenging, it is important to mention that team diversity can also stimulate creativity and innovation (Paulus et al., 2016), 'because cultural differences are associated with differences in mental models, modes of perception, and approaches to problems, they are likely to provide strong inputs for creativity' (Stahl et al., 2010, p. 692). The combination of the team members' knowledge, experience and skills provides access to a large pool of competences, but also to more social (business) networks, which can benefit the group as a whole. Mutual exchange and social interaction then lead to synergy effects that can result in improved problem-solving ability, creativity, innovation and adaptability to external pressures.

Constructive intercultural management thus draws attention to the functional effects of cultural differences: divergent working styles might form a considerable potential for complementarity and synergy (Chapter 10). It is also possible that a third (hybrid) culture emerges, which is created or negotiated through mutual adaptation and learning processes. The involved team members might need to change their initial goals, adapt their behaviours and revise their usual ideas about work processes. This can be problematic, especially when their own goals can no longer be pursued. A 'win–win' constellation takes place only when team members contribute to the achievement of goals with their core competences and, at the same time, experience personal satisfaction from the established cooperation.

Within teams, cultural diversity is thus both a resource *and* a challenge (Stahl et al., 2010). Diversity does not lead *per se* to increased performance but needs to be used constructively under the right conditions and at the right time: 'just putting different individuals together in teams may not yield creative teams' (Reiter-Palmon et al., 2012, p. 301). Diversity can therefore be perceived as two sides of a coin, with possibilities for creative thinking and action, and with risks due to dissatisfaction and conflicts.

Intercultural teams can associate several departments and functions, and it is possible to use these multiple perspectives constructively. This is the case for *cross-functional teams*, whose members have different professional skills. They can bring together people from several departments (for example, research and development, production and marketing) who work on a specific project. They can also associate people from other organizations (for example, suppliers, key customers and consultants). This cross-functional collaboration can stimulate creativity, and multiple competences and perspectives can improve problem-solving processes. For example, in the Renault–Nissan–Mitsubishi alliance, intercultural cross-cultural teams have enabled the alliance partners to foster innovation and to develop new products and processes (Chapter 10) (Barmeyer & Mayrhofer, 2016).

In response to the VUCA world, companies are increasingly using *agile teams* for managing specific tasks and projects. Agile teams are 'organizational forms that allow members to quickly come together, address a problem or opportunity, and then disband when the work is done' (Anderson, 2019, p. 265). They can be formed, altered and dissolved rapidly, and mainly rely on experimentation, prototyping and self-management. Their core characteristic is their flexibility and adaptability to the fast-changing environment. Agile teams can work as physical or virtual teams. They often apply specific management methods such as 'scrum' (a project management practice for developing complex products, which relies on cross-functional teams), 'lean development' (an approach that aims at more efficiency and the reduction of waste) and 'kanban' (a method for controlling production processes, that allows reducing stocks due to just-in-time orders) (Rigby et al., 2016).

2.   INTERCULTURAL VIRTUAL TEAMS

With globalization and digitalization, virtual teams have become increasingly popular in all types of organizations, including start-ups, small and medium-sized enterprises (SMEs) and multinationals. *Intercultural virtual teams* are temporary groups of people whose members come from different cultural backgrounds, who are separated from each other in space and time, and who work towards a common goal by using organizational and digital resources (Gibson & Gibbs, 2006). In international companies and cross-border project teams, digital technologies allow using a variety of geographically distributed resources and core competences (Cagiltay et al., 2015; Maznevski & Chui, 2018). Box 7.1 illustrates the importance of virtual teams at Google.

BOX 7.1   VIRTUAL TEAMS AT GOOGLE

As one of the largest global technology companies, Google employs more than 100 000 people in 170 cities across 60 countries. The group relies on an important number of intercultural virtual teams, with team members working in different parts of the world. Google sets guidelines for distributed work behaviour for employees, 'buddies' (trustworthy contact persons), managers and leaders. For example, for leaders, the 'distributed work playbook' sets the following recommendations:

1. 'Set team visions at work': clarify expectations, document norms and communication rules, and set guidelines for travel;
2. 'Reach out': connect with team members on a personal level and organize regular physical meetings;
3. 'Traverse time zones': respect different time zones and working hours;
4. 'Appreciate differences': reflect behaviours due to cultural norms and values, listen to support and include Google employees from all over the world.

Source: Google (2020).

Virtual teams have their own characteristics, and it is thus necessary to adapt management practices accordingly. They are often temporary and decentralized and require more flexibility and coordination. It is essential to agree on the objectives and to delegate precise tasks to all team members who then work relatively autonomously. It is often more difficult to build trust since team members do not know each other personally. Box 7.2 provides an example of an intercultural virtual team.

BOX 7.2 POCKETCONFIDANT, A START-UP WITH AN INTERCULTURAL TEAM

Located in Nice in the South of France, PocketConfidant AI is a start-up proposing digital coaching powered by artificial intelligence (AI). The company was founded in 2016 by three entrepreneurs, with backgrounds in coaching, human-machine interaction, neuro-science, innovation, and enterprise and education management. The three founders had the idea to develop a digital coaching experience, which would listen to people and help them question themselves to discover their own solutions. The management team works as an intercultural virtual team, with the ambition 'to be attentive listeners, life-long learn-ers and to pioneer capacity building through AI'. The Chief Executive Officer (CEO) is French, with professional experience in Europe, Asia and the United States, and lives in France. The Chief Technology Officer (CTO) is Ukrainian, with study experience in Italy and France, and lives in Ukraine. The Chief Learning Officer (CLO) is British-American, with work experience in Europe and the United States, and lives in France and the United States. The three entrepreneurs have been working as a virtual team since the creation of the company. Due to their intercultural profiles, they were able to raise funds from the United States, the United Kingdom, France and Australia, and to market the innovative self-coaching services globally.

Source: Mayrhofer et al. (2020).

2.1 Advantages and Challenges of Virtual Teamwork

Virtual teams enable organizations to work with the most competent people in their respective areas without the need to travel. In addition, they allow for considerable time savings since the entire 24 hours of a day can be utilized: for example, the Japanese engineer who has worked eight hours on the project can transfer the work to his colleague in Spain, who also spends eight hours on it, and then passes the work on to her American colleague, who passes her tasks back to the Japanese colleague after completion.

Intercultural virtual teams can be challenging, mainly due to misunderstandings at the organizational (for example, considering delays) and communicative levels (for example, the lack of personal and verbal exchange, and ambiguous interpretation contexts). Therefore, it is necessary to put in place coordination mechanisms. Table 7.3 indicates major advantages and challenges associated with intercultural virtual teams.

Managing communication and knowledge sharing appears to be particularly challenging in intercultural virtual teams, mainly because of the risks associated with misunderstanding and misinterpretation. Therefore, it is necessary to carefully choose the media used: rich media such as videoconferencing facilitate conversations, verbal and non-verbal signs of support, and reactions of disagreement with other team members. They are more suitable for complex (or equivocal) messages, which concern information about questions with unclear answers and discussions with divergent opinions. In contrast, lean media such as emailing remove social

Table 7.3   Advantages and challenges of intercultural virtual teams

Advantages	Challenges
• Expertise from around the globe can be integrated and combined to foster creativity and innovation • Multiplicity and diversity of perspectives and ideas enhance performance • Spontaneous calls and meetings accelerate search for information and decision-making • Time savings: working 24h around the globe, fast exchange via digital communication tools • Cost savings: saving travel costs • Fast adaptability and flexibility to respond to external pressures (accelerating solution finding and new product development)	• Lower employee commitment and identification with the organization • Coordination and leadership challenges • Team managers often lead several teams at the same time • Lack of intercultural leadership competence • High complexity can slow down decision-making • Misunderstandings due to missing personal dialogue • Technological problems due to missing resources, infrastructure or slow Internet connection

presence cues and thus a joint contextual background. They are more useful for sharing simple and explicit (or canonical) information, for example reporting on numbers and other type of data. However, when differences in the proficiency of the shared language are important, lean media can be more effective for both types of knowledge because they formalize and downplay distinct uses of the common language. This can be the case for intercultural virtual teams who choose English as the common language, but in which certain participants face pronunciation difficulties and lack language proficiency (Klitmøller & Lauring, 2013; Maznevski & Chudoba, 2000). Box 7.3 provides an example of franco-chinese virtual teams.

BOX 7.3   COMMUNICATION AND KNOWLEDGE SHARING IN FRANCO-CHINESE VIRTUAL TEAMS

Mixel Agitators is a French SME, specialized in industrial mixers, which has established a production and sales subsidiary in Beijing (China). The company designs, manufactures and sells mixers to industrial companies such as Areva, Bayer, Solvay, Sanofi, Total and Veolia. The products have specific technical specifications and need to be customized for each client. The Chinese subsidiary thus has to interact regularly with the French headquarters to monitor local operations and respond to customer demands. The company uses videoconferencing (rich media) and emailing (lean media) to manage communication and knowledge sharing between the Chinese and French teams. The French CEO and the Chinese subsidiary manager, who are both fluent in English, mainly rely on videoconferencing to coordinate business operations, but the other team members prefer to use email communication, mainly because of their lack of English proficiency. In the Chinese subsidiary, there are only three employees who speak English, and they have to translate the messages of their colleagues and contact the French headquarters. The use of email communication facilitates the translation into English, but the use of lean media also generates misunderstandings. For example, the time requested for answering emails and providing solutions is negatively perceived by the Chinese team, who has to respond quickly to requests from local customers and who fears to lose potential orders. They sometimes have the impression that their French colleagues are deliberately slowing down the processes. However, for the French team, the time spent for responding to their Chinese colleagues shows that requests are handled seriously. In fact, it can take them several days to understand the questions and to find the solutions, which are often technically complicated.

Source: Based on Dominguez and Mayrhofer (2018b).

In intercultural virtual teams, it is therefore necessary to consider the way team members experience cultural differences. Micro-interactions, that is interactions between two or several actors, are likely to influence team-level dynamics. Organizations should pay particular attention to cultural differences that can be perceived as stressors and attempt to understand how individuals cope with this stress. In cross-border teams, stressors often derive from language and communication difficulties, knowledge and professional gaps as well as geographical distance. It can be useful to enhance the team members' awareness of such issues and to implement learning processes based on their respective reflections (Zaidman & Cohen, 2020).

2.2   Working in Multiple Teams

People in organizations are sometimes working in several teams at the same time. So, for example, a person can be part of a cross-national team and at the same time be part of a cross-functional team. The different teams build the network of the whole organization, which connects and combines teams to reach organizational objectives. The existence of

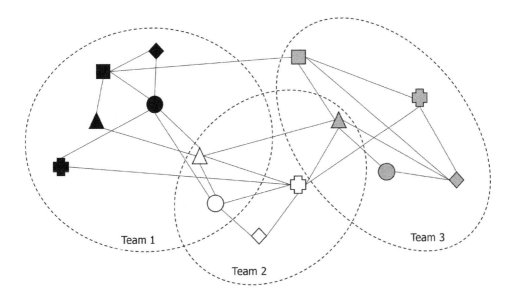

Source: Adapted from Maznevski and Chui (2018, p. 292).

Figure 7.1   Team networks in organizations

multiple teams increases the complexity of organizations because of shared and overlapping responsibilities, but the constructive combination of resources and competences also facilitates the development of synergies. As shown by Figure 7.1, team members from different national cultures (expressed in grey, black and white) can belong to the main project team (marked by circles), but also share their knowledge with regard to their function (marked by symbols) in other project teams.

In contrast to 'offline' teams, virtual teams often do not have classical hierarchical structures; they can be depicted as intertwined networks in which actors can take central or peripheral positions and be closer or further away from each other, depending on the frequency and intensity of interaction. Networks can thus show different degrees of density (Maznevski & Athanassiou, 2003). It is possible that members from the same cultural or linguistic background have more intensive contacts since they share common values and meaning systems.

However, as for non-virtual teams, research has revealed that it is mostly the weak ties that support creativity and innovation in multicultural teams (Perry-Smith & Shalley, 2014), the so-called 'strength of weak ties' (Granovetter, 1983). This is because individuals tend to connect faster and more frequently with people who share the same worldviews and opinions than to those with different worldviews. Although connecting with people from different backgrounds is less comfortable, potentially weak ties might bring about new knowledge and ideas. This is because individuals are exposed to multiple perspectives from other worldviews. Peripheral members of multicultural (virtual) teams can therefore bring fresh ideas and new perspectives into the team.

Virtual teams rely on strong communication and interaction, and this is particularly important in intercultural teams, when team members have different communication styles. It is essential to foster regular communication from the start of the project since people do not necessarily know each other. Some organizations even work with virtual team facilitators whose role is to address group dynamics, foster participation and face-to-face meetings, identify expectations, uncover anxieties and provide constructive feedback to the team (Lisak & Erez, 2015). Virtual teams must also adopt a common language that can be understood by all team members. Even if English is often used as a lingua franca, some members may have a better command of English than others, which might provoke unbalanced power relations within the team. It is therefore recommended to pay specific attention to the language choice (Chapter 9) (Tenzer et al., 2014).

In principle, efficient cooperation is based on mutual understanding and a good knowledge of all parties involved (DiStefano & Maznevski, 2000). In the sense of *constructive intercultural management*, team managers should attempt to organize regular physical meetings with all members, at least at the beginning of virtual team cooperation, since such meetings are essential for developing a common team spirit.

3. CONSTRUCTIVE INTERCULTURAL TEAM DEVELOPMENT

Intercultural team development is a central goal of *constructive intercultural management*. The objective is to develop the intercultural competences of team members in order to increase the quality and efficiency of teamwork, as well as performance and satisfaction. Intercultural team development can take place at different stages, for example at the start in the form of teambuilding or later during ongoing projects to provide continuous support for arising intercultural difficulties. It can be facilitated by formal (*on-the-job*) and informal (*off-the-job*) teambuilding measures such as leisure activities. In this way, it is possible to establish trust relationships and to strengthen the feeling of being part of the team.

There are four possible leadership modes in intercultural teams: (1) single leadership, (2) paired leadership, (3) rotated leadership and (4) shared leadership. The choice depends on whether activities are centralized or distributed and whether authority is vertically or horizontally organized (Zander & Butler, 2010) (Table 7.4).

Table 7.4 Four leadership modes in intercultural teams

Type	Definition	Major advantages	Major disadvantages
Single leadership	Leadership is appointed to one person. Decision-making and coordination lie in the responsibility of the team leader.	Centralized and fast decision-making.	Cultural dilemmas when team members expect different leadership styles.
Paired leadership	Leadership functions are carried out by two persons. They share responsibilities and make joint decisions.	Leaders can share responsibilities and lead team members according to their culturally based leadership expectations.	Disagreements in decision-making. Takes more time.
Rotated leadership	Leadership activities are distributed among several team members. Decision-making authority shifts over time from one member to another.	Inclusion of multiple team members.	Contradictory leadership styles. Unsuitable for certain cultures (for example, high power distance cultures).
Shared leadership	The team is self-responsible for leadership activities. Self-management ('holacracy').	Involvement and active engagement of all team members.	Contradictory leadership styles. Unsuitable for certain cultures (for example, high power distance cultures).

Source: Based on Zander and Butler (2010).

In intercultural virtual teams, team members should exchange their respective – usually divergent – expectations and ideas regarding teamwork (Barmeyer & Haupt, 2016). This includes the awareness of individual roles in the team (expert, communicator, decision-maker, etc.), and jointly negotiated and accepted working practices. There are three phrases for the intercultural design of team processes: (1) mapping, (2) bridging and (3) integrating (Maznevski & DiStefano, 2000) (Figure 7.2). Team members tend to concentrate on tasks and project goals; however, interpersonal and group dynamics as well as intercultural processes are often neglected. It is possible to control them through a moderator or consultant.

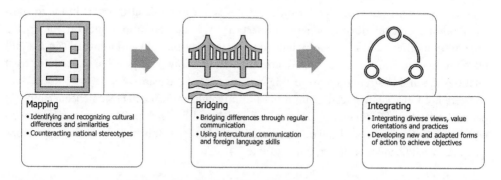

Source: Adapted from Maznevski and DiStefano (2000).

Figure 7.2   MBI (mapping – bridging – integrating) process model

Moreover, it is also possible to organize temporary meetings to establish a 'heartbeat', which can increase the efficiency of virtual teams: 'rhythmically pumping new life into the team's processes before members circulated to different parts of the world and task, returning again at a predictable pace' (Maznevski & Chudoba 2000, p. 486). The meaning of the 'heartbeat' emphasizes the 'heart' as a human component of social interaction, mutual appreciation, sympathy and empathy. It is necessary to consider design structures and processes interculturally, but also human interactions. Regular physical meetings play an essential role to achieve the common goal. Furthermore, organizations can adopt rule-oriented formalizations such as a 'code of conduct' or a 'team charter', which have proven themselves in Anglo-Saxon cultures (Schneider et al., 2014). It is necessary to take into account the intercultural constellation of the team so that the team members can share the developed orientation (Maznevski and Chui, 2018). Box 7.4 provides the example of project teams at Google.

BOX 7.4   UNDERSTANDING TEAM EFFECTIVENESS AT GOOGLE

In 2012, Google started the project 'Aristotle' to study 180 project teams in order to understand what makes cross-functional teams more effective. The conducted interviews focused on team characteristics such as group dynamics, skill sets, personality traits and emotional intelligence. The findings indicate that the most important factors concern team collaboration:

1. Psychological safety: the team members feel safe to take risks within the team without feeling embarrassed when they make mistakes, ask questions and propose their ideas.
2. Dependability: effective teams are reliable, that is, they complete work on time and with high quality.
3. Structure and clarity: the members understand their job expectations and how to accomplish their tasks.
4. Meaning: team members find a sense of purpose in their work and in the team output.
5. Impact: team members feel that they are making a difference with their work and that it is important for the organization.

Source: Rework (2020).

Table 7.5   Factors stimulating creativity in intercultural and virtual teams

Category	Factors applying to all teams	Factors applying to virtual teams
Leadership	Setting clear objectives and a sense of purpose Identifying the potential of the intercultural team Recognizing the strengths of all team members Motivating the team Openness to cultural diversity Boundary management between team members of different cultures Open communication and positive atmosphere Managing and solving conflicts	Providing clear instructions Leaving autonomy to team members Regularly encouraging group dynamics Developing a sense of belonging Creating a climate of psychological safety Continuous communication and exchange
Team structure	Defining the team size and composition (according to intercultural skills and experience) Establishing a culturally balanced team structure Structuring tasks and processes Using intercultural individuals as boundary spanners	Choosing a variety of communication tools that can be used by all team members (for example, email, telephone, videoconferences and online platforms) Implementing a culturally sensitive interface design for digital communication Considering time differences between locations of team members
Team processes	Developing positive attitudes and beliefs Creating collaborative engagement, team cohesion and team identity Trust-building between team members Organizing regular team meetings Making efforts to share diverging opinions and viewpoints Structuring tasks and assigning roles as well as responsibilities Similarities facilitate the start of teamwork, but differences and friction might then stimulate creativity	Developing a 'sense of urgency' to maintain discipline Regular face-to-face meetings ('heartbeat'), especially at the start of the project Establishing personal relationships and trust Intercultural competences to interpret verbal and non-verbal communication

Sources: Based on Cagiltay et al. (2015); Lisak et al. (2016); Maznevski and Chui (2018); Paulus et al. (2016); Schneider et al. (2014).

Constructive intercultural teamwork varies according to the type of team and the context in which the team operates. *Boundary spanning* can also be used for intercultural team development (Di Marco et al., 2010). In this context, boundary spanners do not necessarily hold a leading position, but often perform several functions within the team. Boundary spanners can fulfil the following three functions in intercultural teams: (1) representation, (2) information procurement and (3) coordination of tasks. Boundary spanning, a global mindset, cultural intelligence and biculturalism are important competences for intercultural teams (Zander et al., 2012). In fact, intercultural individuals can improve intercultural interactions in multinational teams and adopt behaviours that bridge cultural gaps, namely facilitating, translating, integrating, mediating and empathetic comforting (Backmann et al., 2020).

Table 7.5 indicates strategic, structural and processual prerequisites, which can positively stimulate creativity in intercultural teams.

SUMMARY

In this chapter, we have focused on intercultural teams, which can take the form of virtual teams. Compared to monocultural teams, they are likely to increase the complexity of cooperation, but they can also generate multiple solutions due to complementary competences. However, the potential of team members and intercultural group dynamics is not always fully exploited and it is necessary to pay particular attention to intercultural leadership skills. Organizations need to adopt appropriate mechanisms to stimulate team member collaboration and creativity and we propose several factors that may stimulate creativity in intercultural and virtual teams.

DISCUSSION QUESTIONS

1. What are the differences between monocultural and intercultural teams?
2. What are required leadership skills for intercultural teams?
3. What are the advantages and challenges associated with intercultural virtual teamwork?
4. What are further mechanisms organizations can use to foster intercultural team development? Which mechanisms are appropriate for intercultural virtual teams?

8

Intercultural transfer of management practices

In this chapter, we will explain how organizations transfer management practices constructively across cultures. First, we will present concepts and models of intercultural transfer, and examine how multinational companies can organize knowledge transfer processes between headquarters and subsidiaries. Second, we will study major challenges faced by multinationals in the intercultural transfer of management tools and practices. Third, we will indicate how intercultural transfer can be managed constructively through recontextualization.

CHAPTER LEARNING OBJECTIVES

1. Be familiar with concepts and models of intercultural transfer.
2. Know how multinationals can organize intercultural transfer processes.
3. Understand the concepts of contextualization, decontextualization and recontextualization.
4. Gain an appreciation of how to manage intercultural transfer constructively.

1. CONCEPTS AND MODELS OF INTERCULTURAL TRANSFER

The intercultural transfer of knowledge, ideas and practices is a common and vital activity within and between organizations. It concerns the diffusion and adaptation of artefacts, routines and practices across cultural boundaries. Internationalization and globalization (Chapter 2) have increased the necessity and relevance to transfer management practices interculturally. Transfer processes can take place at the individual, organizational and societal levels. They are subject to culture, institutions and contextual conditions such as asymmetries of interests and power (Ybema & Byun, 2009).

1.1 Intercultural Transfer in Multinational Companies

The success of multinational companies increasingly depends on the effective circulation of knowledge and ideas. Headquarters often attempt to exert direct influence on their subsidiaries through coordination, management and control mechanisms. They are tempted to strive for the harmonization and standardization of their strategies, structures, processes and organizational cultures (Dörrenbächer & Geppert, 2017) to reduce complexity and to create coherence, alignment and transparency.

It is questionable, however, to what extent corporate strategies, structures and processes are converging on a global scale. Companies often have to deal with opposed logics of convergence and divergence, homogenization and heterogenization or standardization and differentiation. Intercultural management shows that globalization has not led to the convergence of values and practices in different economic and organizational systems. Despite a certain degree of 'surface' harmonization, regional and local contexts remain highly diverse, and organizations are simultaneously exposed to processes of convergence and divergence (Chapter 2).

This means that concepts, standards and practices developed in the context of the parent company cannot always be adopted and implemented in foreign subsidiaries. International transfer thus needs to be regarded as an *intercultural* process in which subjective perception and interpretation play a central role (Brannen, 2004; d'Iribarne, 2012). In particular, divergent systems of meaning can lead to difficulties in communication, and local subsidiaries may question the relevance of standards defined by the parent company (Barmeyer & Davoine, 2011). Such processes are even more challenging when they concern different organizations, for example in the case of joint ventures, mergers and acquisitions. It is therefore necessary to actively shape the processes of intercultural transfer within organizations.

According to the three-level model (see Chapter 4), intercultural transfer processes take place on individual, organizational and societal levels (Table 8.1).

Table 8.1 Three-level model and examples of intercultural transfer

Levels	Examples of intercultural transfer
Micro level: Individuals	Migrant workers and expatriates International consulting
Meso level: Organization	Organizational practices Management instruments (for example, corporate values, codes of conduct, ERP – Enterprise Resource Planning)
Macro level: Societies	Models of vocational training Liberalization/hybridization of economic models

In multinational companies, intercultural transfer is often organized from an ethnocentric perspective, which may lead to failure. An interesting example is provided by *Fordlândia*, a city founded by the US Ford Motor Company in Brazil (Box 8.1).

BOX 8.1   FORDLÂNDIA, A FAILURE LINKED TO THE ETHNOCENTRIC TRANSFER OF ORGANIZATIONAL PRACTICES

The city of Fordlândia, named after the founder of the company Henry Ford, is located south of Santarém in the Amazon rainforest. The industrial town was established in 1928 by Henry Ford to secure natural rubber exploitation for the production of car tyres in the United States. The aim was to build a city of 10 000 inhabitants, but the project failed. In fact, Brazilian workers could not get used to the prescribed – puritanically oriented – living and working conditions modelled on the corporate headquarters in Detroit. They had to wear identity badges, keep early working hours (from 6 a.m. to 3 p.m.) controlled with the help of time clocks and adopt the US way of life, including American-style housing and US food in the canteens. Alcohol, tobacco and football were prohibited. In 1930, the workers revolted against the prescribed rules of life and nutrition, and the Brazilian army intervened. The city was abandoned in 1934, and the area was sold back to the Brazilian government. Nowadays, the city is a ghost town in the middle of the jungle.

Source: Grandin (2009).

The three levels of the model may also intertwine. So, multinationals can choose to transfer vocational training systems to foreign countries. For example, German multinationals such as Bosch, Siemens and Volkswagen have exported the German dual education and training system to countries where they face difficulties to recruit skilled labour (Gessler, 2017). They often benefit from the support of public institutions such as the chambers of commerce. Box 8.2 explains how the German company Schuler successfully transferred the German apprenticeship system to Mexico.

BOX 8.2   GERMAN COMPANY SCHULER SUCCESSFULLY TRANSFERS DUAL VOCATIONAL TRAINING TO MEXICO

The German company Schuler is the world's leading manufacturer of presses for the metal forming industry. The presses are used to produce parts for cars and electric motors, beverage and aerosol cans, coins, sinks and large pipes. The company employs 6 000 people in more than 40 countries. Three subsidiaries are located in Mexico where the company has established a vocational training centre. The three-year course is based on the curriculum for apprenticeships in industrial engineering professions, with theoretical and practical phases like in Germany. The company can thus educate apprentices as industrial mechanics. The participants receive a certificate from the German Chamber of Commerce and Industry, the equivalent to the qualification received in Germany. The transfer of the dual vocational training facilitates the supply of a young and skilled workforce, which is essential for the production of high-tech presses and technological system solutions. In the past, Schuler was facing difficulties to recruit qualified staff since the Mexican education system does not offer basic technical training as in Germany. The project is also supported by other companies who can use the training facilities established by Schuler.

Source: Schuler (2013).

For multinational companies, the intercultural transfer of organizational practices appears to be particularly challenging. Organizational practices are '[...] particular ways of conducting organizational functions that have evolved over time under the influence of an organization's history, people, interests, and actions and that have become institutionalized in the organization' (Kostova, 1999, p. 309). They can take multiple forms: strategic or cultural, highly formal or informal, people-embodied or product-embodied, and soft or hard practices. Reflecting the collective knowledge of the organization, they can be accepted or rejected by the employees. The aim of embedding organizational practices is that employees, when performing corporate tasks, take practices, methods and cognitive elements for granted, which then become a kind of 'unwritten law'. Organizational practices are then infused with values and become part of corporate culture and identity. The commitment to values is thus essential for the intercultural transfer of organizational practices.

> Value-infused practices relate to issues of identity, culture, language, rituals and customs which have over time evolved within the local cultural system and which are continuously reconfirmed by the local social environment. The transfer of value-infused practices across MNC sub-units therefore requires not only the transfer of knowledge and behavioural rules but also the change of patterns of meaning, interpretation, symbolic attachment and individual values. (Blazejewski, 2006, p. 66)

Organizations are open social systems in which intercultural transfer processes of practices take place. When multinational companies transfer practices from headquarters to subsidiaries, it is necessary to take into account four major elements of the system: (1) contexts, (2) actors, (3) contents and (4) interactions (Figure 8.1):

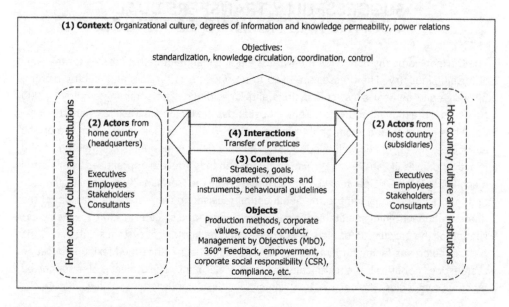

Source: Based on Barmeyer (2018).

Figure 8.1   International transfer of concepts and instruments in multinationals

(1)   There are *contexts* such as countries and organizations, with defined boundaries and different degrees of information and knowledge permeability from other systems. In addition, transfer processes are characterized by subordination and superordination, with (strategic, financial and legal) power being generally more concentrated at the parent company.

(2) *Actors* such as managers, employees, consultants and stakeholders participate in transfer processes. At the headquarters, 'transfer managers' can be responsible for setting up and managing subsidiaries and, in particular, implementing information and production systems. Expatriates and external consultants can play a mediating role in international transfer processes between headquarters and subsidiaries.

(3) *Contents* concern, for example, strategies, goals, management instruments and concepts, behavioural guidelines which are then materialized in the *objects* such as production methods, corporate values and codes of conduct.

(4) Intercultural transfer takes place in *interactions*, with the exchange of knowledge and practices. Interactions can be unidirectional or bidirectional, with varying intensity, and might lead to changes within the whole system. They are often *asymmetrical*, originating from the parent company and being transferred to the subsidiary.

1.2   Analysing Intercultural Transfer Processes

In multinational companies, intercultural transfer processes can concern headquarters and subsidiaries, but also external stakeholders. Transfer processes can take place within the multinational, that is from the parent company to subsidiaries, from subsidiaries to the parent company or between subsidiaries. Since multinationals are increasingly embedded in global networks, transfer processes can also associate other organizations, for example acquired companies, cooperation partners, suppliers, distributors and customers (Mayrhofer, 2013; Valentino et al., 2018). The strategic orientation – ethnocentric, polycentric, regiocentric and geocentric – of the multinational (Chapter 2) often determines to what extent and the way organizational practices are transferred internationally. This orientation refers to the alignment of the organizational culture and the associated decision-making authority, control standards, incentive systems, intensity and direction of communication (Perlmutter, 1969). Intercultural transfer processes in multinational companies have been analysed from institutional and cultural perspectives (Lervik, 2008).

From an *institutional perspective*, the success of transfer processes is determined by the degree and type of 'institutionalization' of practices in foreign subsidiaries. Institutionalization is the 'process by which a practice achieves a taken-for-granted status at the recipient unit – a status of "this is how we do things here"' (Kostova, 1999, p. 311). The transferred practices thus also gain a symbolic meaning for the employees of the receiving company because the diffused set of rules is transmitted with value-infused meanings (Kostova, 1999).

According to Kostova (1999), the transfer of organizational practices takes place in two steps: (1) implementation and (2) internalization.

(1) *Implementation* concerns the way subsidiaries comply with the formal rules of the parent company's organizational practices, and the adoption of behaviours and processes that can be observed objectively.

(2) *Internalization* refers to the fact that employees of subsidiaries consider the transferred organizational practices to be valuable and give them a symbolic meaning. Employees are motivated and committed to put formal rules into practice and they agree with the adoption of the new practice.

The two steps are linked to each other, even if the implementation is not always followed by the internalization of practices. Transfer processes are considered to be successful when organizational practices are implemented and internalized (Kostova, 1999). Box 8.3 explains how the French multinational Danone has adapted lean production practices to the institutional contexts of Argentina and Brazil.

BOX 8.3 DANONE TRANSFERS LEAN PRODUCTION PRACTICES TO ARGENTINA AND BRAZIL

Danone is one of the world leaders in fresh dairy and plant-based products, packaged waters and nutrition. The mission of the company is 'to bring health through food to as many people as possible'. The group employs more than 100 000 people in over 55 countries. The parent company transfers the corporate lean production programme, called 'DaMaWay' (Danone Manufacturing Way) to foreign subsidiaries. 'DaMaWay' is based on three principles: (1) performance management: indicators and tools are used to guarantee continuous and progressive improvement; (2) organizational development: clear and precise tasks are assigned to workers to develop competences and skills; (3) proximity leadership: communication and teamwork are encouraged. The implementation and internalization of the lean production programme require adaptations to local institutional contexts. The examples of Argentina and Brazil show how labour laws, the strength of labour unions and the source of employee motivation can influence the way 'DaMaWay' is implemented and internalized.

In Argentina, following the workers' resistance to the programme, 'DaMaWay' was renamed 'Proyecto Dueños' ('Project Owners'). Instead of applying teamwork, each worker was made an 'owner' of his or her task: 'some machines were divided into pieces in order to ensure that every worker had his or her own individual responsibility' (Friel & de Villechenon, 2018, p. 291). Wage differences between managers and workers are smaller than in Brazil, and a strong labour union secured higher salaries so that workers were motivated by the desire to feel proud of their work, a characteristic of Argentinian culture.

In Brazil, teamwork was introduced, but hierarchies remained the same, so that the company started to promote workers to managerial positions. High wage differentials between managers and workers, and weak labour unions in Brazil led to the fact that workers were motivated by promotion to compensate wage differentials. Moreover, they received year-end bonuses for team performance. Local labour laws, for example severance indemnity funds, cause high turnover in Brazil, since workers are paid upon their dismissal. Workers with low wages therefore often ask voluntarily for dismissal.

Source: Friel and de Villechenon (2018).

The *cultural perspective* pays attention to the multiple types of culture, which are likely to shape organizational practices. The term 'intercultural transfer' suggests that the development of social systems is not only shaped by internal, but also by external influences. Culture and interculturality can thus be considered as a continuous process of construction and deconstruction. In this perspective, language, meaning and interpretation of practices come to the forefront (Brannen, 2004; d'Iribarne et al., 2020). Culture is then defined as an interpretation system (Geertz, 1973) (Chapter 3) and the intercultural transfer of practices involves people using different semiotic and semantic repertoires. Organizational practices originate from one cultural system and are marked by the meaning of that specific system. When transferred to other cultural systems, people make sense of these practices, adapt them to their own reality and can possibly give them new meanings (d'Iribarne & Henry, 2007). In other words, no idea is the same in two peoples' minds.

When organizational practices are transferred internationally, it is necessary to take into account the institutional and cultural contexts of different countries (Lervik, 2008). Parent companies tend to adopt an ethnocentric approach and to standardize processes with the objective to achieve cost-reduction and synergy effects. Foreign subsidiaries and external stakeholders differ in their propensity to adopt new practices, which can be linked to the characteristics of their business environment, but also to the behaviours of involved actors. In fact, receiving organizations can be more or less motivated to participate in transfer processes and use institutional and cultural patterns of their home country to maintain local practices. In practice, multinationals therefore often need to adapt certain aspects of the transferred processes (Beddi & Mayrhofer, 2013).

2.   CHALLENGES IN INTERCULTURAL TRANSFER

Intercultural transfer can be regarded as a process that takes place in different steps. The company first needs to determine the organizational practices that are transferred to the target organization(s). It is then necessary to compose the team responsible for the transfer at the headquarters and the team in charge of the integration of the selected practices at the local level. Both teams should be involved during the whole process, and collaborate and communicate constantly. The adoption of the new practices in the target organizations may require time and adaptations. It is useful to follow up the implemented processes in order to make adjustments and to measure their effectiveness.

Concerning the adoption of new organizational practices in target organizations, three possible reactions can be observed (Barmeyer & Davoine, 2006):

(1) *Resistance*: employees resist the introduced practices and do not implement them.
(2) *Adaptation*: employees adopt the new practices following content-related and linguistic modifications to take into account the local context.
(3) *Integration*: employees accept the new practices without questioning or conflict. It is important to note that practices are never fully replicated, but undergo at least some minor changes.

The three reactions are not mutually exclusive and target organizations can demonstrate diverging reactions according to the organizational practices being transferred. An example is provided in Box 8.4.

BOX 8.4 TRANSFER OF CORPORATE VALUES FROM US AND CANADIAN MULTINATIONALS TO FRANCE AND GERMANY

US and Canadian multinationals attempted to transfer their corporate values to their French and German subsidiaries. The French subsidiary rejected the common American value of 'compliance' to report misbehaviour, irregularities and infringements, which was interpreted as denouncement and whistleblowing (*resistance*). Corporate values were translated into French and German, but words like 'integrity' and 'excellence' adopted new connotations in France and Germany and had to be changed (*adaptation*). The corporate values were displayed in the subsidiaries, but they were not integrated and internalized by local employees.

Source: Based on Barmeyer and Davoine (2006).

The reactions of target organizations can evolve over time and companies can take measures to facilitate the local adoption of practices. For example, employees may demonstrate *resistance* for a limited time, and then change to *adaptation* or even *integration*. They can voluntarily give up resistance if they realize that the transferred practices make sense for their daily work. The *adaptation* and *integration* of new practices at the local level can also be achieved by human resource management actions. Finally, top management and the parent company can use authority, coercion and sanctions to impose new practices.

Organizational culture and human resource management instruments, especially values and codes of conduct, play an important role in the transfer of management tools and practices (Tréguer-Felten, 2017) since they influence organizational learning and development. A 'strong' organizational culture is likely to contribute to the added value of the organization, namely through coherence. This is particularly true for multinational companies, which often strive for uniformity in their global operations.

Multinationals thus can face important challenges when transferring their practices to foreign locations. Boxes 8.5, 8.6 and 8.7 explain the difficulties faced by Western multinationals who attempted to transfer organizational practices to Japan, Lebanon and Vietnam.

BOX 8.5 TRANSFERRING ORGANIZATIONAL PRACTICES FROM GERMANY TO JAPAN

The transfer of organizational practices from a German multinational to its Japanese subsidiary illustrates the potential for conflicts, linked to diverging institutional and cultural contexts. The respective entities are described as 'typically German' and 'typically Japanese'. They are confronted with various challenges. Four organizational practices in particular led to incomprehension and conflicts in the Japanese subsidiary:

1. The corporate value of 'integrity': according to the German understanding, the term was evidenced with guidelines of conduct relating to price agreements, negotiation tactics and corruption. For Japanese managers, this value clashed with local practices, since the exchange of gifts between business partners is an important ritual. In Japan, exchanging gifts is not an illegal practice or assimilated to corruption, but rather a gesture of courtesy that strengthens the quality of relationships between business partners.

2. English as the common corporate language: this challenge refers to the conflict between young English-speaking Japanese employees and older employees with little knowledge of English, but with higher hierarchical positions. The latter complained that they were increasingly unable to participate in meetings, misunderstood written and verbal information, and were becoming more isolated in regard to the parent company.

3. Quality standards set by the German parent company: the objective was to reduce costs, but the new standards clashed with the Japanese understanding of quality. In Japan, quality has a high symbolic meaning, leading to proudness and identification with the company and its products. Cost reduction cannot take place at the expense of quality.

4. A global evaluation and feedback system for managers: the proposed system is in contrast with the traditional seniority principle in Japanese organizations. Evaluation as open criticism and confrontation between colleagues or superiors is not a common practice in Japan due to the value of 'saving face'.

Source: Blazejewski (2006).

The example described in Box 8.5 shows that employees in host organizations can be exposed to dual constraints and may have limited scope for shaping their own actions. If the employees of the Japanese subsidiary behave according to the guidelines of the German parent company, they might jeopardize their relationship with Japanese business partners. In the same way, preserving their behaviour according to the Japanese norms can provoke conflicts with the German headquarters. This situation triggers frustration among employees and eventually leads to resistance. The transfer and alignment of management practices in the Japanese subsidiary was discarded in favour of a more flexible regional adaptation. Both sides could thus find mutually acceptable solutions.

BOX 8.6 TRANSFERRING CODES OF CONDUCT FROM THE UNITED STATES AND EUROPE TO LEBANON

Western multinationals are often facing difficulties when they attempt to transfer codes of conduct to the Arab world. For example, several US and European companies observed that their codes of conduct had been adapted to the Lebanese context, characterized by cultural diversity, the coexistence of religious groups and a high proportion of women in leading positions. Even if local employees did not express criticism or resistance to the parent companies, they interpreted and adapted several rules of the transferred code of conduct. For example, private discussions were allowed at work since social relationships are paramount in the Lebanese culture. In the same way, the recruitment of family members was possible, since this is a widespread practice in Lebanon.

Source: Nakhle and Davoine (2016).

BOX 8.7 TRANSFERRING PIZZA HUT'S GLOBAL CODE OF CONDUCT FROM THE UNITED STATES TO VIETNAM

Pizza Hut is the world's largest pizza chain, operating more than 18 000 restaurants, mainly through franchising contracts. The US headquarters propose a global code of conduct, which employees need to sign to ensure that they will follow the established rules. In Vietnam, the implementation of the company's code of conduct presented several challenges for local managers. Although the majority of principles were adopted and employees adhered to the core values of Pizza Hut in their daily work. Certain ethical rules clashed with the Vietnamese business culture. For example, commissions and gifts from suppliers, illicit payments to local authorities and personal favours appeared to be critical issues. Local managers thus had to explain the importance of the code of conduct for long-term profitability and sustainability, and train local employees to respect the rules and principles established by the US headquarters.

Source: Claes (2019).

3.   CONSTRUCTIVE INTERCULTURAL TRANSFER OF MANAGEMENT PRACTICES

Management and control instruments are culture-specific and their transfer to other contexts might be problematic. For this reason, *recontextualization* helps to explain how companies can constructively transfer their organizational practices (Brannen, 2004). Recontextualization allows a more adequate and meaningful, and thus more successful reception of the transferred practices, by adapting and negotiating their meanings. For a better understanding of international transfer, it is necessary to differentiate three forms (Table 8.2): (1) contextualization, (2) decontextualization and (3) recontextualization.

Table 8.2   Forms of contextualization for intercultural transfers

Concept	Time	Challenge
Contextualization	Past	Concepts make sense in their context of origin, but there is a lack of awareness of one's own cultural characteristics
Decontextualization	Present	Irritation if practices do not fit to the context or seem senseless
Recontextualization	Future	Confrontation with the existing and the new, and dialogical creation of meaning to be effective

Source: Based on Barmeyer (2012b, p. 110).

3.1   Contextualization

Organizational practices that are regarded as universal are neither culture-free nor value-free. They are created in a specific cultural and institutional context, at a specific time and in a specific space, due to underlying challenges or problems. They are conceived, designed and developed by people whose thinking and actions are based on certain basic assumptions and values, before being tested and integrated in organizations. Management practices are therefore meaningful and effective in specific contexts. If they prove themselves, they are retained. If they do not prove themselves, they are discarded. Contextualization can be defined as the consideration of meaningful elements of the actors' organizational environment, which influence the framework for action, that is the interactions, and thus contribute to their development and interpretation. Shared contextual knowledge is shaped by multiple factors, for example the cultural affiliation of interaction partners, institutions, professional cultures, social classes, organizational structures and processes, as well as the actors' strategies, tactics and interests.

3.2   Decontextualization

Implementing management practices in other cultural contexts is a difficult task (d'Iribarne et al., 2020). In contrast to their context of origin, these practices may not be correctly understood and they may not fit the local institutional and cultural context.

> (1) Countries differ in their institutional context; (2) organizational practices reflect the institutional environment of the country where they have been developed and established; and, therefore (3) when practices are transferred across borders, they may not 'fit' with the institutional context of the recipient environment, which, in turn, may be an impediment to the transfer. (Kostova, 1999, p. 314)

When transferred to other cultural and institutional contexts, organizational practices are not always understood since their meaning and sense are likely to change. Decontextualization then describes the state in which practices no longer make sense to local employees. Intercultural misunderstandings lead then to resistance, and practices remain ineffective. Box 8.8 shows two examples of the decontextualization of codes of conduct.

BOX 8.8   EXAMPLES OF DECONTEXTUALIZATION IN INTERNATIONAL TRANSFER PROCESSES

Walmart in Germany

In the United States, codes of conducts require a commitment to the rules of conduct specified by the company, which is expressed by a signature. Any breaking of the rules of conduct can lead to sanctions, including dismissal. In Germany, the US retail company Walmart made headlines with transferring these rules: two employees were fired because their collegial relationship developed into an intimate one and eventually led to marriage. Several months later, the ethics guideline was declared void by the German labour court, and Walmart had to rehire both employees.

Rio Tinto in Brazil

North American codes of conduct often start with a passage stating the prohibition of carrying firearms within the company. This is mostly contained in other versions of foreign subsidiaries, although national weapons bans apply in most countries by law. While the passage was surprising for European employees of Rio Tinto, an Anglo-Australian metals and mining corporation, the situation was very different in Brazil. The ban led to the fact that previously armed and socially weak workers, who received their salaries in a wage bag at the end of the month, were attacked on the company site and had to hand over their monthly salaries, defenceless.

Source: Barmeyer (2012b, p. 104).

Therefore, organizational practices have to be 'made to fit', that is, recontextualized to make sense in the target context.

3.3   Recontextualization

Despite their challenges, transfer processes can also bring about constructive outputs in multinational companies. They provide new knowledge, ideas and elements to organizations, and they initiate change and learning processes which contribute to organizational development. To be effectively implemented, they should be recontextualized (Brannen, 2004; Søderberg, 2015). Recontextualization refers to a cognitive process in which involved actors provide new meaning and sense to signs (such as language) and objects in social systems: 'recontextualization is a notion derived from anthropology that tackles the semantic dimension of internationalization by examining how meanings shift and change in differing cultural contexts. As the term suggests, recontextualization focuses on the context that gives meaning to language, objects, and systems' (Brannen, 2004, p. 604).

Recontextualization leads to the situation in which central elements (for example, organizational practices) of the context of origin (for example, the parent company) are made to fit the context of application (for example, the subsidiary) in such a way that they are understood and perceived as meaningful and accepted as a common frame for action. They can thus become effective in the whole organization (d'Iribarne & Henry, 2007). Local interpretations and new combinations of meaning take place, and organizational practices are then perceived as useful.

Recontextualization is influenced by institutional (for example, laws, educational systems and employer–employee relationships), cultural (for example, values and practices) and linguistic (for example, semantics and interpretation) factors. It is also necessary to consider cultural and institutional proximity or distance (Moalla & Mayrhofer, 2020), which can lead to the desired 'fit'.

> The social context also influences transferability [...]. Communication and diffusion is more likely between actors that share similar characteristics or perceive themselves to be similar, whereas more arduous relationships limit transfer [...]. The lack of congruence or fit [...] in relation to its cultural or institutional context is not considered. (Lervik, 2008, p. 302)

Box 8.9 and Table 8.3 show how recontextualization takes place at foreign locations of Walt Disney Company, one of the world's leading mass media and entertainment companies. The case highlights diverging meanings and perceptions of products, organizational practices and ideologies in the United States, Japan and France (Brannen, 2004).

BOX 8.9   RECONTEXTUALIZATION IN THE CASE OF WALT DISNEY COMPANY

The international experience of Walt Disney Company shows that products (cartoon character Mickey Mouse, the figure of the cowboy and souvenirs), organizational practices (service orientation, human resource management and training) and ideologies (the concepts of Disneyland and 'foreignness') can take on different meanings when transferred to foreign markets. For example, in the United States, souvenirs are 'fun' and 'part of the experience', whereas in France, souvenirs are rather regarded as a waste of money. In Japan, they must fit into the *senbetsu* system, that is the traditional gift giving custom, and represent a legitimating memento.

Source: Based on Brannen (2004).

Table 8.3 Perception of Walt Disney Company's organizational practices in the United States, Japan and France

Transferred organizational practices	United States	Japan	France
Perception of service orientation	Hypernormal The 'what' and 'how' of services including food reflects American norms and values (for example, alcohol is prohibited).	Normal Pronounced service and harmony orientation are also present in everyday life.	Abnormal Service orientation is perceived as exaggerated.
Human resource management practices	Hypernormal American standards and labour regulations. Strict 'Disney' dress code and behaviour.	Normal Standards are regarded as patronage by employers who prescribe how to dress.	Illegal and invasive Labour regulations are perceived as an invasion of privacy and personal expression.
Training practices	Hypernormal Disney has its own rules, for example, 40 days of training at Disney University.	Normal No special training is necessary, since rules and service-orientation are taught in all other jobs.	Totalitarian Rules are perceived as totalitarian.

Source: Adapted from Brannen (2004).

Box 8.10 explains how a Danish multinational in the biotechnology industry transferred corporate values to its Indian subsidiary, with local adaptations taking place through recontextualization. The concerned values were interpreted by local employees and took on new meanings in the Indian context.

BOX 8.10 LEADERSHIP AND CORPORATE VALUES

The Danish biotechnology company attempted to implement corporate values, which were defined uniformly throughout the company, in the Indian subsidiary located in Bangalore. The two values *work-life balance* and *empowerment* show that local adjustments were made at the subsidiary. By reinterpretation the Indian workforce made the corporate values fit into their work context:

- The value *work-life balance* is a general concern for the well-being of employees in Scandinavian countries and, for the Danish multinational, means that the company takes care of employees and encourages professional growth. The value was quickly and easily accepted by Indian employees, but adapted to the local context. In line with the prevailing 'nurturant leadership', Indian employees reinterpreted the value *work-life balance* as the nurturing of their personal and professional development, including the well-being of their families. Consequently, they left the workplace relatively early, even if the work to be done had not been finished yet.
- The value *empowerment* encourages the autonomy of employees. In the Scandinavian context, marked by flat hierarchies, the value refers to the employees' responsibil-

ities and expansion of their scope of action for the benefit of the organization. For the Danish company, it involves developing leadership skills, taking initiatives and encouraging innovation. In the Indian subsidiary, the value *empowerment* was interpreted as a lack of interest and support from managers. In fact, Indian employees expect a rather directive leadership style, with managers taking initiatives, giving orders and controlling their execution. They respect hierarchy and are reluctant to provide feedback to superiors. Therefore, local employees waited for their managers to enable them to work with more autonomy.

The two examples suggest that recontextualization is influenced by national and corporate cultures, but also by the actors' individual strategies and interests.

Source: Based on Gertsen and Zølner (2012).

3.4   Practical Recommendations

In the context of the VUCA (Volatility, Uncertainty, Complexity and Ambiguity) world (Chapter 2), multinational companies need to find meaningful solutions that bridge the tensions between globalization and regionalization, standardization and differentiation, and ethnocentrism and ethnorelativism. Like other intercultural processes, negotiated culture (Brannen & Salk, 2000) (Chapter 5) also plays an important role in the cross-border transfer of organizational practices. Opposites must not be ignored, but rather combined as strengths to become effective in a complementary way. *Constructive intercultural management* can therefore contribute to the successful design of international transfer processes.

Based on previous work, we can propose several recommendations for the constructive transfer of organizational practices, which can be helpful for corporate and human resource management policies. We believe that multinational companies should opt for an *ethnorelativist recontextualization*, which allows combining existing practices with new elements. Recontextualization facilitates the generation of novel ideas as well as the conceptualization and implementation of management instruments in joint working groups. Actors from different cultural backgrounds can thus elaborate and introduce new, unexpected and innovative solutions. If managers and employees understand diverging meanings as a resource and not as a disturbance factor, learning, development and innovation become possible within and between organizations. These, in turn, contribute to intercultural creativity that organizations need for their survival. Three factors can help companies to constructively transfer organizational practices:

(1)   *Ethnorelativist attitude:* actors should develop an awareness of cultural differences to better understand intercultural issues and their consequences for management. They need to build intercultural competence to lead transfer processes constructively and synergistically (Chapter 11). This includes an awareness of one's own cultural background and the questioning of context-related management instruments.

(2) *Strategic impulses:* the organization should provide strategic support and shape the organizational culture to promote an ethnorelativist attitude. Actors will then be able to recognize the practices of host companies as equal in terms of knowledge and skills, and possibly leverage them for the entire organization. Strategic impulses can be supported by intercultural organizational development (Chapter 12).

(3) *Institutional anchoring:* an ethnorelativist stance can be promoted through increased contact and exchange with actors from other cultures, for example by short-term assignments, discussion forums and workshops on specific topics. Management can thus address and promote interculturality with institutionalized practices within the organization.

The *constructive design* of intercultural transfers can take place at different stages and concerns both home (for example, headquarters or the acquiring company) and host organizations (for example, subsidiaries or acquired companies): (1) negotiated conception, (2) negotiated mediation and (3) negotiated implementation (Figure 8.2).

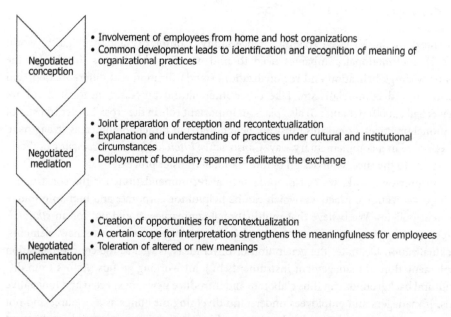

Figure 8.2   Three steps for designing cross-border transfers constructively

(1) *Negotiated conception:* the conception and development of management instruments should associate employees from home and host organizations. In the sense of multiple cultures and diversity (Özbilgin & Chanlat, 2018), it is then possible to consider and integrate a wide range of cultural ideas, positions and meanings. In this way, management concepts and instruments can be elaborated by different participants with an ethnorelativist approach instead of being developed and prescribed ethnocentrically by the home organization. Employees of host organizations can thus identify themselves with management concepts and instruments, and recognize them as meaningful (Chapter 12).

(2) *Negotiated mediation:* actors from home and host organizations should jointly prepare and accompany the implementation and recontextualization of organizational practices. This includes explaining and understanding organizational practices, which take into account institutional and cultural specifics. Expatriates and intercultural profiles, who are familiar with both systems, can act as boundary spanners (Chapter 2) to facilitate negotiated mediation (Søderberg, 2015).

(3) *Negotiated implementation:* the implementation of organizational practices should leave space for recontextualization to allow a certain scope for interpretation (Barmeyer & Davoine, 2011). Employees then have the possibility – to a certain extent – to give management concepts a new meaning that makes sense to them. These meanings should then be tolerated and accepted by the home organization.

Box 8.11 provides the example of two Finnish multinationals who succeeded to constructively transfer organizational practices to their Russian subsidiaries. Box 8.12 shows how recontextualization led to organizational learning and development (Chapter 12) at a large German car manufacturer.

BOX 8.11 TRANSFERRING ORGANIZATIONAL PRACTICES CONSTRUCTIVELY FROM FINLAND TO RUSSIA

Two Finnish multinationals experienced significant cultural differences when transferring four organizational practices (corporate culture, human resource management, management training, intercultural and linguistic training) to their Russian subsidiaries. The Finnish culture is characterized by egalitarianism, participation and advanced English language skills, whereas the Russian culture is marked by the post-Soviet period, the preference for a strong leader and limited English language skills. Nonetheless, they were able to overcome cultural barriers by two internalization mechanisms: boundary spanning and the reliance on local competence, that is the recruitment of local managers. The two multinationals proposed training sessions at the Finnish headquarters to eliminate the mistrust Russian managers initially showed towards Finnish managers. They also used translation and boundary spanners to compensate for the lack of language and cultural knowledge. The companies decided to rely on local, Russian managers in the Russian subsidiaries. Moreover, they were able to create a new corporate culture which was neither shaped by Finnish nor by Russian culture. The negotiated corporate values facilitated trust building, lowered the perception of cultural differences and enhanced employee motivation.

Source: Koveshnikov et al. (2012).

BOX 8.12 CULTURALLY ADAPTED IMPLEMENTATION OF 'STORYTELLING' SALES PRACTICES

The example of a large German car manufacturer reveals how the transfer of 'storytelling' as a sales practice to Spanish retail organizations led to intercultural organizational development and learning through recontextualization and through the shift from an ethnocentric to an ethnorelative mindset. At the beginning of the transfer, the discourse at the headquarters was dominated by phrases such as 'We [Germans] need to show them [Spanish] how it works!' and 'Every single element of the new practice needs to be implemented!', but over time terms such as 'co-creation' and 'flexibility' became popularized among the German workforce. Realizing that the transfer initiative was going to fail without local adaptations, the German managers noticed that tolerance for recontextualized meanings, practice adaptations and interest in ideas from the recipient unit was necessary to succeed in the transfer. In the following, recontextualization took place, and the Spanish, local meanings were integrated into the main practice, which, in turn, was then shared with other subsidiaries. Employees recontextualized storytelling as 'telling stories of personal experiences and interactions with other customers' instead of 'stories about the car brand's history and design' as intended by the German headquarters. In this case, intercultural organizational development was facilitated by an ethnographic action researcher who initiated joint reflections on the learning outcomes during and after the transfer. Consequently, the shift from an ethnocentric to an ethnorelative transfer strategy influenced further intercultural cooperation, such as the set-up of joint workshops. To summarize, employees recontextualized storytelling as 'telling stories of personal experiences and interactions with other customers' instead of 'stories about the car brand's history and design'.

Source: Based on Stumpf (2021).

SUMMARY

In this chapter, we have studied how organizations transfer management practices interculturally. We have presented concepts and models of intercultural transfer, and explained how multinational companies can coordinate knowledge transfer processes between headquarters and subsidiaries. Moreover, we addressed the challenges linked to the intercultural transfer of management tools and practices. We have defined the concepts of contextualization, decontextualization and recontextualization, and emphasized the facilitating role played by recontextualization for the constructive transfer of management practices between home and host organizations. We have also elaborated a set of practical recommendations of how to manage intercultural transfer processes successfully.

DISCUSSION QUESTIONS

1. What are the main challenges linked to the intercultural transfer of management practices?
2. How can multinationals coordinate intercultural transfer processes between headquarters and subsidiaries?
3. Explain the concepts of contextualization, decontextualization and recontextualization. Find your own examples.
4. What are the key success factors of intercultural transfer in multinational companies?

9
Intercultural communication and language

Multinational companies are multilingual organizations, and language plays an important role in meetings, teamwork, negotiations, knowledge transfer and subsidiary coordination. Language and communication are often 'taken-for-granted' in business practice, and organizations do not always draw on the rich language resources from their diverse workforce. In this chapter, we will first shed light on the interplay between communication, language and culture. We will then explain how organizations can deal with multiple languages and communication styles before developing the solutions they can adopt for the constructive design of multilingualism.

CHAPTER LEARNING OBJECTIVES

1. Understand the interplay between communication, language and culture.
2. Be aware about the multiple forms of language in organizations.
3. Identify challenges associated with the use of English as lingua franca.
4. Know how organizations can deal constructively with multilingualism.

1. COMMUNICATION, LANGUAGE AND CULTURE

Communication, language and culture are closely interwoven. Language permeates everyday life, and, as a visible part of communication, expresses and reflects cultural values, artefacts and practices (Szkudlarek et al., 2020).

1.1 Communication and Culture

Language is a constitutive element of culture and enables people to express and share thoughts and emotions. It forms the basis of human communication, defined as the exchange and creation of common meaning between actors through the production, reception and interpretation of signs. Signs are material manifestations to which meanings are assigned (de Saussure 1916[2011]), and sign meanings arise in specific social and cultural environments, influenced by historical, political and economic conditions. The overall goal of communication is to influence the communication partner and to generate understanding. A communicative action is therefore only successful if all involved actors reach a common understanding. Communication expresses either orally or written (Ting-Toomey & Dorjee, 2018) and can take multiple forms (Table 9.1).

Table 9.1   Communication forms in cultural contexts

Communication forms	Definition	Examples
Verbal communication	What is explicitly said in a conversation in a specific language Written text in a specific language	Direct verbal communication in Anglo-Saxon, Germanic and Scandinavian cultures Indirect verbal communication in Asian, Latin American and Mediterranean cultures
Non-verbal communication	Kinesics (gestures and mimics): body movements, facial expressions, oulesics (eye contact), posture and haptics (body contact) in oral communication Pictures, diagrams and colours in written communication	Necessity to keep eye contact with the conversation partner to signal attention in Western cultures 'Appropriate' eye contact and its length depending on the relationship between the conversation partners in some African cultures
Para-verbal communication	Prosody (tone) of the voice, intonation, volume, tempo, rhythm and pauses in oral communication Punctuation, spelling and typography in written communication	Tendency of Romance language speakers to speak louder than Germanic language speakers
Extra-verbal communication	Time and space of sign transmission, proxemics (spatial distance), chronemics and the meaning of time, olfactory stimuli (smell) and clothing	Tendency of Romance language speakers to touch more often during a conversation than English and German language speakers

Sources: Based on Bolten (2015); Ting-Toomey and Dorjee (2018).

These different forms of communication systemically intertwine. They appear together in communicative acts, influence and condition each other. When analysing language in organizations, it is necessary to consider conversations as well as documents such as strategy formulations, contracts, annual reports, codes, guidelines and patents.

Communication can take place either analogically or digitally (Chapter 7). Digital tools can take the form of 'rich media', such as videoconferences, and 'lean media', such as emails. Depending on the complexity of the message, the need for non-verbal reactions and the desired response time, these two types of media have been shown to facilitate information exchange within and between organizations across cultures (Dominguez et al., 2017; Klitmøller & Lauring, 2013).

1.2   Communication in Culture Comparison

Communication styles vary across cultures. They are notably apparent in intercultural situations in which interaction partners experience 'foreign' cultural communication patterns, and thus become aware of their own cultural imprints and communication habits. In the following, we will present two differences in communication styles.

On the one hand, there are different ways of how information is transmitted. The context dimension of culture – high-context or low-context – describes the amount of information that interlocutors should explicitly express to be understood properly (Hall & Hall, 1990) (Chapter 3). In *low-context* cultures, group members assume that most information is already stored in the message. Communication is therefore rather *explicit*. Examples are Anglo-Saxon and Germanic cultures. In *high-context* cultures, group members assume that contextual information is less stored in the message, and thus *interpret* the verbally said and written. Communication is rather *implicit* and informal communication can play an important role. Examples are Arabic, Asian and Latin American cultures (Box 9.1).

On the other hand, communication styles differ with regard to thought patterns and logics of expression (Kaplan, 1966). There are differences in how actors from different cultures express their thoughts, either verbally or written. Native English speakers think and communicate linearly with the Platonic-Aristotelian logic of dichotomies. Paragraphs usually start with a topic sentence, followed by details of the topic content and examples which highlight the claim of the topic sentence. The sentence flow is marked by the repetition of the key idea. The topic sentence may either introduce or close the paragraph, which reflects deductive or inductive thinking. In contrast, Romance language speakers tend to 'digress' from the main topic, repeat specific ideas of the topic and include ideas which do not necessarily contribute to the main idea. Speakers of many Asian languages (Japanese excluded) are characterized by a circular thought pattern. This type of communication has been found to circle around the subject, without ever explicitly mentioning the subject. 'Things are developed in terms of what they are not, rather than in terms what they are' (Kaplan, 1966, p. 17), which appears to English speakers as 'indirect' communication. Speakers of Arabic languages often use parallelisms in sentence constructions, linked with connectors ('and', 'but', 'therefore'), which may express positive and negative thoughts, synonyms and antitheses within one sentence. Tendentially, there is no super- or subordination of ideas in sentence and paragraph structure, which might appear 'archaic' to English native speakers.

BOX 9.1 INFORMAL INFORMATION CIRCULATION DURING THE ITALIAN COFFEE BREAK

In Latin cultures, informal and dialogic forms of communication are of particular importance. A practice that expresses this importance is the Italian coffee break in which employees come together spontaneously and circulate information informally. In Italian companies, the coffee break can be regarded as a dynamic, inter-divisional and heterarchical organizational practice, with several essential functions: personal information sharing, coordinating work processes, temporal structuring of the working day, problem-solving, strengthening relationships, reducing hierarchies, social networking, and gaining knowledge about processes and structures. The Italian coffee break can reduce organizational complexity in an informal and fluent way by connecting individuals from different departments and hierarchical levels in a relaxed atmosphere. This can increase the willingness to share information within organizations and is consistent with the high-context communication style that characterizes Latin cultures.

Source: Barmeyer et al. (2019c).

1.3   Intercultural Communication

Intercultural communication is a process of exchange and interaction between individuals and groups from different cultural backgrounds who exchange ideas, emotions and meanings verbally or non-verbally. From this perspective, culture functions as an interpretation system (Chapter 3). Members of the same cultural system share a common stock of ideas, signs, symbols and meanings that are taken for granted and that create unambiguity. This, in turn, enables the creation of common meaning and shared knowledge for goal-oriented communication and cooperation. Culture in this sense is a 'semantic inventory' (Geertz, 1973) that forms the basis for successful communication. Semantics, the study of sign meanings, is concerned with the underlying content of expressed language.

Human language is characterized by the symbolic nature of its signs, whereby the relationship between signs and their meaning is arbitrary (de Saussure 1916[2011]). We distinguish between the word, which represents a sequence of signs (in French *signifiant* = significant, linguistic expression), and the content of meaning, that is the idea that the word or linguistic sign represents (in French *signifié* = signifier, linguistic content). Expression and content are two sides of a coin. The meaning (content) of a linguistic sign is culture-bound: ideas and concepts arise in a specific cultural environment and develop according to prevailing conditions. Due to the culture-bound nature of the sign, the same expression (word or phrase) can evoke different ideas (meanings) across cultures. Box 9.2 illustrates that the word 'concept' can have different meanings in the French and German contexts.

BOX 9.2   DIVERGENT MEANINGS OF 'CONCEPT' IN FRENCH AND GERMAN

In an international project meeting held in English, French and German, managers agree to work out a 'concept' in separate groups. In the following meeting a few weeks later, the German project managers bring an elaborate folder with them, while the French bring a draft. Annoyance and prejudices emerge on both sides. The Germans think: 'these Frenchmen haven't done anything! They probably don't want to work with us!' The French think: 'these Germans behave like a steaming machine and have overtaken the project. They did all the work without us – it seems they don't want to collaborate!'

This critical incident shows that German and French managers have a different conception of the word 'concept'. Despite their similarity – 'Konzept' in German, 'concept' in French and 'concept' in English – the contents diverge: in Germany a 'concept' evokes a first plan for a solution, whereas in France a 'concept' is a first, informal collection of ideas.

Source: Barmeyer (2011b, p. 49).

Likewise, English terms that seem similar in translation can lead to misunderstandings in international project teams and, consequently, provoke frustration and annoyance. Examples include the terms 'teamwork', 'cooperation', 'quality', 'decision-making' and 'deadline'.

Differences in meanings can also arise *within* national cultures, between people from different ethnicities, professional cultures, generations or gender. Box 9.3 presents the example of divergent meanings of the term 'social responsibility' in ethnic groups in Australia.

BOX 9.3 DIVERGENT MEANINGS OF 'SOCIAL RESPONSIBILITY' IN AUSTRALIA

Ongoing tensions within an Australian minerals company between non-indigenous and indigenous employees (belonging to the aboriginal community) reveal that 'social responsibility' takes on different meanings in the intercultural context. Depending on the meaning system, an interdiscursive construction of terms and realities takes place, which influences the legitimacy of the organization and thus its ability to act. In the end, the two groups could not agree on shared meanings.

Term	Non-indigenous employees	Indigenous employees (aboriginal community)
Indigenous/ Native	Static and non-negotiable, unproblematic and generally accepted, homogenization	Demarcation/identity, problematic (political, economic and social gaps), integration efforts
Land	Economic resource	Central focus of identity, connection, dispossession, rights
Respect	Sense, regard, mutuality	'What keeps people and things in balance and harmony'
Development	Natural progress, something inherently desirable (development opportunities, sustainable development)	Sustainable (social and community) development, critical, inequality (privileges Western, capitalist ideas)
Industry	Unproblematic, provider of employment (something implicitly desirable)	Something that offers economic opportunities, but also disrupted traditions, destruction, exploitation, disadvantage/loss

Source: Parsons (2008).

Whenever the meanings from different cultural and linguistic origins resemble each other, information can be conveyed and interpreted in the same or similar way. Communication then succeeds. However, if the meanings diverge, a common understanding is more difficult because conversation partners interpret the signs differently (Adler & Gundersen, 2008). As a result, communication and cooperation may fail.

Even though many cultural-specific meanings are incommensurable, that is, they are not fully translatable, actors in intercultural communication must negotiate a common language to work together *constructively*. In a globalized and diverse multilingual work setting, language must be considered as a social practice through which actors constantly create and innovate new forms of hybrid 'interlanguages' (Janssens & Steyaert, 2014). Within organizations, actors belong to multiple linguistic identities and thus 'negotiate' new forms of communication in interaction with other actors (Figure 9.1).

Language is fluid and dynamic, and represents the social worlds of its speakers. Due to internationalization, migration and digitalization, national languages increasingly intermingle.

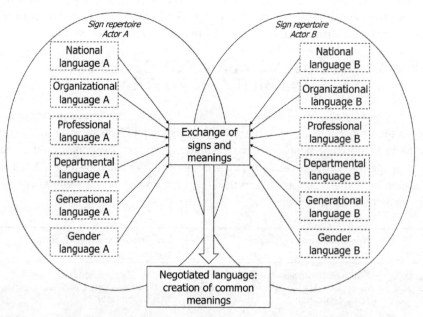

Figure 9.1 Negotiated language and meaning in intercultural communication across multiple cultures

Famous examples are 'Sheng', a Swahili-English hybrid language spoken by young people in Kenya who mix up both languages to create a new, modern identity (Janssens & Steyaert, 2014, p. 629) or 'Spanglish', a mixture of Spanish and English, spoken by the descendants of Latin immigrants in the United States. Furthermore, national languages are nowadays penetrated by Anglicisms, notably from technical lexemes and computer language. These types of linguistic syncretism have led to neologisms and hybrid forms of languages.

2. MULTILINGUALISM IN ORGANIZATIONS

Language in organizations is multifaceted and diverse (Brannen & Mughan, 2017; Horn et al., 2020). The cultural diversity of employees determines the extent of linguistic diversity in companies. According to the multi-layered cultural and identitary affiliation of actors, it is necessary to take a closer look at the many languages spoken within an organization in order to use language diversity constructively.

2.1 Multiple Layers of Language

Organizations do not only combine different national languages, but also dialects, regiolects and sociolects, professional languages (for example, those used by physicists, computer scientists and consultants), technical languages of certain departments (for example, research and development, human resources and marketing), and special vocabulary regarding the hierarchies, generations and gender (Piekkari et al., 2014). These languages constantly intertwine and influence each other (Brannen et al., 2017; Church-Morel & Bartel-Radic, 2016).

National and regional languages are the most salient language types in organizations. Although some multinational companies choose to introduce English as a common 'standard' corporate language, most companies stick to the language of the country where they are located. This type of 'everyday language' (Piekkari et al., 2014), spoken between colleagues and with business partners, manifests itself primarily in the national language of the country, but also in regional languages and dialects. Regionally embedded companies are often known for their organizational language, which is strongly influenced by the local culture and language. For example, the German Daimler Group is also known for the Swabian dialect (a dialect spoken in the area of Stuttgart), which is sometimes used in press releases and international negotiations ('Swabian-English').

Organizational (or corporate) language can emerge over time as part of organizational culture. It is characterized by acronyms and abbreviations (for example for positions, departments and processes), organization-specific denominations, technical terms and newly assigned meanings to existing terms (Aichhorn & Puck, 2017). Organizational language is often used internally for faster and more efficient communication based on a common pool of understanding. From a *constructive intercultural management* perspective, an organization-specific language can foster internal organizational identification, lead to improved formal and informal communication, serve internal and external marketing purposes, and strengthen the brand recognition value. However, organizational language may also hinder the integration of new members since they do not have the necessary knowledge of acronyms and meanings. Box 9.4 provides the example of the organizational language used at Google.

BOX 9.4   ORGANIZATIONAL LANGUAGE AT GOOGLE

At Google, the campus is called 'Googleplex', a neologism made up of 'Google' and 'complex', and employees simply call it 'Plex'. New employees are called 'nooglers' (pronounced 'new-gler'); 'xooglers' are employees who leave the company (pronounced 'zoo-gler') and 'googlegeist' is the annual survey in which Google employees rate managers and life on the Google campus.

Source: Carson (2015).

Professional language develops along with professional, technical and industry cultures, with a specific use of vocabulary, concepts and meanings. In addition to the domain-specific vocabulary, it can also include regular expressions that are used in a domain-specific way (Piekkari et al., 2014). Prominent examples are the language of computer scientists, engineers, consultants and researchers. For example, the excessive use of information technology language can lead to communication difficulties between software developers and business professionals who do not share the same semantic inventory. At the same time, professional cultural affiliation and mastery of the respective professional language can enable intercultural communication when communication across national languages fails. An example is provided in Box 9.5.

BOX 9.5   PROFESSIONAL LANGUAGE IN ENGINEERING

The affiliation to the engineering culture creates a unique, global identity (Chevrier, 2003) which can facilitate intercultural communication in spite of national language barriers: 'engineering communities can be viewed as a transnational and de-localized community of experts with global, partly virtual practices that are considered to be highly universal' (Mahadevan, 2011, p. 91). This is because engineers speak a rather 'mathematical language', which is understood all across the world: accuracy, precision, efficiency and ease of use are, for instance, important characteristics of engineering language, along with a mathematical vocabulary such as 'measuring', 'testing' and 'verifying'.

Team language arises in working groups within organizations, whose members collaborate for a certain amount of time on a specific task. Especially in intercultural teams (Chapter 7), language plays an extremely important role. A common team language fosters formal and informal communication, the diffusion of knowledge, trust-building and identification with the team, and can lead to faster socialization within the organization (Hinds et al., 2014; Tenzer et al., 2014). Moreover, a team language can positively influence the building of a hybrid team culture. Nevertheless, these positive effects only unfold if all members share a certain level of language skills and agree with the chosen team language. Otherwise, differences in language fluency might lead to the formation of subgroups within the team, resulting in asymmetrical power relations, emotional conflicts and barriers of trust that hinder communication and team performance (Ciuk et al., 2019). This also holds true for virtual teams.

Language choice and language competences can reflect power relationships (Beeler & Lecomte, 2017): individuals who have a better command of the common national, organizational or team language can express themselves more freely and diversely, and are therefore attributed more legitimacy and power. This is particularly the case in teams in which one nationality predominates in number or in which native speakers collaborate with non-natives in the respective team language. To meet such challenges, it is necessary to balance the team structure and to choose a language that is mastered and accepted by all team members. If English is chosen as the team language, the team leader should consider that native speakers may be perceived as more competent than non-native speakers. Especially in bicultural teams, leaders should ensure that the number of team members from the two cultures is balanced in order to prevent power asymmetry.

2.2   Language Choices within Multilingual Organizations

Multinational and multilingual companies can adopt different language choices, which influence intercultural collaboration and performance (Janssens & Steyaert, 2014). They can be linked to Perlmutter's (1969) international orientations (Chapter 2).

Ethnocentric organizations might opt for the top-down introduction of a lingua franca, which can be the language of the corporate headquarters or the majority shareholder in international joint ventures, or a third language such as English. This choice parts from a homogenous approach to culture and assumes that texts, ideas and practices are mechanically translatable from one language to another. However, organizations 'do not become monolingual through the introduction of a corporate language' (Tietze & Piekkari, 2020, p. 185). Individuals have a diverse range of languages and language competences, which have an impact on their position and power within the organization, and top-down approaches might thus lead to resistance (Lønsmann, 2017).

Polycentric organizations can make a culture-sensitive language choice, which considers multiple local languages and aims for multilingualism. This approach leverages cultural differences and allows the simultaneous adoption of several languages within organizations. For example, subsidiaries may adhere to their local languages, and intercultural teams can choose the desired language flexibly, depending on the linguistic backgrounds of their members.

Geocentric organizations might opt for a bottom-up approach, in which language use is constantly negotiated by employees, with the introduction of a 'multilingua franca': rather than opting exclusively for universalism (lingua franca) or particularity (multilingualism), a 'multilingua franca' integrates both of them in a *constructive* way. This choice considers language as a negotiated, situated practice, which is embedded in a specific socio-political context. It allows 'translingual practices', in the sense of linguistic bricolage, in which actors draw on their individual resources and multiple language varieties to communicate within and across borders (Barner-Rasmussen & Langinier, 2020). Box 9.6 provides an example of language choices in Switzerland.

BOX 9.6 LANGUAGE CHOICES IN SWITZERLAND

Switzerland is well-known for its multilingualism, with four official languages: German, French, Italian and Romanish (a minority language spoken in the Swiss canton of Graubünden). In addition to many regional dialects (Swiss-German, for example), English is considered as the first second language for many Swiss people. In such complex linguistic environments, people can adopt different language choices:

- Adapting the spoken language to the location (for example, German in the German part of Switzerland)
- Adopting the language of the communication partners (depending on their language proficiencies)
- Negotiating a common language according to the situation (for example, in form of a re-negotiation in every meeting)
- Using several languages simultaneously (in terms of 'intercomprehension')
- Finding a compromise through a third language (for example, a 'simplified English')
- Improvising, that is active mixing of several languages (in terms of 'code switching')

Source: Steyaert et al. (2011).

It follows that language choices can influence intra- and inter-organizational processes at various levels. Table 9.2 summarizes major factors related to language and their effects on organizations.

Table 9.2 Factors relating to language and their effects on organizations

Level	Factors related to language	Effects on organizations
Organization	Internal and external communication within and between organizations Information flows and knowledge transfer Forms of information procurement Translations Power resources and power relationships Trust Choice of communication media	Communication quality among employees Speed of communication and decision-making Coordination and control Effectiveness, efficiency and performance Communication with customers Entry barriers to foreign markets
Team	Shared cognition as a basis for communication Trust among team members Team dynamics Power relationships and hierarchical positions in teams	Establishing contact and building personal relationships Effectiveness and efficiency of teamwork Team climate and team member well-being
Individual	Formation of social identities through possibilities and limitations of communication Social position within the organization Perception of and by others Relationship to others	Satisfaction at work Motivation Individual efficiency

2.3 The Challenge of English as Lingua Franca

Multicultural and multilingual organizations often introduce English as the common lingua franca to create a shared communication basis (Tietze, 2008). English is one of the world's most widespread languages with almost 370 million native speakers and approximately 900 million speakers learning it as a second language (Ethnologue, 2020), The historical reasons why English is practised as the most common corporate language can be found, among other things, in the hegemony of the British Empire and the adoption of modern information technology language (Fredriksson et al., 2006). The origin of the term lingua franca is explained in Box 9.7.

BOX 9.7 ORIGIN OF THE TERM LINGUA FRANCA

The term lingua franca stems from the pidgin language which developed in the Middle Ages between merchants and traders of Southern Europe (especially Spain, Italy and Portugal) and speakers of non-Romance languages of the Mediterranean such as Arabic, Greek and Turkish. The name lingua franca was first mentioned in 1612 by Fray Diego de Haedo, and in the eighteenth century, it was transferred to other widespread languages such as English, which served as a basis for communication between speakers of different languages.

Source: Bergareche (1993).

Many organizations work effectively across cultures with English as lingua franca, but the reality of everyday work often turns out to be difficult, notably in countries where English is less widespread. Employees then only have limited English skills and prefer to communicate in their national language or dialect.

Too often, there are discrepancies between the desired corporate policy vision of introducing English as the 'official' language and the practical reality of employees who are technically proficient, but whose language proficiency is insufficient to meet corporate policy objectives. Moreover, the imposition of language 'from the top' has shown severe issues of acceptance among the workforce in practice (Neeley, 2017). Box 9.8 provides the example of the Japanese company Rakuten who introduced English as lingua franca.

BOX 9.8   RAKUTEN INTRODUCES ENGLISH AS LINGUA FRANCA

Rakuten, Japan's largest e-commerce company, decided to introduce English as lingua franca in foreign subsidiaries, namely in the United States, Brazil, France, Germany, Indonesia, Japan, Taiwan and Thailand. Initially, the English-speaking natives (US employees) enjoyed advantages in cooperation and felt more powerful. However, with increasing language proficiency by the Japanese, the headquarters transferred their Japanese organizational culture, charged with Japanese values, to foreign subsidiaries. As a result, a fragmentation of employees into three types happened:

1. Japanese employees became 'linguistic expats' in their own country, obliged to adhere to English but living with Japanese values.
2. Americans became 'cultural expats' in their own country, speaking their mother tongue, but obliged to follow Japanese practices. For example, Americans were supervised by Japanese over whether they wore their company badges properly.
3. Employees who were neither Japanese nor American became 'linguistic-cultural expats' or 'dual expats', who had to speak English and adhere to Japanese organizational culture.

After initial struggles to adapt to the new culture and language, the third group demonstrated the highest openness and tolerance. They adjusted fast to language changes and were thus seen as the most effective group in a multinational company operating in a globalized and digitalized context.

Source: Neeley (2017).

In summary, we can emphasize that introducing English as lingua franca might bring potential benefits to the surface such as common organizational identification ('we are all the same because we speak the same language'), but can also lead to deeper-level challenges due to local employees' lack of proficiency, comfort and missing identification, which might result in asymmetrical power relationships and problems regarding translations due to missing equivalence of words and expressions (Tenzer & Pudelko, 2015). Language standardization in multinational companies can provoke anxiety in intercultural communication, which triggers emotions that are likely to affect communication behaviours (Wang et al., 2020). In certain contexts, it may be preferable to employ regional lingua francas (Box 9.9).

BOX 9.9   ADOPTING REGIONAL LINGUA FRANCAS IN EAST AFRICA

When multinational companies implement corporate social responsibility policies, they are facing pressures from local stakeholders to obtain legitimacy. This is the case for foreign mining companies operating in East Africa where local stakeholders belong to communities of place. Such communities steward the land of their ancestors and have increased their voices of how the land should be used. Foreign multinationals need to dedicate specific attention to their relationships with powerful communities of place, and language appears to play a major role in the communication with the local population. Some multinational mining companies have thus adopted regional lingua francas such as Swahili to improve the communication and build sustainable relationships with local stakeholders. This practice enables them to bridge linguistic and cultural boundaries, to gain legitimacy in the local environment and to improve the outcomes of their corporate social responsibility policies.

Source: Selmier et al. (2015).

2.4   Translation in Multicultural Work Settings

Translations show that meanings are culture-bound. *Constructive intercultural management* assumes that each language has its own system of words (lexemes), sounds (phonemes) and sentences (syntax), and thus cannot simply be translated literally. Meanings arise in specific contexts: they are shaped by cultural, institutional and linguistic influences (Box 9.10). Context sensitivity and intercultural experience are therefore indispensable prerequisites for deciphering and interpreting meanings 'correctly'. If speakers transfer the logic of their mother tongue to other languages or interpret foreign language lexemes using 'their' linguistic rules, we speak of 'lingo-centrism', a form of ethnocentrism in language use. In contrast, 'lingo-relativism' assumes a reflection on one's own linguistic system, and the appropriate use of lexemes and expressions in other linguistic systems (Chanlat, 2013). Dealing with translation issues constructively calls for a shift from a technicist view, based on the lexical transfer of meaning, to a more contextualized approach that considers translation as a process of intercultural interaction (Chidlow et al., 2014).

BOX 9.10   THE TRANSLATION OF US MANAGEMENT LITERATURE INTO RUSSIAN

The translation of US management literature into Russian shows that some ideas were not translatable while others were translated and interpreted differently. For example, the term 'management' was translated into *menedzhment*, a word already existent in

Russian vocabulary. However, the term for a decentralized coordinator and manager in the American sense did not exist because the post-Soviet Russian society is still marked by centralized structures. Therefore, the word was re-interpreted in a centralized sense. In the translation, *menedzher* was rather interpreted as the *organizer* of a centralized system than an independent *decision-maker*. The word *upravlayat* was considered the equivalent of *manager*, although it referred rather to the process of *decision implementation* than to that of *decision-making*.

Source: Holden and Michailova (2014).

Translations can be challenging for three reasons: (1) ambiguities (multiple meanings of lexemes within one language), (2) interference between languages (shifts of meaning) and (3) lack of equivalence (missing terms in the target language) (Table 9.3).

In recent years, artificial intelligence has helped to bridge language gaps. Providers such as Google Translate and DeepL allow translating documents and texts within seconds. At first glance, the translations appear to be correct, but it can happen that expressions are translated in the wrong way, since the logics of the translated text will reflect the original language. This reveals that language is highly human-dependent and bound to cognitive processes, which are shaped by contextual factors such as culture.

3. CONSTRUCTIVE USE OF LANGUAGE IN MULTILINGUAL ORGANIZATIONS

To design multilingualism constructively, organizations can adopt several solutions: (1) the introduction of a '(multi)lingua franca', (2) intercomprehension, (3) simultaneous and consecutive interpreting, (4) language training, and (5) the use of intercultural and multilingual individuals.

(1)   A (Multi)Lingua Franca for Multilingual Organizations

Organizations can choose to use a 'standardized' lingua franca when employees show high proficiency in the selected language, or build on multilingualism and adopt a 'multilingua franca' (Janssens & Steyaert, 2014) when employees speak various languages with different levels of proficiency. In the first case, 'lingo-centrism' facilitates coordination and reduces translation costs. In the second case, organizations move away from 'one language only' to 'all languages at all times' and aim to leverage the plurilingualism of a diverse workforce in the sense of 'lingo-relativism' (Chanlat, 2013; Yanaprasart, 2015). This type of lingua franca is negotiated from the ground, and considers the needs and interests of all employees as well as the situational contexts in which communication is embedded. Through a constantly negotiated language, organizations are then able to build their own 'linguistic landscape' (Steyaert et al., 2011) which creates an own corporate identity and unique sense of belonging. The 'multilingua franca' may then evoke a shared language, common stories and neologisms which

Table 9.3   Challenges in translation

Phenomenon	Refers to	Examples
(1) Ambiguity	Certain words (lexemes) have several meanings	French: *Il est gentil* ↔ German: *Er ist nett* ('He is nice') / *Er ist harmlos* ('He is harmless')
(2) Interference, manifests itself on different levels:	Shifts of meaning	
Lexical	Single words, also 'false friends'	English: *delay* ↔ French: *délai* ('deadline') Spanish: *éxito* ('success') ↔ English: *exit* ('salida')
Semantic	Meaning of words	Spanish: *exquisito* ('delicious') ↔ Brazilian Portuguese: *exquisito* ('strange')
Syntactical	Sentence structure	'Denglish' (German-English): German: *I mean* ('Ich meine') instead of English: *I think*
Prosodic	Intonation	The country's typical speech melody encodes emotions and irony in different ways
(3) Lack of equivalence	Translatability of expressions	
Lexical	Missing terms and conceptions in the target language	Brazilian Portuguese: *o jeitinho brasileiro* Finnish: *Sisu* Hebrew: *Chutzpah* German: *Mittelstand / Zeitgeist / Gemütlichkeit*
Idiomatic	How idiomatic expressions are translated	English: *I feel cold.* ↔ German: *Mir ist kalt* ↔ French: *Il fait froid* (literally 'it makes cold')
Grammatical-syntactical	How word orders interfere in translations	In Romance languages, the verb is usually at the beginning of the sentence, whereas in German, it is positioned at the end of the sentence (this is why Germans are less likely to interrupt each other in conversations)
Experiential	How translated expressions are re-interpreted in everyday language	The concepts of 'responsibility', 'decision-making' and 'face keeping' are experienced differently in East and West

Sources: Holden and von Kortzfleisch (2004); Usunier (2011); Usunier et al. (2017).

strengthen organizational identification. The adoption of a 'multilingua franca' is appropriate for organizations who follow a geocentric strategy across all units.

(2)   Intercomprehension

Intercomprehension is a communication technique that allows all people to speak in their own mother tongue (Pinho, 2015). The idea is to bring languages from the same or similar language families together and to communicate without having a complete command of the language. In this case, employees need to have at least a passive understanding of the other languages. For example, intercomprehension can be applied for Romance languages, since French, Spanish, Italian, Romanian and Portuguese speakers are able to communicate with each other without having profound proficiency in the other languages due to the shared Latin roots. Therefore, some words may be quite similar (Table 9.4). Box 9.11 illustrates intercomprehension in the Franco-German organizations ARTE and Alleo.

Table 9.4   Intercomprehension of Romance languages

English	French	Italian	Portuguese	Romanian	Spanish
Project	Projet	Progetto	Projeto	Proiect	Proyecto
Community	Communauté	Comunità	Comunidade	Comunitate	Comunidad
Economy	Économie	Economia	Economia	Economie	Economía
Objective	Objectif	Obiettivo	Objetivo	Obiectiv	Objetivo
Strategy	Stratégie	Strategia	Estratégia	Strategie	Estrategía

BOX 9.11   INTERCOMPREHENSION AT ARTE AND ALLEO

In the Franco-German organizations ARTE and Alleo, meetings take place in both languages, German and French, and intercomprehension is actively practised, which means that all employees can speak their mother tongue. People from border regions, such as Alsace and Lorraine, show a high level of double language competence and a stronger willingness to adapt. Thus, some terms are taken from German, others from French. For example, French ARTE employees use the German abbreviation PK ('Programm-Konferenz') for 'conférence des programmes' and the German word 'Vorstand' ('board of directors') for 'comité de gérance'. In the same way, the Germans use the French word 'habillage' for the channel design. The application of intercomprehension has also led to the emergence of neologisms. For example, the term 'Schwerpunktisation', which means 'priority setting', was created from the combination of the German word 'Schwerpunkt' and the French ending '-isation'.

Sources: Barmeyer and Davoine (2019); Barmeyer et al. (2019b).

(3)   Simultaneous and Consecutive Interpreting

Simultaneous interpreting means that an interpreter translates what is said at the same time, and consecutive interpreting involves a time gap in translation. In the second case, the interpreter takes notes and translates into the target language. Both types of interpreting require high linguistic and cultural competences. It is important to do the formal translation correctly and to convey the content to the target language. Simultaneous interpreting promotes immediate conversation between communication partners and requires a high level of concentration. Consecutive interpreting supports attention, active listening, reflection and understanding, but takes more time.

(4)   Language Training

Organizations should also invest in the language skills and language training of their workforce. This can be done with language courses, offered in-house or externally, which should also focus on professional language competences, especially when English is introduced as lingua franca. It is necessary that executives have proficient language and communication skills to effectively manage employees with different linguistic backgrounds. Language skills provide opportunities for career development since language proficiency allows leading employees in a constructive way. Language skills – especially in English – are an indispensable requirement to enter management positions and for promotion (Peltokorpi, 2015). They can also facilitate the selection of expatriates and the success of the assignment (Piekkari, 2008). A high level of language skills among leaders also helps to build trust with employees from different cultures and promotes the positive perception of leaders abroad (Barner-Rasmussen & Björkman, 2007).

(5) Supporting Multilingual Individuals

Companies can rely on multilingual individuals to facilitate translation and communication within and across organizational boundaries. Identifying language competences of the workforce strengthens knowledge circulation and serves constructive communication. These 'bicultural-bilinguals' (Barner-Rasmussen, 2015) can then act both as 'language nodes' (Marschan et al., 1997) and 'boundary spanners' (Barner-Rasmussen et al., 2014) between different meaning systems. They can ensure the cohesion of the organizational network because of faster relationship building across countries and departments. However, it is important to underline that these individuals should possess language skills as well as cultural knowledge and sensitivity to overcome the challenges of translation. Practice shows that cultural competences help to bridge the gaps in intercultural communication (Tréguer-Felten, 2017). *Constructive intercultural management* thus encourages organizations to identify, hire and support multilingual individuals, and to use their intercultural and linguistic backgrounds for cross-border communication and coordination.

In conclusion, language is crucial for social communication. As an inherent part of culture, it shapes and influences social relationships and determines the success of intercultural interaction. Language is subject to the dynamics and changes of a globalized and diverse world (Angouri & Piekkari, 2018; Szkudlarek et al., 2020), and is constantly negotiated among actors in multilingual organizations. In the light of *constructive intercultural management*, language therefore requires special attention in multinational and multilingual settings.

SUMMARY

In this chapter, we have explained that communication, language and culture are closely intertwined. Language is a visible part of communication, and reflects cultural values, artefacts and practices. Organizations are facing multiple challenges when dealing with language issues, and they often use English as lingua franca in cross-border communication. *Constructive intercultural management* considers language diversity as an asset that can enrich interactions between individuals and teams. Organizations can adopt several solutions to deal with multilingualism constructively: (1) the introduction of a '(multi)lingua franca', (2) intercomprehension, (3) simultaneous and consecutive interpreting, (4) language training, and (5) the support of intercultural and multilingual individuals.

DISCUSSION QUESTIONS

1. How do communication, language and culture interplay?
2. Which different types of languages are represented in organizations? Provide examples.
3. What are the challenges associated with the use of English as lingua franca?
4. How can organizations deal constructively with multilingualism?

PART III
DESIGNING CONSTRUCTIVE
INTERCULTURAL MANAGEMENT

10
Intercultural complementarity and synergy

This chapter focuses on the concepts of intercultural complementarity and intercultural synergy, which are central for the *constructive interculturality* in organizations. They rely on the fact that the combination of differences can create added value in social systems. If cultural differences are considered as enriching and complementary rather than inhibiting and conflictual, then interculturality becomes a valuable resource for creativity and innovation, which are likely to improve employee satisfaction and corporate performance. Five emblematic case studies will be presented to illustrate how organizations can develop intercultural complementarity and synergy: Airbus, Cirque du Soleil, Fiat Mio, Renault–Nissan–Mitsubishi and West-Eastern Divan Orchestra.

CHAPTER LEARNING OBJECTIVES

1. Understand the concept of intercultural complementarity.
2. Be familiar with the concept of intercultural synergy.
3. Be aware that interculturality can be a valuable resource for creativity and innovation.
4. Know how organizations can build intercultural complementarity and synergy.

1. INTERCULTURAL COMPLEMENTARITY

The term 'complementarity' originates from the Latin words *plenus, complere* and *complementum*, and means 'fulfilment' or 'completion'. Intercultural complementarity is primarily about people or groups and their characteristics, which complement each other. At first glance, the characteristics of people or groups of different cultural systems are on an equal footing, that is without any claim to superiority or subordination, whether they match naturally or whether they are in apparent contradiction. These characteristics can be attributes of personalities, ways of thinking or behaviours which, from an intercultural perspective, represent relative differences between individuals. Intercultural complementarity seeks to combine these differences and integrate them in such a way that they complement each other (Barmeyer, 1996). The concept spread with Goethe's theory of colours (German: *Farbenlehre*), presented in Box 10.1.

BOX 10.1   GOETHE'S THEORY OF COLOURS (*FARBENLEHRE*)

From a historical point of view, the term 'complementarity' first developed in natural sciences, especially physics, and then progressively found its way into social and cultural sciences. Until then, complementarity was mainly known through Goethe's (1810) *Farbenlehre*, the 'theory of colours'. It is based on the elementary, polar opposition of light and dark, with colours being considered as phenomena between light and darkness. Yellow is at the border to light ('first at light') and blue is at the border to darkness ('first at darkness'). Complementary colours are opposite to each other in the colour circle and are therefore also referred to as counter colours. Painted side by side, complementary colours reinforce each other and enhance the visual impression in a picture. Complementarity in intercultural contexts is also based on this idea: specific elements and characteristics can be reinforced by combination.

Source: Goethe (1810).

Complementarity takes into account the systemic and holistic elements of cultural systems, which interact in circular polarity. There are several approaches to complementarity (Crouch, 2010):

(1)   Complementarity is based on opposites, differences and contradictions: individual elements are combined to *compensate deficits*. That means that individual elements require other elements in order to exist.

(2)   Complementarity is based on commonalities and similarities: elements influence each other and *reinforce certain effects*.

(3)   From an economic perspective, complementarity is understood as the addition of resources such as production factors. Meaningfully combined elements (whether opposites or similarities) lead to system *stability*, so as well in social systems such as organizations.

Figure 10.1 visualizes the concept of complementarity with the example of achieving performance and effectiveness within a project team associating members from two cultures. The axes represent two opposite, possibly contradictory solutions for achieving the goal, which are usually influenced by certain values. On the one side, a person or a group may reach the goal through 'planning and organization'. On the other side, they may attain the goal through 'improvisation and flexibility'. Both solutions might succeed, and they have their strengths and weaknesses. However, too much improvisation and flexibility might lead to disordered and inconsistent processes, which, at worst, result in chaos. Conversely, too much planning and organization results in rigidity and bureaucracy and leaves no room for the meaningful adaptations required by uncertain and rapidly changing environments.

Cultural complementarity is placed on a continuum that ranges from 'cultural differences as an advantage' to 'cultural differences as a source of friction'. The position on the continuum depends on the tasks being performed and the relationships established. Cultural specifics can

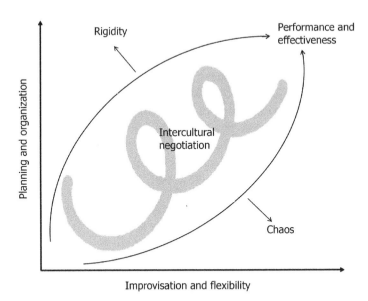

Source: Based on Barmeyer et al. (2011a, p. 24).

Figure 10.1 Complementarity of opposites using the example of goal attainment

thus positively or negatively affect tasks and relationships (Chua & Jin, 2020). *Constructive intercultural management* aims to contribute to the positive outcomes of intercultural complementarity.

Intercultural complementarity focuses on resources and strengths, and advocates the conscious combination of differences and contradictions. In the abovementioned example (Figure 10.1), intercultural complementarity means that improvisation and flexibility as well as planning and organization are combined in a circular process. Within a project, improvisation can be appropriate for the phases of idea generation and conception, whereas planning is needed for the phases of coordination and execution. At the start of the project, a high degree of improvisation might generate unexpected ideas and solutions and, in subsequent phases, planning is usually necessary to provide structure and order. The space between the two problem-solving possibilities is of particular importance for interculturality: participating actors can actively shape this intercultural space through negotiation, so that the combination of apparently contradictory behaviours becomes possible.

Nevertheless, several prerequisites are necessary to develop intercultural complementarity:

(1) All involved individuals adopt an open and value-free attitude. There is an attitude of *both-and*, with no polarities such as *either-or* and *wrong-right*.
(2) They consciously recognize the respective cultural characteristics as qualities and strengths.
(3) They use and combine the respective cultural characteristics according to the situation.

2.   INTERCULTURAL SYNERGY

While complementarity primarily concerns the *combination* of opposites, synergy focuses on the *added value* and the *creation of something new* in this combination. Intercultural complementarity therefore serves as a preliminary stage of intercultural synergy.

The term *synergy* originates from Greek, composed of *syn* (together) and *érgon* (work), and refers to the *interaction* of different elements. Synergy means that the whole is more than the sum of its parts. This means that the synergetic effect, resulting from the interaction of several elements, is quantitatively higher or qualitatively different than the mere addition of the partial effects. Synergy can be characterized by three attributes (Scherm, 1998, p. 64):

- *Creativity*: the creation of new and original things.
- *Supersummativity*: the result is more than the sum of its individual elements and certain characteristics cannot be explained by the function of the parts.
- *Added value*: the result is of higher quality than it was before.

To understand the concept of synergy, it is necessary to briefly address its genesis: it was primarily the psychologist Abraham Maslow (1954) who spread the term in the 1950s, building on unpublished manuscripts by the anthropologist Ruth Benedict (1887–1948), specifically with regard to social and cultural systems: 'I shall call [it] synergy, the old term used in medicine and theology to mean the combined action. In medicine it meant the combined action of nerve centres, muscles, mental activities, remedies which by combining produced a result greater than the run of their separate actions' (Maslow & Honigmann, 1970, p. 326). Box 10.2 explains how synergies develop in native North American tribes.

BOX 10.2 SYNERGY DEVELOPMENT IN NATIVE NORTH AMERICAN TRIBES

The American cultural anthropologist Ruth Benedict conducted a comprehensive study of native North American tribes and the Pacific Islands. She intuitively felt that some tribes – Zuñi, Arapesh and Dakota – had something vital, secure and sympathetic, while other tribes – Chuckchee, Ojibwa, Dobu, Kwakiutl – represented the opposite. The collected data on individual tribal members and the different tribes as a whole did not explain such differences. She concluded that certain social systems allow people to live together peacefully and develop harmoniously (in the sense of 'high synergy'), while other social systems are characterized by discord and conflict (in the sense of 'low synergy'). Benedict developed the concept of synergy, based on a holistic and systemic understanding, and primarily referring to communities (Benedict, 1934; Maslow, 1964, p. 153).

From all comparative material the conclusion emerges that societies where non-aggression is conspicuous have social orders in which the individual by the same act and at the same time serves his own advantage and that of the group ... not because people are unselfish and put social obligations above personal desires, but when social arrangements make these identical. (Benedict, cited in Maslow & Honigmann, 1970, p. 325)

Benedict identified several factors that facilitate collective and social synergies and that lead to clarity, stability and continuity within social communities: generosity, the ability to build relationships, the application of cooperative practices and the development of social institutions. Communities with these characteristics manage to reconcile values (what people want) and norms (what is expected of the community). Synergetic societies thus have specific cultural patterns: they create social relationships where individual actions serve *both* the personal *and* the collective. This is not about altruistic behaviour where individual needs are put behind those of the group, but about individual needs being put on an equal footing with the collective.

Reciprocity appears to be the basic principle of synergy. This might be the case *between* individuals – 'two people have arranged their relationship in such a fashion that one person's advantage is the other person's advantage rather than one person's advantage being the other's disadvantage' (Maslow, 1964, p. 162) – or in so-called stable communities – 'it is stable as long as the different groups are really interdependent upon each other for mutual necessities and recognize that they are receiving benefits from the others' (Maslow & Honigmann, 1970, p. 324).

These cultural patterns can also be found in organizations. Individuals and social systems act in a synergistic way if they succeed in integrating and leveraging (value) opposites: 'high synergy from this point of view can represent a transcending of the dichotomizing, a fusion of the opposites into a single concept' (Maslow, 1964, p. 163).

Transferred to *constructive interculturality*, this means that intercultural synergy refers to the cooperation and interaction of people from different cultures, having specific abilities, experiences, attitudes, values, ways of thinking and behaviours (Barmeyer, 2012a, pp. 153-154), which leads to better performance than the sum of homogeneous groups or individual actions (Barmeyer & Franklin 2016). Cultural differences, values and solution-finding behaviours are combined and integrated without forcing individuals to abandon their own values and behaviour patterns. Intercultural synergy thus leverages cultural differences while respecting the values and behaviours of all involved cultures. This leads to a feeling of well-being for all interaction partners, and is likely to increase creativity and innovation.

Intercultural synergy arises through the communicative interaction of individuals from different cultures. Synergy is constructed or negotiated through cultural contact and mutual processes of interpretation and adaptation in specific contexts. Thereby, the diversity, whose potentials and strengths are used, serves as a basis for the multitude of perspectives. Diversity favours intercultural creativity in the sense that individual expertise and experience, perceptions, information and emotions are combined to achieve goals of intercultural communication, negotiation and cooperation (Stein, 2010, p. 69), and to find new and unexpected solutions. Complementary perspectives and competences can create added value for social systems in general and for organizations in particular, for example in the field of innovation management.

Interaction partners can adopt different behaviours to deal with interculturality. The matrix proposed by Adler and Gundersen (2008) is based on two dimensions – one's own culture

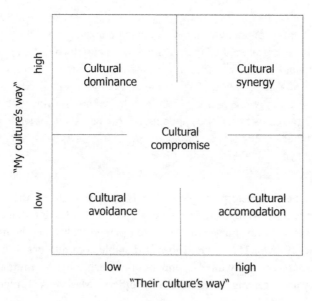

Source: Adapted from Adler and Gundersen (2008, p. 118).

Figure 10.2   Strategies of intercultural action

('my culture's way') and foreign culture ('their culture's way') – and differentiates five options (Figure 10.2).

(1)   *Cultural avoidance:* cultural differences and conflicts are minimized or negated, and interaction partners behave as if there were no major discrepancies. This option is rarely possible in organizational contexts.

(2)   *Cultural dominance:* individuals are strongly oriented towards their own culture and try to implement their ways over the other cultures' ways. This is the case in unbalanced relationships of influence and power, where some individuals have more resources and decision-making sovereignty than others. This option can also result from an individual's – unconscious – ethnocentric attitude.

(3)   *Cultural adaptation:* individuals put back their own cultural positions because they are hierarchically subordinate. For example, individuals in minority groups can only assert themselves to a limited extent against the majority, if the latter has strategic, financial, human or organizational resources.

(4)   *Cultural compromise:* people attempt to balance their own and the foreign culture's way, and search for a middle ground accepted by both sides.

(5)   *Cultural synergy:* individuals consider their own and the foreign culture, and target their mutual integration. Both cultures are combined to achieve higher quality than the separate cultures alone.

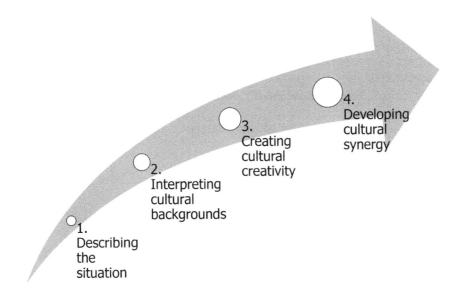

Source: Based on Adler and Gundersen (2008, p. 112).

Figure 10.3   Developing intercultural synergy

Individuals and organizations can develop intercultural synergies in four steps (Adler & Gundersen, 2008, p. 112) (Figure 10.3):

(1)   *Describing the situation*: what is the situation from your own and the foreign culture's perspectives?
(2)   *Interpreting cultural backgrounds*: which cultural assumptions explain one's own and the foreign culture perspectives? What are similarities and differences between the cultures?
(3)   *Creating intercultural creativity*: what new alternatives could be created, based on the positive use of the actors' cultural potentials?
(4)   *Developing intercultural synergy*: does the possible solution consider basic assumptions of all involved cultures? Is the solution new? How can the synergetic solution be implemented and what is the reaction of each cultural group? How can the solution be adapted according to the multicultural feedback?

Intercultural synergy represents the desired 'positive' and constructive side of interculturality, which tries to leverage cultural diversity as an advantage and to understand opposites as supplements and enrichment. Synergy is understood as a creative 'synthesis', a social process of human development. Intercultural synergy is a process of interculturality at a high stage of development through the integration and compatibility of cultural diversity.

3. CASE STUDIES ON INTERCULTURAL COMPLEMENTARITY AND SYNERGY

In the following, we will present five emblematic case studies to illustrate how organizations can develop intercultural complementarity and synergy: (1) Airbus, (2) Cirque du Soleil, (3) Fiat Mio, (4) Renault–Nissan–Mitsubishi and (5) West-Eastern Divan Orchestra.

3.1 Airbus, Intercultural Complementarity in the European Context

The European Airbus company – formerly named EADS (European Aeronautic Defence and Space Company) – was created through the merger of the French company Aerospatiale-Matra, the German company DASA (Deutsche Aerospace Aktiengesellschaft) and the Spanish company CASA (Construcciones Aeronáuticas Sociedad Anónima). Airbus is a leading company in the aerospace sector, with total sales of 70.5 billion euros in 2019 and 134 931 employees worldwide (140 nationalities). The group is organized in three strategic business units: (1) commercial aircraft (77 per cent of total sales), (2) helicopters (15 per cent), (3) defence (military transports) and space (satellites and launch vehicles) activities (8 per cent of total sales). Airbus has the ambition to leverage its European roots while pursuing a global strategy through local actions. The corporate values are customer focus, integrity, respect, creativity, reliability and teamwork.

The merger of Aérospatiale-Matra, DASA and CASA was a great challenge and benefited from the support of national governments. It was necessary to define a clear vision, common goals and core competences to succeed in combining of the companies' respective strengths. The three companies agreed to constructively combine their values and basic assumptions to develop a new 'European' corporate culture. Box 10.3 explains how intercultural complementarity was developed for the construction of civil aircraft.

BOX 10.3 AIRBUS AIRCRAFT AS AN EXAMPLE OF INTERCULTURAL COMPLEMENTARITY

The strategic goal of the merger was to build European civil aircraft as a counterweight to the US competitor Boeing. The history of EADS is marked by diverging cultural assumptions, particularly between the French and the German, which influenced strategic decision-making. On the French side, strategic positioning and the 'honour' of building high-performance aircraft were vital. In contrast, on the German side, business success, that is revenue and costs, was of primary importance. These value orientations have their origins in social history and sometimes find their justification in educational systems. In France, strategic thinking has a strong tradition and is taught at the *Grandes Ecoles*, the French elite higher education institutions. The 'logic of honour' plays an important role in organizations in France (d'Iribarne, 1994). In Germany, accounting has strongly shaped business administration and management, thus leading to the 'logic of profitability'.

These two diverging value orientations have caused conflicts of interest between French and German actors. However, both sides combined their points of view, resources and core competences to achieve the common strategic goal. The construction of the Airbus A321 provides an example of this complementarity in the sense that areas of responsibility and production were allocated according to the respective interests and core competences of the associated companies. The French side was responsible for cost-intensive but strategically important aircraft parts, namely the cockpit, the fuselage and the wing box (which holds the wings together), in accordance with the 'logic of honour' and the importance of strategy; the German side rapidly realized significant economies of scale with the mass production of sanitary facilities, thus showing its economic expertise.

Source: Barmeyer and Mayrhofer (2008, 2014).

3.2   Cirque du Soleil, Intercultural Creativity in Entertainment

Established in Montreal, Cirque du Soleil has become the world leader in live entertainment. In 2020, the company employs 4 000 people, including 1 300 artists, who originate from about 50 countries. The Canadian organization has reached over 180 million spectators worldwide, with productions presented in 450 cities in 60 countries. The artistic and acrobatic circus provides an emblematic example of intercultural synergy: it integrates image, music, movement and people into an aesthetically appealing symbiosis, and motivates artists to perform at their best.

The original and imaginative vision of this unusual circus was developed by Guy Laliberté, the French-Canadian son of a steel worker, who had worked as a fire-eater and street artist. The history of the company is presented in Box 10.4. Several factors facilitated the successful development of Cirque du Soleil as a creative organization: (1) the tradition of street artists in the festival city of Montreal, which made it possible to draw on complementary skills and resources; (2) the lack of an established circus model, which favoured the development of a new unconventional form of circus because, unlike in Europe, there was no competition; (3) the governmental support of the cultural sector in the Quebec province, which coincided with the 450-year celebrations of the discovery of Canada by Jacques Cartier.

BOX 10.4 HISTORY OF CIRQUE DU SOLEIL

Early 1980s: A troupe of artists performed eclectic shows, with jugglers, dancers, fire-eaters and musicians in the streets of Baie-Saint-Paul, a village along the St. Laurent River near Quebec City.

1984: Creation of the Cirque de Soleil (the sun symbolizes youth, energy and strength) which offers a travelling show in the province of Quebec, reflecting the history of Canada (1984 marked the 450th anniversary of the discovery of Canada) and the future of circus arts, with outrageous costumes, magical lighting and original music.

1987:	First tour in the United States, starting in California, with a refined template: detailed set design, a stage flanked by seating on all sides and dynamic audience interaction.
1990:	First overseas tour in Europe.
1993:	First permanent Cirque du Soleil show, called 'Mystere', in Las Vegas, followed by new shows in large arenas in Asia, Europe and South America.
From 2010:	Entertainment continues to create and perform new shows, with a forward thinking spirit, for example 'Beatles Love', 'Crystal' and 'Zumanity', pushing boundaries and stunning fans worldwide.
2015:	The founder Guy Laliberté sold the circus to the investment fund *Caisse de dépôt et placement du Québec* and two private investment companies from the United States and China.
2020:	The *Caisse de dépôt et placement du Québec* acquired the shares of the founder Guy Laliberté, who continues to participate in the creative processes of the company.

Source: Cirque du Soleil (2020a).

The case of Cirque du Soleil illustrates that cultural diversity can lead to intercultural creativity that is considered genre-forming for a new kind of circus. The image and reputation of the company are based on multiculturalism, favouring creativity and leading to singular artistic and acrobatic performances. Internal intercultural processes enable the organization to negotiate new cultures, and to develop creativity and synergy through diversity. As a global start-up, Cirque du Soleil found itself in a pioneering phase of growth and development, before achieving the phase of consolidation and being sold to investors from Quebec, the United States and China. Box 10.5 indicates how intercultural creativity is developed at Cirque du Soleil.

BOX 10.5 INTERCULTURAL CREATIVITY AT CIRQUE DU SOLEIL

The success of Cirque du Soleil is built on the constructive combination of audacity, creativity and imagination. Since its creation, the company considers that intercultural creativity generates limitless possibilities and unique performances. The corporate headquarters in Montreal are considered an 'international think tank' where 400 artists, craftsmen and experts in creative fields work together on new projects. The creative synergy allows the company to push its boundaries and continuously reinvent itself. Each show is developed by a core creative team, which is composed of a creative director, a writer-director, choreographers as well as costume, lighting and set designers.

The creative energy of the shows is based on the talent of athletes, acrobats and artists who can flourish creatively while being part of the creative team. They can surpass themselves to create new art, thus contributing to the originality and uniqueness of the circus. 35 per cent of the company's cast come from sports disciplines, 34 per cent from circus arts disciplines and 31 per cent from other artistic backgrounds such as dance, music, physical theatre and street arts. Each show features between 50 and 100 artists. The multifaceted teams aim to develop ideas and dreams in memorable shows that are performed worldwide. The company considers that everyone's contribution is important for the success of the cast. Musicians and singers need to adjust their tempo and follow the pace of the artists on stage.

The synergetic approach developed by Cirque du Soleil also concerns the creation of stage outfits and sets by the textile design team, with the objective to produce special effects on the stage. The sets and stage equipment are created to convey the theme and atmosphere of the shows, with many pieces being developed from scratch by the in-house design team.

Source: Cirque du Soleil (2020b).

3.3   Fiat Mio, Crowdsourcing at Fiat Brazil

The Brazilian subsidiary of the Italian car manufacturer Fiat had the ambition to create a new innovative car by the project 'Fiat Mio' (Portuguese for 'My Fiat'). The main idea was to engage customers in the development of a new product, the third Fiat concept car (Saldanha et al., 2014). Fiat Brazil observed that most automotive companies did not respond to customer needs because the time-to-market (period between market surveys and launch of new car model) appeared to be too long. Moreover, they were inspired by crowdsourcing practices used by US companies such as Google (Box 10.6).

BOX 10.6   CROWDSOURCING AS A DIGITAL TOOL

Crowdsourcing has become a popular tool for new product, process and service development, since a large and evolving group of people, with different cultures, positions and professional backgrounds, can engage in the development of creative and innovative output. The tool allows companies to use the Internet to 'outsource work to the crowd', that is to people anywhere in the world, thus providing access to a wide array of skills and expertise. Crowdsourcing can take place within organizations, but also between different groups of stakeholders, for example managers, employees, customers and suppliers. Companies can thus leverage the knowledge and perspectives of various stakeholders to create new ideas, and to develop customer-tailored solutions and innovations. The participants can submit their ideas through websites, social media and smartphone applications.

Source: Based on Saldanha et al. (2014).

The team of Fiat Brazil decided to start an online blog on their website where customers from all over the world could engage in discussions about the development of the new car. They launched 21 topics of discussion, including fuel efficiency, noise cancelling and cabin space. For example, they posed questions about the number of seats that should be available in the new car. In total, 17 000 people from 160 different countries engaged in online discussions over fifteen months, generating more than 7 000 blog posts.

The crowdsourcing project was developed in six phases: (1) the original idea, (2) scenario mapping, (3) idea generation, (4) design, (5) modelling and (6) launch of the prototype. Each phase was characterized by lively discussions, questions, comments and votes from the global online community. Although some of the automotive experts believed that 'laymen' could not provide useful input for developing a new car, the co-creation process led to fruitful results. The Brazilian subsidiary succeeded in managing the discussions between customers with different cultural backgrounds and expectations. They were able to develop a synergistic approach by integrating multiple perspectives, knowledge and ideas from both experts and laymen, which led to the creation of a prototype for the new car.

Customers felt that the Fiat Mio project made the car 'theirs', and Fiat Brazil received new ideas for solving potential problems. As mentioned by a member of the organizing team, 'surprising innovations come from the periphery; as they are embodied, an innovative project then moves towards more central positioning in the organization' (Saldanha et al., 2014, p. 31).

The case of 'Fiat Mio' can provide several useful implications for companies:

(1)   The need of an 'in-house collaborative mindset', that is, the willingness of the company executives to engage in the crowdsourcing project;
(2)   The need for determination: some ideas must be discarded in the innovation process;
(3)   The co-created prototype might not be the final product, but crowdsourcing can be a tool to get in touch with customers;
(4)   Customers are able to stimulate new ideas and perspectives for the future.

The case study shows how an established company can leverage the diversity of ideas and perspectives from a large group of people with different backgrounds (professionals and non-professionals) and customer expectations from all over the world to create a completely new product.

3.4   Renault–Nissan–Mitsubishi, a Global Automotive Alliance

The alliance formed between the French car manufacturer Renault and the Japanese car manufacturers Nissan and Mitsubishi is the world's leading automotive partnership. The successful management of the cooperation allows the three companies to develop important synergies and to face global competition. The automotive industry has been marked by significant re-structuring, with the multiplication of strategic alliances, mergers and acquisitions, and the need to attain a critical mass on the global scale.

The alliance was initially established between Renault and Nissan in 1999, and Mitsubishi joined the cooperation in 2016. The three companies are linked through cross-shareholding investments: Renault holds a 43.4 per cent equity stake in Nissan, Nissan holds a 15 per cent equity stake in Renault and Nissan holds a 34 per cent equity stake in Mitsubishi Motors. The alliance is managed by a company that is equally owned by Renault and Nissan, and located in Amsterdam (the Netherlands). This form of cooperation allows the three partner companies to maximize synergies while remaining independent and keeping their corporate cultures and brand identities.

With more than 11 million vehicles produced in 2019, the Renault–Nissan–Mitsubishi alliance is the largest car manufacturer in the world, ahead of its competitors Volkswagen, Toyota and General Motors. The current strategic vision of the alliance partners is 'Mobility for all. Building clean, affordable and safe cars for everyone.' The alliance has also become a global leader in electric vehicles, with the two popular car models Nissan Leaf and Renault Zoe. Table 10.1 provides some key figures on the alliance.

Table 10.1 Key figures of the Renault–Nissan–Mitsubishi alliance (2020)

Information	Figures (in 2019)
Number of employees	450 000
Number of production plants	122
Number of vehicles produced	11 million
Part of world automotive production	11.5%
Brands	Renault, Nissan, Mitsubishi, Dacia, Renault Samsung, Lada, Alpine, Infiniti, Venucia and Datsun

Since its creation, the alliance has been considered a successful case of organizational synergy (Barmeyer & Mayrhofer, 2016), despite the existence of significant cultural differences between partner companies. Strategies, structures and processes have been designed to favour reciprocal enrichment between the associated cultures. The strategic alliance reveals a high level of mutual respect for the particularities of national and corporate cultures. Thus, the three companies remain independent in many aspects of their organizational culture and development. The establishment of the headquarters of the alliance in the Netherlands reflects a 'neutral' location which is a symbol for equal power relationships. The alliance board is composed of four Renault senior executives and four Nissan senior executives, and chaired by Makoto Uchida, Chief Executive Officer (CEO) of Nissan, after the dismissal of Carlos Ghosn in 2018 (Box 10.7). The alliance board focuses on strategic orientation and is constantly looking for new opportunities for collaboration.

BOX 10.7 CARLOS GHOSN, THE ARCHITECT OF THE RENAULT–NISSAN–MITSUBISHI ALLIANCE

Born in Brazil, to parents of Lebanese origin (his mother had French and his father Brazilian citizenship), Carlos Ghosn was raised in Brazil and Lebanon where he received a French Jesuit education. After graduation from the prestigious engineering schools *Ecole Polytechnique* and *Ecole des Mines* in Paris, he started his career at the French Michelin group, Europe's largest tyre maker, where he became managing director of the Brazilian subsidiary and then of the US subsidiary.

The cosmopolitan manager Carlos Ghosn has three nationalities (French, Brazilian and Lebanese), speaks four languages (English, French, Portuguese and Arabic) and has gained important international experience. This multicultural background allowed him to become the lead architect of the Renault–Nissan–Mitsubishi alliance.

When he joined Renault, he was asked to redress the financial situation of Renault before being successively nominated Chief Operation Officer (COO) and CEO of Nissan. He was the leader of the Renault–Nissan alliance and managed the recovery of Nissan. Carlos Ghosn then also became Chairman and CEO of Renault and the Renault–Nissan (later Renault–Nissan–Mitsubishi) alliance. In 2018, Carlos Ghosn had to quit his functions following financial misconduct.

Source: Based on Barmeyer and Mayrhofer (2016).

Within the alliance, core competences of the partner companies are consciously valued and combined to develop mutual learning by sharing best practices. For example, as a Japanese company, Mitsubishi has a strong reputation in engineering and manufacturing, while Renault has developed strong skills in communication and finance. Several core competences of the alliance partners can thus be considered as complementary. The success is also facilitated by the complementary market positions, with Renault having a strong position in Europe, and Nissan and Mitsubishi in Asia and North America.

The companies attach particular importance to the balance of power within the alliance. Projects are conducted with a high degree of autonomy by local management teams before being implemented in several departments. For joint projects, intercultural and cross-functional teams are set up to facilitate the use of complementary resources and competences. This flexibility promotes mutual learning and understanding, thus reducing the risk of intercultural conflicts within the teams. In this way, synergies could be maximized in core functions, namely in engineering, purchasing, human resources, manufacturing and supply chain management. Synergies are reflected in cost reductions and revenue increases. These are regularly reviewed by the financial and management controllers of each company.

The Renault–Nissan–Mitsubishi alliance has broadened its scope and signed partnerships with other car manufacturers, namely the German Daimler group, the Chinese Dongfeng company and the Russian AvtoVAZ corporation. The alliance has also launched new industrial projects in Indonesia, Myanmar, Nigeria, Algeria, Mexico and Argentina. The alliance partners can build on their intercultural cooperation experience to manage these additional partnerships.

3.5   West-Eastern Divan Orchestra, Symphonic Synergy

Based in Sevilla (Spain), the West-Eastern Divan Orchestra is known worldwide for its high-quality concert performances and audio recordings, but also for its intercultural character. The ensemble is formed by Arab, Israeli and Spanish musicians who meet each summer for rehearsals before going on an international concert tour.

The orchestra was founded in 1999 by Daniel Barenboim, a pianist and conductor, who was born in Argentina, and Edward W. Said, a professor of literature at Columbia University in New York and founder of postcolonial studies, who was born in Palestine. The two founders created the orchestra for young musicians to promote coexistence and intercultural dialogue

(Barenboim & Said 2002). The name and direction of the orchestra were inspired by Johann Wolfgang von Goethe's collection of poems 'West-Eastern Divan' (1819), which can be regarded as a central work for the concept of 'world culture': 'who knows himself and others, will also recognize: Orient and Occident are not dividable anymore.' The orchestra's first workshops and rehearsal sessions were organized in Weimar (Germany) and Chicago (United States).

The orchestra is famous for its strong symbolic character, which exemplifies international understanding and calls for peace in the Middle East, marked by the conflict between Israel and Palestine. Box 10.8 presents the underlying philosophy and concert highlights of the orchestra.

BOX 10.8 UNDERLYING PHILOSOPHY AND CONCERT HIGHLIGHTS OF THE WEST-EASTERN DIVAN ORCHESTRA

The West-Eastern Divan Orchestra shows that music can help to overcome barriers that appear insurmountable. The repertoire covers symphonic works, opera and chamber music. The founders are convinced that there is no military solution to the Arab-Israeli conflict. The orchestra aims to encourage people to express themselves while listening to their neighbours and to build bridges between the two cultures. This way of thinking expresses the values of equality, cooperation and justice. The ambition of the West-Eastern Divan Orchestra is to perform in Arab countries, whatever their position concerning the Arab-Israeli conflict, for example in Abu Dhabi, Doha, Rabat and Ramallah.

Other concert highlights include performances at the Philharmonie in Berlin, the 'Musikverein' in Vienna, the 'Teatro alla Scala' in Milan, the 'Carnegie Hall' in New York, the 'Tchaikovsky Conservatory' in Moscow, the 'Hagia Eirene Museum' in Istanbul and the 'Centro Cultural Kirchner' in Buenos Aires. The orchestra regularly plays at the BBC Proms (British Broadcasting Corporation), and the festivals of Salzburg and Lucerne. The orchestra also gives concerts at the United Nations (UN) and, in 2016, it was nominated a UN Global Advocate for Cultural Understanding.

Source: West-Eastern Divan Orchestra (2020).

The two founders of the orchestra, Daniel Barenboim and Edward W. Said, worked as an intercultural 'tandem' with complementary skills, notably with their (1) professional, (2) intercultural and (3) language competences.

(1) *Professional competence*: As a pianist and conductor, Daniel Barenboim contributed with his musical talent and his particular charisma. As a professor of literature and public intellectual, Edward W. Said participated with his comprehensive knowledge, analytical competence and ability to make abstract assessments about the situation in the Middle East.

(2) *Intercultural competence*: Daniel Barenboim was born in Buenos Aires, to Argentinian-Jewish parents, and his family moved to Israel when he was ten years

old. His education was marked by bicultural socialization, and he worked as a music director in Berlin, Chicago, Milan and Paris. Edward W. Said was born in Palestine, with a Palestinian father and a Lebanese mother, and educated at British and American schools in Palestine and Egypt. After his studies at Princeton University and Harvard University, he became a professor of literature at Columbia University in New York.

(3)   *Language competence*: Daniel Barenboim holds Argentinian, Israeli, Palestinian and Spanish citizenship, and speaks Hebrew, Spanish, English and German. Edward W. Said received US citizenship by his father, a US army veteran, and was fluent in Arabic, English and French.

Daniel Barenboim and Edward W. Said share the humanistic view that education in general, and musical education in particular, can help people to get to know each other and to contribute to mutual intercultural understanding, and thus to peace.

The annual summer workshops of the West-Eastern Divan Orchestra take place in Sevilla, Andalusia, where rehearsals are complemented by readings and discussions. Andalusia symbolizes a special territory, which is marked by the peaceful coexistence of three religions (Islam, Christianity and Judaism) as well as the creative and symbiotic interaction of intellectuals, for example in the fields of philosophy, mathematics and medicine, during the time of the *Convivencia* ('living together') (711–1492).

During the intensive workshops organized in Sevilla, young musicians learn to overcome their prejudices and to experience peaceful interculturality. They live together for several weeks, discussing and working towards a common goal: a concert. Thereby, the musicians are constantly involved in intercultural negotiation processes, which concern the creative handling of practices and norms to make music together, but also the exchange on subliminal themes such as power, religion and politics. As suggested by the founders of the orchestra, intercultural learning begins with gaining knowledge and raising awareness about one's own and other cultural systems. This paves the way for collective intercultural learning and networking, thus contributing to synergies, since Israeli and Arab musicians can share their passion.

The West-Eastern Divan Orchestra has become a *third space*, which, detached from local discourses and prejudices, enables negotiation processes about political and cultural values, and creates synergy by playing music together. The workshops and concert tours thus create an intercultural 'exile' where the participants negotiate national identities and stereotypes, and emphasize synergetic identity characteristics.

Table 10.2 summarizes the factors that facilitated intercultural complementarity and synergy in the five case studies.

SUMMARY

This chapter was dedicated to the concepts of intercultural complementarity and intercultural synergy, which can be considered as prerequisites for *constructive interculturality* in organizations. Intercultural complementarity deals with resources and strengths of a diverse workforce, and advocates the constructive combination of cultural differences. Intercultural synergy focuses on the creation of something new in the combination of cultural differences.

Table 10.2 Facilitating factors of intercultural complementarity and synergy

Case study	Countries	Facilitating factors
Airbus	France, Germany, Spain	Decentralized organizational structure Combination of core competences Division of work processes Creation of a new, 'European' corporate culture Support from national governments
Cirque du Soleil	Quebec, International	Influence of founder's creativity International, diverse and interdisciplinary workforce Combination of audacity, creativity and imagination Autonomous creative teams Embeddedness in wider ecosystem: government support
Fiat Mio	Brazil, International	Global and interdisciplinary cooperation Interaction between 'laymen' and experts Open discussion of creative ideas Use of digital resources Trust in customers and customer involvement
Renault–Nissan–Mitsubishi	France, Japan	CEO's intercultural background and competences Equally owned company structure Alliance headquarters at a 'neutral' third location Mutual respect for the particularities of national and corporate cultures
West-Eastern Divan Orchestra	Palestine, Israel	Founders' international and professional background Founders' intercultural and language competences Founders work as an intercultural 'tandem' Workshops at a 'neutral' third location Using music (arts) as the combining element Local displacement and variety of show places

Intercultural complementarity can therefore serve as a preliminary stage of intercultural synergy. Both concepts rely on the fact that the combination of cultural differences can create added value in organizations. Cultural diversity should thus be considered as enriching so that interculturality becomes a valuable resource for creativity and innovation. Five emblematic case studies illustrated how organizations can develop intercultural complementarity and synergy: Airbus, Cirque du Soleil, Fiat Mio, Renault–Nissan–Mitsubishi and West-Eastern Divan Orchestra.

DISCUSSION QUESTIONS

1. How can organizations develop intercultural complementarity? Find examples.
2. How can organizations build intercultural synergy?
3. Why can interculturality foster creativity and innovation in organizations?
4. What recommendations would you provide to organizations who wish to develop intercultural complementarity and synergy?

11

Intercultural competence

This chapter focuses on intercultural competence, which plays a central role for *constructive intercultural management*. First, we will differentiate between the concepts of intercultural competence and intercultural intelligence, and highlight the affective, cognitive and behavioural components. Second, we will examine the methods that can be used for intercultural competence building, and more specifically intercultural training, coaching and consulting. Third, we will study the challenges as well as facilitating factors for constructive intercultural competence development.

CHAPTER LEARNING OBJECTIVES

1. Distinguish the concepts of intercultural competence and intercultural intelligence.
2. Define the affective, cognitive and behavioural components of intercultural competence.
3. Be familiar with intercultural training, coaching and consulting methods.
4. Know the facilitating factors for intercultural competence development.

1. INTERCULTURAL COMPETENCE AND CULTURAL INTELLIGENCE

In organizations, individuals often interact with people from other cultural backgrounds. They have a variety of resources and competences, including professional but also social and intercultural competence. In order to shape intercultural interactions constructively, individuals should develop intercultural competence and intelligence. Organizations can use certain methods to support actors in improving their intercultural skills, which are essential for *constructive intercultural management*.

1.1 Intercultural Competence

Intercultural competence is the ability (1) to understand the values, ways of thinking and behavioural patterns of individuals from other cultures, (2) to communicate one's own point of view transparently in intercultural interactions and (3) to think about alternative solutions in intercultural situations (Barmeyer & Mayrhofer, 2020; Bartel-Radic & Giannelloni, 2017). Intercultural competence allows for culturally sensitive, constructive and effective interaction.

Two models explain the development of intercultural competence: the three-component model and the developmental model of intercultural sensitivity.

1.1.1   The three-component model

The *three-component model* originates from social psychology (Rosenberg & Hovland, 1960) and structures the characteristics of intercultural competence into three components, which are mutually dependent and which need to be addressed for building intercultural competence (Gertsen, 1990, p. 346) (Table 11.1):

(1)   The *affective* component describes emotional attitudes of individuals towards cultural differences, which are expressed in personal attitudes and social competences such as empathy and openness.
(2)   The *cognitive* component refers to cultural knowledge, which facilitates the individual perception of commonalities and differences between cultures as well as their values and ways of behaving.
(3)   The *behavioural* component expresses the behaviour required for appropriate interaction. Emotional attitudes and cultural knowledge are put into practice, for example by foreign language use or willingness to communicate.

Table 11.1 Key components of intercultural competence

Affective Attitudes, values and sensitivity	**Cognitive** Terms, knowledge and understanding	**Behavioural** Skills, aptitudes and actions
Empathy Openness Flexibility Respect Value-free attitude Ethnorelativism Multiple perspectives Ambiguity tolerance Frustration tolerance	Knowledge of political, social and economic systems Knowledge of cultural dimensions and cultural standards Foreign language skills Self-awareness	Ability to apply cognitive knowledge Communication skills Ability to put language skills into practice Metacommunication skills Flexible behaviour Self-discipline

Source: Adapted from Barmeyer (2000); Spitzberg and Changnon (2009).

Study and work experience in foreign countries foster the development of intercultural competence: individuals who decide to work or study abroad usually possess social competence such as empathy and openness (affective component), they learn about other cultures (cognitive component) and know how to put their cultural knowledge into practice (behavioural component). Box 11.1 explains how international corporate volunteerism programmes contribute to intercultural competence development.

BOX 11.1   GAINING INTERCULTURAL COMPETENCE THROUGH INTERNATIONAL CORPORATE VOLUNTEERISM PROGRAMMES

Multinational companies, such as Dow, IBM and PepsiCo, offer international corporate volunteerism programmes to achieve corporate social responsibility goals and provide employees opportunities for intensive intercultural experiences. They send highly skilled employees to host countries where they work on projects for non-profit partner organizations. Two longitudinal case studies, conducted at an American insurance company proposing corporate volunteerism programmes in Indonesia and Thailand, and a European pharmaceutical group offering corporate volunteerism programmes across the world, provide interesting insights about intercultural competence building. Their findings indicate that the development of the volunteers' intercultural competence is shaped by (1) the contextual novelty (working in an unfamiliar cultural environment), (2) the project meaningfulness (significance attributed to the employees' work) and (3) the social support (socially supportive learning environment) associated with such work experiences. They reveal that the participants had the highest intercultural competence after the assignment in two situations: when employees with high intercultural competence prior to their volunteer experience work in high contextual novelty and when employees with low intercultural competence prior to their volunteer experience competences work in low contextual novelty.

Source: Caligiuri et al. (2019).

When used simultaneously, the three components of intercultural competences can become a 'mega competency' which refers to the appropriate combination of intercultural competences to increase effectiveness and the adaptation of these competences to the specific situation and context (Caligiuri & Tarique, 2016, p. 281). For example, cultural agility is a useful 'mega competency' in today's globally interconnected world, which requires increased flexibility and adaptation to external circumstances. It refers to the ability to use specific competences according to the intercultural situation, by choosing between cultural adaptation, minimization and integration (Caligiuri, 2012; Caligiuri & Tarique, 2016) (Table 11.2).

Table 11.2 Dimensions of cultural agility

Solutions	Behaviours	Examples
Cultural minimization	Downplaying cultural differences and seeking commonalities	Maintaining values and codes of conduct defined by the organization Preserving quality standards and processes
Cultural adaptation	Adapting behaviours to the expected norms in each culture	Motivating colleagues from different cultures Developing trust with customers from other cultures
Cultural integration	Integrating cultures to create something new which is acceptable for all cultures involved	Encouraging work in intercultural teams Fostering creative ideas and innovation

Source: Adapted from Caligiuri and Tarique (2016, p. 283).

1.1.2 Developmental model of intercultural sensitivity

The *developmental model of intercultural sensitivity* allows classifying the intercultural sensitivity of individuals. The model assumes that intercultural sensitivity can be developed through guided learning processes and that individuals can change their behaviours. They can increase their intercultural sensitivity by moving from three ethnocentric stages (related to one's own culture and with a limited ability to interact interculturally) to three ethnorelativist stages (with tolerant and respectful openness for other cultures) (Bennett, 1986, 2017).

Ethnocentric stages are:

(1) *Denial* of differences: cultural differences are not perceived; individuals have limited or no intercultural contacts, and therefore little experience with diverging values, ways of thinking and working.
(2) *Defence* against differences: cultural differences are perceived, but (unconsciously) classified as threatening; defence is expressed in prejudice, for example, against people from different religious, ethnic or national groups.
(3) *Minimization* of differences: cultural differences are neither denied nor ignored but considered insignificant; similarities are emphasized so that one's own worldview cannot be questioned.

Ethnorelativist stages are:

(1) *Acceptance* of differences: instead of a negative or positive evaluation, there is a value-free acceptance and recognition of cultural differences.
(2) *Adaptation* to differences: individuals change their own communication and behavioural patterns while maintaining their own identity.
(3) *Integration* of differences: cultural differences are dealt with in a constructive and critical way, with cultural attitudes and practices being integrated into the development of one's own personality.

The *developmental model of intercultural sensitivity* helps to determine to what extent individuals have already gained intercultural sensitivity and contributes to a better understanding of intercultural competence development. The model allows setting specific development goals for each stage and to implement practical measures to achieve them (Table 11.3). It can be used as an instrument for designing *constructive interculturality*.

Box 11.2 provides the example of African entrepreneurs who developed their intercultural competence during their study-abroad period in China.

Table 11.3 Developing intercultural sensitivity

Stage		Development goal	Development measures
1.	Denial	Carefully creating awareness of cultural differences	Culture-specific events Knowledge transfer (for example, history, country information and travel reports) Activities to raise cultural awareness Avoiding discussions about cultural differences
2.	Defence	Increasing cultural self-esteem	Focus on commonalities between people Discussion on the respective strengths of one's own and the foreign culture(s)
3.	Minimization	Recognizing relativity	Personal stories and experiences Simulations of cultural awareness Presentation of cultural differences as relevant elements for intercultural communication Integration of representatives from other cultures 'to help'
4.	Acceptance	Recognizing and respecting behavioural and cultural differences	Acceptance and respect of different communication styles, verbal conventions and body language Understanding of values being perceived as offensive as part of the respective cultural worldview
5.	Adaptation	Applying knowledge about cultural differences through interactions with actors from other cultures	Exchange of intercultural experience with people from other cultures Discussion and interaction in multicultural groups Activities related to communication situations
6.	Integration	Establishing one's own cultural value system	Reflection on one's own culture-specific frame of reference Developing intercultural mediation skills

Source: Bennett (1986, 2017).

BOX 11.2   GAINING INTERCULTURAL COMPETENCE THROUGH STUDY-ABROAD PROGRAMMES

Entrepreneurs can benefit from their study-abroad period to acquire academic knowledge, intercultural competence and other social skills. A qualitative study shows that African entrepreneurs (from Benin, Côte d'Ivoire, Ghana, Guinea Conakry, Niger, Senegal and Togo) who had studied in China could develop their intercultural competence and managerial skills associated with Chinese soft power. Their study-abroad period enabled them to gain in-depth knowledge about the Chinese culture (Chinese language, society, managerial culture, history and politics) and to put their knowledge into practice. Their exposure to Chinese soft power also helped them to become more network-oriented, less risk-adverse, more optimistic and more pragmatic. African entrepreneurs could thus learn how to optimize networking relationships, based on their knowledge of the Chinese networks (*Guanxi*). They also developed risk-taking behaviours despite the limited propensity of African managers to take risks. African entrepreneurs who had studied in China demonstrated more positive attitudes when starting their business and, through their interactions with the Chinese, they developed the capacity to construct relationships and share knowledge in a more pragmatic way, which had a positive influence on their business in Africa.

Source: Abodohoui and Su (2020).

1.2 Cultural Intelligence

The concept of *cultural intelligence* refers to the multiple abilities which enable individuals to adapt to different cultural contexts (Ang & van Dyne, 2015; Thomas & Inkson, 2017): 'we define cultural intelligence as: A person's capability for successful adaptation to new cultural settings, that is, for unfamiliar settings attributable to cultural context' (Earley & Ang, 2003, p. 8).

Culturally intelligent individuals are able to find their way in different cultures. The culture-free concept of cultural intelligence has four components (Ang & van Dyne, 2015) (Table 11.4) and can play an important role in global teams (Box 11.3):

Table 11.4 Four components of cultural intelligence

Cognitive cultural intelligence	Metacognitive cultural intelligence	Motivational cultural intelligence	Behavioural cultural intelligence
Knowledge and understanding of one's own and other cultural systems Orientation framework for one's own and other cultural values and behaviours Knowledge and expertise enable accurate interpretations and attributions of different cultural behaviours	Awareness of one's own and other cultural specifics Distance helps to gain a more objective and value-free view of different positions and to identify rules for action Ability to continuously analyse one's own situation, to rethink one's own behaviour and to learn from it	Motivation helps to activate new skills to expand and use cultural knowledge to control one's own actions in a culturally appropriate way Motivation and enthusiasm are used as driving forces to learn and engage in intercultural contexts	Implementation of knowledge and skills into practice in intercultural situations Capability to show appropriate verbal and non-verbal actions Ability to adapt actions to achieve agreed results Ability to identify and control the impression left to others

Sources: Adapted from Ang and van Dyne (2015); Earley and Ang (2003).

(1)   *Cognition*: this component is necessary to acquire new knowledge, that is *declarative* knowledge about cultural differences (for example, rules shaping social relationships and foreign language competences) and *procedural* knowledge about processes and procedures in different cultures (for example, meeting conduct and business negotiations).

(2)   *Metacognition*: this component refers to cognitive strategies that are developed to master intercultural interaction situations. Finding one's own way in another cultural context requires continuous analysis and rethinking of one's own situations, including the active observation of one's own behaviour. Individuals can thus learn from their own experience.

(3) *Motivation*: this component is necessary so that individuals are motivated to put their knowledge into practice. Motivation is partially rooted in cultural values and reflected in the extent to which people are committed to engage in certain actions.

(4) *Behaviour*: this component shows that knowledge is not sufficient to behave appropriately in other cultures. The acquired knowledge must be applied in real life. Culturally intelligent individuals are able to successfully translate their knowledge and intentions in particular behaviours.

BOX 11.3 CULTURAL INTELLIGENCE IN GLOBAL TEAMS

Cultural intelligence is an important driver for successful collaboration in multicultural teams.

A quantitative study on virtual research and development (R&D) project teams in a Scandinavian multinational, which had the ambition to decentralize business operations at the global level, shows that motivational cultural intelligence is of particular importance. Motivation (the attention and energy directed towards intercultural situations) facilitates the alignment of communication norms and the clarification of team member roles, which, in turn, is likely to increase team member satisfaction and overall performance.

Another study on multicultural teams in three companies highlights the effects of cultural intelligence on the integration and adaptation of team members. Results show a positive correlation between team and individual motivational cultural intelligence with team acceptance and integration for new members. Cognitive cultural intelligence is likely to strengthen self-reported feelings of acceptance and the integration by team members. Successful team integration and adaptation do not only rely on cultural intelligence, but also on the prior knowledge of team members, technical competence and common team events.

Sources: Flaherty (2015); Henderson et al. (2018).

To develop intercultural intelligence, individuals must first acquire knowledge about other cultures and understand the underlying mechanisms of intercultural interactions. It is then important to reflect on observed and learned situations (mindfulness) before acquiring a repertoire of skills to apply in new cultural contexts. This process is iterative (Thomas & Inkson, 2017). For example, the cultural intelligence of expatriates can facilitate their embeddedness in foreign subsidiaries and their ability to engage in knowledge sharing with local teams (Stoermer et al., 2021).

1.3   Intercultural Competence as a Meta-competence

The meta-level, in the sense of metacognition, plays a central role for constructive interculturality: a meta-level is a 'superordinate' abstract level and viewpoint that individuals adopt to observe structures, objects and interactions from a distance, and thus to better understand and question them (Barmeyer et al., 2020). It is suitable for reflecting on one's own and on other cultures, especially with regard to diverging attitudes, expectations, perceptions, values and practices. The objectives are to evaluate intercultural reality from a neutral perspective, and to adjust actions and shape intercultural situations *constructively*. The meta-level can also be useful for individual self-control and collective control, as shown by the example provided in Box 11.4.

BOX 11.4 INTERCULTURAL COMPETENCE AS A META-COMPETENCE FOR PROBLEM-SOLVING AT SWAROVSKI

The assistant to the manager of the Austrian Swarovski group, a leading manufacturer of high-quality crystal, reported:

> There was a customer visit from China to our company in Austria and we had planned a lunch with our managing director. I accompanied the customers to the restaurant, but the managing director was not there yet. The Chinese customers stopped in front of the table and looked at each other with surprise. Then, I remembered that there were seating arrangements in China, especially for business lunches, which also explained why nobody chose a free seat. Since I did not know the rules of seating arrangements in China, I explained that it was common practice in Austria to choose a free seat and that they could all take a seat, what they did after my explanation. So, by explaining our habits and cultural customs, I was able to avoid any possible mistakes in the seating arrangement.

Source: Barmeyer (2018, p. 300).

For intercultural individuals, it is usually easier to adopt a distanced perspective due to their intercultural experience and intercultural background (Barmeyer et al., 2020). These individuals often have the ability to implement, communicate, and, if necessary, adapt company interests to the target culture in a more reflected and differentiated way. Due to their involvement in multiple cultural systems, they have a higher intercultural sensitivity and might thus, for example, demonstrate more efficient leadership styles for global teams (de Waal & Born, 2020).

Similarly, a good sense of humour can also help to relativize one's own position and those of the interaction partners and thus elevate intercultural issues to a meta-level (Kohls, 1994). However, in intercultural situations, the idea is not to be humorous and to make jokes, which are often contextualized and require culture-specific knowledge. It is more the humorous attitude towards other cultures or incomprehensible behaviours in intercultural situations that allows dealing with differences constructively. A good sense of humour indicates that the person involved can step back from the current situation and look at it from a distance.

It is particularly interesting for *constructive interculturality* in organizations when several persons from different cultures have the ability to reflect on meta-levels. They can then discuss intercultural experiences and conflicts from different perspectives and agree on working practices (*metacommunication*). For example, participants in mixed cultural teams can discuss on a meta-level about the most suitable methods as well as the significance and importance of adhering to certain rules.

2.   METHODS FOR INTERCULTURAL COMPETENCE DEVELOPMENT

For *constructive intercultural management*, it is necessary that international companies provide professional, that is strategic and sustainable, intercultural support for their managers and employees. The objective is to foster intercultural qualifications and align them with existing requirements and competence profiles. Among the existing methods, we will focus on (1) intercultural training, (2) intercultural coaching and (3) intercultural consulting.

2.1   Intercultural Training

Intercultural training is the most frequently used method for intercultural competence development. The educational tool aims to create awareness of cultural differences among participants and to promote skills for constructive adaptation and effective action in intercultural situations. Intercultural trainings are used to develop intercultural competence of managers and employees, namely, to support them for foreign assignments (expatriation), multicultural project teams and organizational changes such as cross-border alliances, mergers and acquisitions. Training programmes are usually organized in several steps: (1) analysis of company situation (business context, corporate needs and target group), (2) training programme proposal (objectives, contents and learning format), (3) implementation of training sessions and (4) training programme evaluation (feedback from participants and company).

Table 11.5 Goals, methods and learning outcomes of intercultural training

	Affective Attitudes, values and sensitivity	**Cognitive** Terms, knowledge and understanding	**Behavioural** Skills, aptitudes and actions
Goals	Developing positive attitudes towards people from other cultures Reduction of fear and stress	Acquiring basic cultural knowledge Acquiring knowledge about specific cultures	Being motivated and interested to interact with people from other cultures in a goal-oriented and enriching way
Methods	Cultural simulations Self-awareness exercises Discussions about values Critical incidents	Publications (books, articles) Presentations Movies and (short) videos Webinars Massive open online courses (MOOCs) Field reports Case studies Country studies	Communication exercises Role plays (Online) serious games Experiments Interactions in multicultural groups
Desired learning outcomes	Participants are confronted with different values and perspectives, and reflect on their own cultural 'self-evident facts'	Participants understand the connections and meanings of different cultural systems	Participants achieve goals and adopt appropriate and respectful behaviours with their interaction partners from other cultures

Source: Adapted from Fowler and Blohm (2004, p. 46).

Table 11.5 presents the goals, methods and learning outcomes of intercultural training using the three-component model of intercultural competence.

Intercultural training provides the necessary space for participants to temporarily address specific topics from their daily work on a meta-level. Individuals have the opportunity to take day-to-day work interactions to a higher level of abstraction, to reflect on them and to discuss them with others. It can be helpful to hold training sessions in neutral places, for example seminar and conference venues where participants can more easily detach themselves from their daily job environment. It is also possible to organize online training sessions, which can facilitate the participation of employees from different locations. Intercultural trainers should act as neutral knowledge experts and moderators for group learning processes. They can answer questions about intercultural work situations, understand related problems and explain possible solutions.

2.1.1   Intercultural training goals

The main goal of intercultural training is to prepare people for intercultural work situations, so that they can deal with intercultural challenges and avoid *critical incidents* (Chapter 5). Training objectives are often based on components of *intercultural competence*, such as cultural awareness, knowledge transfer and behavioural change. Training goals can be:

- Raising the awareness of participants' cultural imprint and cultural differences, which facilitates the development of an ethnorelativist attitude
- Understanding different cultural logics and gaining an appreciation of cultural specifics
- Building and stabilizing trust-worthy relationships with partners from other cultures
- Developing skills for the constructive adaptation and effective action under different cultural circumstances.

For employees, the development of intercultural (action) competence is a central goal of intercultural training. For organizations, the focus is on minimizing (transaction) costs, for example in case of the failure of foreign assignments and multicultural project work.

2.1.2   Intercultural training contents

Training contents are as diverse as intercultural contexts and situations. In principle, intercultural training should address organizational functions and processes that are likely to affect teams, leadership and communication. There is a general consent that training content should be tailored to specific target groups, functions and tasks. Topics should be related to everyday professional experiences and accompany intercultural irritations or critical incidents faced by the participants.

The contents of intercultural trainings can cover general characteristics of culture (as a system of values, orientation and action) and their influence on work behaviour. They should also include the concepts of interculturality (as a mutual process of communication, negotiation, interpretation, action and adaptation) and stereotypes (as a subjective exaggerated representation of national characteristics). Intercultural trainings foster cultural awareness and ethnorelativism among participants and highlight cultural differences by comparing cultural dimensions such as time, hierarchy and uncertainty avoidance. Box 11.5 provides an example of intercultural training.

BOX 11.5 EXAMPLE OF AN INTERCULTURAL TRAINING PROGRAMME

Introduction
Presentation of participants
Clarification of expectations and goals
Analysis of previous experiences with target culture(s) and with interculturality

Culture
What is culture?
Cultural dimensions and standards (for example, time and communication)
Simulations and role plays

Intercultural communication
Trust-building
Perceptions and stereotypes
Intercultural communication and communication patterns across cultures

Intercultural management
Organizational structures and cultures
Time, processes and projects
Leadership and authority

Reflective and interactive learning
Reflection on one's own experiences
Role plays or simulations
Models and conditions of intercultural competence

Developing complementarities
Identifying success factors and developing 'good practices'
Dealing positively with critical interactions
Analysing strengths and building synergies

Transfer: reflection and feedback
Reflection on newly acquired knowledge
Behavioural change exercises
Feedback and evaluation

Intercultural trainings can raise the general awareness of cultural differences and address the specific characteristics of certain cultures. To improve the understanding of national cultures, it can be useful to highlight the interrelatedness between cultural and institutional elements (for example, laws and employer–employee relationships) and analyse their effect on intercultural situations. It is also necessary to explain that cultural diversity can present a valuable resource for organizations and to encourage the participants to adopt a constructive attitude.

2.1.3 Intercultural training methods

There are numerous training methods and we will focus on three of them: (1) the cultural assimilator (which addresses the *cognitive* dimension), (2) intercultural simulations (which focus on the *affective* and *behavioural* components) and (3) serious games (which concern all three components of intercultural competence).

The *culture assimilator* (or *intercultural sensitizer*) is an intercultural training method (Bhawuk, 2017; Brislin, 1986) that presents and analyses *critical incidents*. It is based on the description of intercultural situations in which individuals from different cultural backgrounds interact without understanding the behaviour of each other. In such situations, the desired goal is not achieved, and mutual irritation and problems arise. It is often not the culturally different behaviour *per se* that is problematic, but the attribution and interpretation of this behaviour. Attribution refers to the ascription of causes and effects of human behaviours (Box 11.6).

BOX 11.6 ATTRIBUTIONS IN INTRACULTURAL AND INTERCULTURAL SITUATIONS

Attributions are ascriptions to behaviour individuals make mostly implicitly. They serve to explain behaviour in everyday life, thus providing orientation. In *intracultural* interaction situations, the attributions of individuals are usually correct. The ascriptions are thus reciprocal, which means that the behaviour-related self-perception corresponds to the perception of the other and vice versa. This correspondence of action and reaction, and the mutually applicable interpretations *within* a cultural system are possible due to the shared patterns of interpretation, thinking and behaviour. In *intercultural* interaction situations, attributions are not always accurate because the behaviour of an individual from a different culture is often explained from one's own cultural perspective, usually in an ethnocentric way. This can lead to fundamental errors in attribution and misinterpretations.

Source: Triandis (1972).

The culture assimilator can present culture-general contents to sensitize for intercultural situations and culture-specific contents to convey essential information about certain cultures. The training method might enable participants to know the underlying values of specific cultures by the description and subsequent analysis of an intercultural situation. An example is provided in Box 11.7. After presenting the case, the participants need to select the most appropriate answer and explain their choice. This is followed by feedback on the answer and a discussion on the reasons.

BOX 11.7   EXAMPLE OF A CULTURE ASSIMILATOR

Mr. Miller has been working for four years in a large organization in Santiago de Chile when he applies for an unlimited residence permit. He submits all necessary documents to the responsible office, which confirms the receipt. He doesn't hear anything for a long time. After several months, he calls and receives the answer: 'Yes, we are working on it!' He has almost forgotten about the application, when his superior, Mr. Muñoz, asks him about it. Mr. Miller says he doesn't know, whereupon Mr. Muñoz requests the name of the official in charge. When Mr. Miller tells him the name, Mr. Muñoz just nods his head and replies: 'I know him. I'll call him'. After two weeks, Mr. Miller receives his new passport and residence permit. He can hardly believe it.

If you analyse this incident exactly as it is reported, which one of the following statements would best describe the behaviour of the people involved?

1. Mr. Muñoz must have given the responsible official a financial 'grant'.
2. As a foreigner in Chile, it is generally more difficult for Mr. Miller to have his administrative affairs handled.
3. Public administrations in Chile work slowly and decision-making structures are not very transparent. Only a local person can understand them.
4. Mr. Muñoz and the responsible official know each other well, perhaps from a joint study experience. Thus, they are committed to each other.

Answers:

1. A very poor choice.

With this explanation, you are very likely succumbing to a general stereotype about Latin America. However, you are on the wrong track with regard to Chile. Officials and police officers in Chile are well known for not being corrupt, and such an assumption can be replied with indignation.

2. Not entirely correct.

In Chile, bureaucracy is a burden even for people from very bureaucratic countries. Simple procedures might take a long time. However, this is equally true for Chilean citizens. They also often despair because of the opaque and lengthy decision-making structures. In this respect, the explanation that this is a 'foreigner's issue' is not entirely correct.

3. Rather a good choice.

It is true that the decision-making structures in the Chilean bureaucracy are not very transparent – both for foreigners and Chileans. Even some locals do not understand them. However, the situation shows that it suddenly became possible to process the application. So, this explanation is partly true, but not sufficient.

4. A very good choice.

In Chile, personal contacts and relationships are very important. Social networks reflect one's status in society. The social network is either present from birth through family relationships or it develops during the time spent together at school, university or other time-intensive activities. Trust, respect and standing-up for each other from this net work is reflected by the cultural characteristic of 'compadrazgo' (Spanish for 'fellowship'), the creation of quasi-familiar, often life-long friendships. Another concept – 'amigismo' (Spanish for 'friendhood') implies that, within these social networks, 'favores' (Spanish for 'favors') are shown among 'amigos'. This is an important part of Chilean life. 'Amigismo' was already widespread in ancient Spain and was reflected in the general predominance of the principle of friendship over the principle of justice. By colonialism, it was transferred to Chile.

Source: Adapted from Ellenrieder and Kammhuber (2009).

There are numerous *intercultural simulation* games that allow participants experiencing and reflecting on interculturality interactively (Fowler & Pusch, 2010; Romero et al., 2015; Wiggins, 2017). Table 11.6 presents some examples.

Table 11.6 Examples of intercultural simulations

Name	Description
BaFáBaFá	The game simulates culture shocks between members of fictitious 'synthetic cultures' by prescribing behavioural rules.
Albatross	The game simulates the meeting of participants with natives from several cultures on the island 'Albatross'. The participants take part in a ceremony where they observe foreign rites and habits, which are usually misinterpreted.
Barnga	The simulation is performed with playing cards and special rules. Each participant moves from one group to the next after each round. It is implicitly assumed that everyone has the same rules and although this is not the case, participants have to interact with each other, without communicating verbally.
CultuRallye	Similar to Barnga, participants internalize slightly different rules of the game in different groups. The participants do not know about the differences. After a few rounds, one participant of each group changes the group that therefore experiences different rules. Since speaking is forbidden, players are quickly irritated and must cope with the new rules.

Intercultural simulations enable individuals to experience the reality of cultural differences in interactions as well as the emergence of misunderstandings and conflicts in a playful way. They can learn about intercultural challenges in a relatively short amount of time and train new skills that they may then apply in their daily work. Simulations usually address the affective and behavioural dimensions of intercultural competence. The interaction partners can belong to different cultures or they are given special 'roles' and 'rules' for interaction (Fowler & Blohm, 2004). The debriefing following the simulation should focus on the analysis of the participants' experiences and their transfer into practice.

The use of intercultural serious games offers an integrative and holistic method which fosters all three components of intercultural competence (Barmeyer & Schirrmacher, 2013). Serious games simulate model-like images of reality and attempt to reduce complexity in order to present the essential components of a system, an organization or a process. Participants take on different roles and perspectives from which they then interact with other participants to reach a certain goal. Due to high personal involvement and individual experience, serious games enable participants to activate cognitive, affective and behavioural elements of intercultural competence. Thus, intercultural serious games contribute to holistic and effective learning and meet the requirements of intercultural competence development by using an integrative method (Barmeyer & Schirrmacher, 2013). Cultural differences and intercultural conflicts, and their effects on processes can thus be represented in such a way that the players experience direct consequences on their behaviour in the form of success or failure. An example is provided in Box 11.8.

BOX 11.8 'MOVING TOMORROW', A SERIOUS GAME FOR INTERCULTURAL COMPETENCE DEVELOPMENT

'Moving Tomorrow' is a serious game that aims at developing the players' intercultural competence in order to deal with an international and diverse work setting. In the game, the players follow the footsteps of Lucy, an ambitious young woman with a fascination for technology and social entrepreneurship. With Lucy, they embark on a virtual journey to the start-up company 'Runergy'. They interact with other characters to make important decisions that affect the course of Lucy's and Runergy's stories: can they convince their (international) friends and colleagues to work for Runergy because the corporate culture is characterized by flat hierarchies? Or because Runergy is particularly successful in the Chinese or Russian context? What is more important for the player: private life or working life? How important is gender when it comes to international collaboration?

In a total of eight hours, the players find themselves in the midst of numerous challenges that threaten not only themselves but also the entire company. Decisions must be made in a culture-sensitive and strategic manner. 'Moving Tomorrow' aims at learning the contents of intercultural management in a playful way by giving insights to various concepts and models, for example, cultural dynamics, cultural diversity, multiple cultures, multicultural teams and global leadership.

Source: ESCP Europe (2020).

2.2   Intercultural Coaching

Intercultural coaching is an individualized and process-based development method for intercultural competence development, which aims to initiate intercultural learning processes with the help of a coach. The goal is to sensitize the coachee to cultural differences and to provide an understanding of cultural systems. The coach leads the coachee to experience reality from different cultural perspectives, which helps to analyse similarities and differences, and to better understand intercultural interactions (Rosinski, 2003). The method encourages the coachee to self-reflect and then to act more proactively in intercultural situations. The coachee should thus be able to recognize intercultural conflict situations and to solve potential difficulties in a more suitable way.

Intercultural coaching can be preparatory, accompanying or following an intercultural encounter. The focus is on the processing of experiences and the *dialogical and interactive* development of meaningful strategies for action. The coach helps to structure and advise the process, and the coachee has to find solutions according to his/her personality and the specific situational context (Barmeyer, 2002).

Coaching can be carried out with emphasis on content and on processes: *content coaching* (expert coaching or specialist coaching) aims to impart knowledge and skills (cognitive dimension); *process coaching* promotes the coachee's behavioural self-reflection to better understand and develop the relationship to other cultural systems (affective dimension). Content coaching and process coaching are not mutually exclusive but complement each other (Figure 11.1).

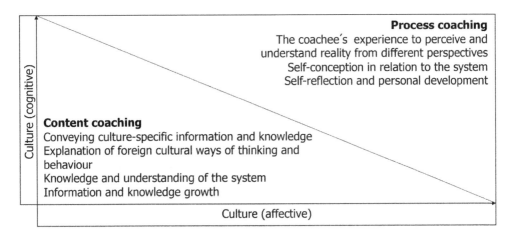

Source: Based on Barmeyer and Haupt (2007, p. 789).

Figure 11.1   Characteristics of content and process coaching

Through the individualized, confidential, dialogue-based and process-oriented approach, coaching can better promote personal self-reflection than a selective content-oriented intercultural training. Intercultural coaching – in the sense of *constructive interculturality* – requires a culture-reflexive approach (Nazarkiewicz, 2018, p. 34).

Psychometric instruments, most of them originating from the US, can serve to analyse and develop intercultural competence. The use of such self-assessment instruments has proved to be useful for specialists and managers, especially to obtain a primary assessment of competences and to subsequently initiate developmental steps (for example through coaching) (Brinkmann & van Weerdenburg, 2014; Spencer-Oatey & Franklin, 2009). One of the tools that has been developed for assessing intercultural competence is *The International Profiler* (Kempf & Franklin, 2016) (Box 11.9).

BOX 11.9   THE INTERNATIONAL PROFILER

The International Profiler is a psychometric questionnaire developed by WorldWork, which offers the opportunity to assess intercultural competence and to recognize strengths and weaknesses with regard to developing international work abilities. The questionnaire can either be done individually, or with groups and teams. The questions are based on ten competences and 22 behavioural dimensions, with a scale from 1 to 100:

1. Openness: new thinking, welcoming strangers, acceptance
2. Flexibility: flexible behaviour, flexible judgement, learning languages
3. Personal autonomy: inner purpose, focus on goals
4. Emotional strength: resilience, coping, spirit of adventure
5. Perceptiveness: attuned, reflected awareness
6. Listening orientation: active listening
7. Transparency: clarity of communication, exposing intentions
8. Cultural knowledge: information gathering, valuing differences
9. Influencing: rapport, range of styles, sensitivity to context
10. Synergy: creating new alternatives

Sources: Spencer-Oatey and Franklin (2009, pp. 185–187); WorldWork (2020).

2.3   Intercultural Consulting

Intercultural consulting can also contribute to *constructive intercultural management* within organizations. Intercultural consulting can take place with individuals and in organizations (management consulting) (Rathje, 2007). Intercultural management consulting concerns organizational issues located at a meso level, in the sense of intercultural organizational development (Chapter 12). Table 11.7 shows core areas of intercultural management consulting as well as associated examples and involved corporate units.

For *constructive intercultural management*, it is necessary to place interculturality in the context of the organization. Interculturality should be made an issue concerning all individuals in internationally oriented companies.

3.   CONSTRUCTIVE INTERCULTURAL COMPETENCE DEVELOPMENT

Intercultural competence development is important for *constructive intercultural management*, because it enables individuals to interpret misunderstandings, irritations and conflicts from various perspectives (Barmeyer & Franklin, 2016). To avoid that the predominant 'cultural differences' and the often unpredictable complexity are in the foreground, it is important to consider multiple cultures and dynamic interculturality. The multiple cultures perspective (Chapter 3) integrates organizational, sectoral, departmental and professional cultures, but

Table 11.7 Core areas of intercultural management consulting

Core areas	Examples	Corporate units
Human resource management	Selection of employees to be assigned abroad (expatriation) Conception of intercultural personnel development	Human resources
Internal corporate communication	Creation of intercultural corporate vision, mission and values	Corporate communication Strategy
External corporate communication	Adaptation of marketing and communication tools to local cultures International public relations of companies	Marketing Public relations Sales
Support of internationalization processes	Preparation of cross-border mergers and acquisitions Integration of cultural aspects into due diligence processes	Strategy Business development
Organizational development	Concept development to optimize intercultural cooperation and realize intercultural synergies	Depends on the functions
Headquarters–subsidiaries relationships	Definition of coordination and control mechanisms with the consideration of local cultural specifics Composition of global teams for project management	Headquarters Subsidiaries

Source: Based on Rathje (2007, p. 802).

also the characteristics of actors and work contexts, including the distribution of power and resources (Bjerregard et al., 2009).

3.1   Challenges and Solutions for Intercultural Competence Development

There are several challenges for intercultural competence development, for which we present solutions in Table 11.8. With internationalization and digitalization, 'classical' intercultural methods and tools are likely to be replaced by integrated and contextualized tools, which take into account the specific challenges and topics faced by organizations. The choice of methods increasingly depends on the needs of involved participants and the desired outcomes.

3.2   Factors for Leveraging Intercultural Competence

Intercultural competence development can be leveraged by several factors (Barmeyer & Franklin, 2016; Kempf & Holtbrügge, 2020; de Waal & Born, 2020):

(1) *Prior international experience of the trainee*: the participants are aware of the relevance of culture in intercultural situations and can relate the learned training content to own experiences. If the participants show limited international experience, they are not able to link the training content to their own situation. However, if participants show a strong international experience, they might lose the motivation to engage in intercultural trainings. A moderate level of international experience appears most appropriate for effective intercultural trainings.

Table 11.8 Challenges and solutions to intercultural competence development

Topic/concern	Challenges	Solution
Acceptance barriers	Individuals do not behave in a culturally appropriate way in intercultural situations. This 'misconduct' can be seen as a weakness of competence.	Individualized forms of competence development such as intercultural coaching and consulting are particularly suitable.
Consultant and trainer qualification	Consultants and trainers do not always fulfil the high and comprehensive requirements in terms of knowledge, methodology and experience. Efforts to implement uniform quality standards on the intercultural training market have so far been unsuccessful. Companies find it difficult to assess the qualification of intercultural trainers.	Intercultural trainers and consultants should have: • A profound knowledge about culture, society, language and social context • Pedagogical and communicative skills • Work experience in the target culture.
Cultural focus	The knowledge of consultants and trainers about organizations and management might be limited. Trainings tend to have a one-sided focus on culture as an explanation for problems and misunderstandings.	Consideration of other systemic context factors, for example, history, industry, strategies, interests and power relationships.
Evaluation	The effectiveness of intercultural competence development methods is difficult to assess. Numerous situational, personal and context-related factors influence the success or failure of intercultural interactions.	Evaluations should consider multiple perspectives. Self- and external assessments. Comparison of survey results at different times.
Geographical dispersion in virtual teams	Joint intercultural competence development is more difficult for physically dispersed and global teams. Lack of face-to-face interaction and of personal information exchange.	Importance of regular face-to-face meetings and shared trainings sessions. Mixture of physical and online sessions.

(2) *International experience of the trainer*: the trainer has experienced interculturality, and can therefore better understand the participants and convey an ethnorelativist perspective.

(3) *Appropriate methods meeting the trainee's learning style*: since participants differ in their learning style (concrete experience, reflective observation, abstract conceptualization and active experimentation), intercultural training methods must be tailored to suit the participants' preferred learning methods. Trainings with participants who are rather oriented towards active experimentation should include more interaction-based methods (simulations and role games), while trainings with participants who prefer reflective observation and abstract conceptualization should provide more concepts and cultural knowledge input (lectures and videos).

(4) *Cultural distance*: when cultural distance is high, it is more difficult to achieve interaction adjustment between the involved actors. If cultures are too distant, participants might find the training contents too difficult to apply. Conversely, if cultures are too close, participants might not see the need to attend intercultural trainings. Therefore,

a moderate level of cultural distance might be optimal for fostering the motivation of participants to learn.

(5) *Personality factors*: personality traits such as extraversion, emotional stability, agreeableness and openness are likely to increase the effectiveness of intercultural training.

(6) *Personal intercultural competence*: besides cognitive, affective and behavioural competences, cultural agility is increasingly important in a globalized and digitized world. The effects of a globally interconnected world require increased flexibility to adapt to external circumstances and thus to choose strategies of cultural adaption, minimization or integration. In terms of constructive interculturality, cultural integration often represents the best solution for all partners involved. However, in some situations, cultural adaptation or even minimization of cultural differences is needed to achieve the desired output within a short amount of time.

(7) *Leadership*: due to their socialization in multiple cultures, intercultural individuals often demonstrate a higher level of intercultural sensitivity and cultural intelligence. Leaders with higher intercultural sensitivity and intelligence are thus able to see the necessity of intercultural trainings, and feel the drive to put the training contents sustainably into practice. Moreover, they are more apt to establish a climate of tolerance for the diversity of perspectives within teams and open for sharing ideas during the intercultural training.

(8) *Media use*: appropriate media use, which fits cultural and infrastructural requirements.

(9) *Organization type*: organizations that are in constant intercultural exchange perceive a higher need for intercultural trainings, since intercultural challenges occur on a daily basis.

(10) *Difficulty of the task*: individuals who find themselves in challenging environments, due to the task they have to solve, might benefit more from intercultural trainings than individuals in a favourable environment. So, the necessity of an intercultural training might be perceived due to the urgency to solve a certain (difficult) task within an intercultural work context.

SUMMARY

In this chapter, we have explained the importance of intercultural competence and cultural intelligence for *constructive intercultural management* in organizations. Intercultural competence is composed of affective, cognitive and behavioural components, and refers to the ability of individuals to understand other cultures, to communicate their point of view and to think about alternative solutions in intercultural interactions. Organizations can use different methods, namely intercultural training, coaching and consulting, to foster intercultural competence building. The process can be challenging, but it is possible to find solutions by relying on factors that facilitate the development of intercultural competence.

DISCUSSION QUESTIONS

1. What are the differences between intercultural competence and intercultural intelligence?
2. Explain the affective, cognitive and behavioural components of intercultural competence and provide examples for each dimension.
3. What are the benefits of intercultural training, coaching and consulting?
4. How can organizations foster intercultural competence development?

12
Intercultural organizational development

This chapter focuses on intercultural organizational development. We will first explain how culture can affect the development of organizations in a global environment. We will then differentiate several conceptions of organizational development, and emphasize the necessity to adapt organizational instruments and practices to local cultures. Finally, we will highlight the benefits associated with intercultural organizational development, which takes into account cultural aspects such as values, attitudes and practices to shape interculturality in a constructive way.

CHAPTER LEARNING OBJECTIVES

1. Recognize the importance of culture for organizational development.
2. Be aware about diverging conceptions of how organizations develop in cultural contexts.
3. Know how to use process and structural models of organizational development.
4. Appreciate the benefits associated with the constructive implementation of intercultural organizational development.

1. ORGANIZATIONAL DEVELOPMENT AND CULTURE

Organizations are social systems that combine, coordinate and use resources to achieve objectives. Many of them operate internationally and develop their activities in two directions: (1) outwardly, in their strategies with the aim of global competitiveness and (2) inwardly, in their structures, processes and organizational cultures with the aim of efficiency. Organizational development concerns both employees within the organization and stakeholders outside the organization. In general, organizational development helps organizations to cope constructively with the complexity and volatility in international, globalized and heterogeneous environments. Ongoing changes can cause uncertainty among people, as shown by the phenomena of globalization, digitalization and immigration. It is therefore necessary to understand the relationships between factors leading to change and thus to leverage the potential of organizational development in an intercultural context.

1.1   Organizational Development

Organizational development concerns the design of change processes within organizations (French & Bell, 1978). It is a human-centred approach using practices and tools that facilitate change with the purpose of individual and organizational learning. Organizational development helps to alter individual and collective values, attitudes and behaviours, aiming to create a favourable environment within the organization to (1) respond to external and internal pressures for change such as the VUCA (Volatility, Uncertainty, Complexity and Ambiguity) world, (2) foster organizational learning, (3) improve the organization's problem-solving abilities and thus (4) provide opportunities for future development (Schein, 1989). As a holistic and systemic approach, organizational development brings about long-term and sustainable change within organizations (Argyris, 1971; Bradford & Burke, 2005), even in the case of extreme dynamics and crisis. The approach assumes that organizations and people can develop by collective learning (Glasl et al., 2020).

Organizational development is influenced by and influences the cultures of individuals and thus their values, attitudes, beliefs, interpretations and practices, but also their emotions and ideas which can be decisive for their participation and personal involvement (Bartunek & Woodman, 2012). This, in turn, influences organizational culture and corporate identity. Examples of organizational development are change management processes, training and coaching, strategy and organizational culture development, re-structuring, process optimization and personnel development. As a systemic approach, it takes into account the objectives of the company *and* of the employees. Different from change management, organizational development focuses on bottom-up processes and employee participation (Box 12.1).

BOX 12.1   ORGANIZATIONAL DEVELOPMENT VS. CHANGE MANAGEMENT

Organizational development emphasizes the role of individual and human factors in change processes. The systemic approach supports people to find solutions by themselves without necessarily influencing corporate strategy. The focus is on changing attitudes to change behaviours.

In contrast, *change management* aims to change a system with pre-defined methods and tools, and mainly concerns strategic action. The focus is on changing behaviours to change attitudes.

Source: Smither et al. (2016).

1.2   Organizational Development and Globalization

As a response to an increasingly volatile and ambiguous environment, organizations are becoming more agile and dynamic across the world (Anderson, 2019). As discussed in Chapter

2, the VUCA world requires adaptation and change within organizations. Table 12.1 lists some of the triggers for change, and their impact on organizational development.

Table 12.1 Triggers for change and their impact on organizational development in the VUCA world

Triggers for change	Explanation	Impact on organizational development
Change of values and requirements of young generations: millennials, generations Y & Z, digital natives	Generations Y & Z and digital natives strive more for purpose at work than for monetary outcomes	'New work' and 'new capitalism': incentives for employees must be renegotiated 'War for talents': companies compete for the best talents
Interdependency of global value chains: global sourcing and purchasing	Products are more easily interchangeable	New business models: from material-based to service-based digital business models Rise of 'digital nomads'
Technological innovation and advancement: 'platformization', 'gig economy'	Some industries and jobs are replaced Expansion of information technology industry	Increase of agile organizations Hiring of freelancers from all over the world and use of international network capabilities
Accelerated technological innovation	Necessity of organizational creativity and innovation	Use of agile and diverse teams Creativity methods such as 'design thinking'
Rise of emerging market multinationals, for example in China and India	Increasingly more Chinese and Indian information technology companies Cross-border alliances, mergers and acquisitions increase intercultural complexity	Migration of highly skilled employees Increase of cross-cultural teams Bi- and multicultural executive boards
Increased global mobility	Workforce becomes more heterogeneous	Use of multicultural teams

Organizational development is of particular importance in international companies, and in cross-border alliances, mergers and acquisitions, in which methods, instruments and practices are applied in different cultural contexts. Multinational companies tend to apply standardized tools to facilitate centralized control. However, they are facing intercultural challenges: how can strategies, structures and processes be developed without harming their original and successful specifics and by maintaining the effectiveness of the organization?

2. COMPARATIVE CULTURAL ORGANIZATIONAL DEVELOPMENT

The concept of organizational development has emerged in the United States and Western Europe and thus embraces 'Western' values such as openness, collaboration and authenticity (Smither et al., 2016). In general, organizational development relies on attitudes, beliefs, knowledge and skills, which vary across countries and cultures. Due to its focus on human and social aspects, organizational development is value-driven and thus culture-dependent (Anderson, 2019). This is why it is necessary to question its applicability to other cultural contexts and reflect the design of organizational development in different cultures.

In general, we can observe that organizational development takes different forms across cultures. This is because cultures differ in their ideas about organizations, and thus also about organizational development. We will first present well-known metaphors associated with organizations and then differentiate several conceptions of organizational development.

2.1 Four Metaphors of Organizations

Organizational development depends on the way organizations and change are conceptualized across cultures. These conceptualizations of organizations in cross-cultural comparison have been depicted by Hofstede et al. (2010) with the help of metaphors, presented in Table 12.2: (1) The 'pyramid of people' (2) the 'well-oiled machine', (3) the 'village market' and (4) the 'extended family' or 'tribe'. The four organizational metaphors suggest that effective organizational development needs to take into account culture-specific ideas about organizations, and adapt procedures and instruments accordingly.

Table 12.2 Metaphors for organizations

Metaphors	Explanations
'Pyramid of people' (France)	Concentration of power at the top of the pyramid Hierarchical structures in which power relationships are regulated by authority Importance of personal relationships Relatively weak delegation and longer decision-making processes (decisions must pass through the different levels of the pyramid)
'Well-oiled machine' (Germany)	Functional structures and processes regulate responsibilities, tasks and procedures Heterarchical structures governed and controlled by formal rules without personalized authority The machine works when all elements fulfil their function and are coordinated with each other Delegation of tasks and necessity to develop technical competence at all levels
'Village market' (Great Britain)	Flat structures and hierarchies with limited formal rules Decisions are situation- and solution-oriented Interests and goals are negotiated within (financial) contracts Competition between actors, with competences being outsourced if financially reasonable
'Extended family' or 'tribe' (Arabic and Asian countries)	Authoritarian and paternalistic, but person-oriented and caring leadership Rules serve the well-being and protection of employees Personal relationships and quality of relationships are more important than functional tasks and roles Strong social control addresses or even sanctions deviations from socially desirable behaviour

Source: Based on Hofstede et al. (2010, pp. 303–306); Schneider et al. (2014).

2.2 Contrasting Conceptions of Organizational Development

Similar to the conceptions of organizations, organizational development shows significant differences between countries and cultures. For example, with regard to national cultures, organizational development appears to be rather optimistic and positive in the United States, and rather pessimistic and critical in France (Table 12.3).

Table 12.3 Perspectives on organizational development

In the US culture, organizational development 'works' because…	In the French culture, organizational development does 'not work' because…
An organization consists of the voluntary efforts of its freely contracting members.	An organization is a loose assemblage of conflicting group interests struggling against each other.
The growth of individuals is compatible with corporate expectations.	The growth of individuals is largely incompatible with corporate expectations.
Discourse about communication problems and misunderstandings can lead to a better understanding.	Discourse about miscommunication and misunderstandings show fundamental contradictions between socio-political goals.
If individuals are authentic, open and trusting, they will show common need.	If individuals are genuinely open, they will grasp the social reasons of their conflicts.

Sources: Based on Hampden-Turner and Trompenaars (1993, p. 363), following Amado et al. (1991).

According to the cultural heritage of philosophies, it is possible to identify different assumptions about change and organizational development, which can be represented by the following metaphors (Abbas, 1996): (1) Western change as a line, (2) Arab change as an oscillation and (3) East Asian change as a circle (Table 12.4).

Table 12.4 Assumptions of change in Western, Arab and East Asian cultures

Western change is…	Arab change is…	East Asian change is…
A line	An oscillation	A circle
Linear and progressive	A zig-zag pattern and processional	Cyclical and processional
Destination-oriented	Goal-oriented and continuous	Journey-oriented
Assumed to create disequilibrium	Assumed to maintain equilibrium	Assumed to restore and maintain equilibrium
Managed by people who are external to objects and processes on which they act to achieve the desired goals	Managed by people who act according to specific goals	Observed and followed by people who are at one with everything and must act correctly to maintain harmony in the system
Unusual, because stability is valued and pursued. People try to maintain the old normal that 'works'	Normal, because everything is subject to change. People are directing change to serve their own and the community's interests	Usual, because continuity and change is the norm. People constantly adapt to the changing environment

Source: Based on Abbas (1996, p. 14).

We can thus deduce that the conception and the practice of organizational development are not universal: organizational development is based on the willingness of individuals to learn, their values (also influenced by philosophy), their conceptions about organizations, and their assumption on whether and how organizations can develop. Organizational development thus requires high levels of personal responsibility, motivation to change and self-regulation of each individual, as well as aligned goals and interests between individuals and the organization.

3. CONSTRUCTIVE INTERCULTURAL ORGANIZATIONAL DEVELOPMENT

Constructive intercultural organizational development aims to shape interculturality in a positive way, through the development of individuals and organizations, with the consideration of (inter)cultural influences and contexts in terms of values, attitudes, methods and contents (Barmeyer, 2010). In contrast to intercultural competence development of employees on a micro-level (Chapter 11), intercultural organizational development is located at the (collective) meso-level. It involves both individual and collective learning processes in intercultural contexts, for example, in teams and departments. Continuous and sustainable change and development optimize the entire organization, that is, its strategies, structures, processes and resources, with the aim of achieving effective intercultural organizational behaviour. It adds value to the organization and fosters cooperation between employees from different cultures.

Intercultural organizational development tools are often established in national contexts and may not be adaptable to multicultural settings. In the same way, they are difficult to implement in multinational companies where headquarters–subsidiaries relationships are characterized by power asymmetry. A rather low cultural awareness and limited knowledge about cultural systems can lead to an underestimation of such differences and to the 'assumption of similarity'. Ethnocentrism can then inhibit the success of intercultural organizational development.

Therefore, it is necessary to:

(1) Define the clear roles of participants, since organizational development processes are primarily driven by members of the organization.
(2) Give time and space to individuals to accept and recognize culture as a learned reference system of basic assumptions, values and practices. This will enable them to approach and learn from each other to develop interculturality in a constructive way.
(3) Respect diverging values and practices of individuals. Differences should be integrated carefully, always taking into account the characteristics, needs and interests of employees from the cultures involved. It is necessary to avoid that representatives of the dominant culture assert themselves from the outset and to leave time and space for mutual intercultural learning processes.
(4) Support consultants with an intercultural-systemic approach, who give impulses for the development process. Whenever possible, they can offer alternatives and ideas without imposing pre-tailored solutions. Nevertheless, consultants also have their own cultural understanding of organizational development, which may increase irritation and uncertainty for both the members of the organization and the consultants. Consultants might therefore question their own cultural origins and their possible influence on development processes.

Box 12.2 provides the example of an Israeli multinational which succeeded in introducing organizational development practices in South Korea.

BOX 12.2 AN ISRAELI MULTINATIONAL INTRODUCING ORGANIZATIONAL DEVELOPMENT PRACTICES IN SOUTH KOREA

The Israeli company succeeded in introducing participative management and creating commitment among employees in the South Korean subsidiary. Israel and South Korea present significant cultural differences (for example, low vs. high power distance), but they both share collectivist values. Historically, Israel has been marked by collective socialist communities (called 'kibbutz'), with the values of economic democracy, collectivism and mutual responsibility. South Korea is characterized by Confucian influence, with hierarchical, authoritarian and centralized management, and large family conglomerates (called 'chaebol'), with paternalistic leadership styles. Despite the differences, the Israeli multinational was able to build a hybrid workplace, which combined national and corporate cultures. Within the implemented processes, a 'readiness to experiment with change set the workplace culture apart from the collectivist and patriarchal national culture of Korea in general and brought it, in some respects, closer to corporate culture' (Raz, 2009, p. 298). The hybrid culture manifested in the participative *and* authoritative leadership style, with hierarchical elements and egalitarian dynamics, and the organization evening events, where solidarity was created against the traditional Korean divisions of gender and age. Organizational development processes are thus seen as an arena for negotiating a workplace culture that operates at the interface between corporate and national cultures.

Source: Raz (2009).

Constructive intercultural organizational development can be displayed either in process models, or structural models that explain relevant factors for change. In the following, we will present two process models and one structural model of organizational development.

3.1   Process Models of Organizational Development

Process models depict how organizations may develop over time, from their inception, to growth and – possibly – their decline.

The phase model, created by Glasl and Lievegoed (2011), shows how organizations develop over time, assuming that there is a predictable sequence of phases, which integrate the capabilities acquired during the previous ones. The model considers four phases, with each phase revealing higher complexity than the previous one and being characterized by greater awareness and abilities of employees to deal constructively with intercultural complexity.

(1) *Pioneer phase*: this phase is characterized by a spirit of improvisation, and roles and responsibilities are not clearly defined yet. Founders play a central role, actors are convinced by their work, and the organization grows. People orientation is in the foreground: flexibility, intuition, personal relationships and emotions play a central role. Major risks are a lack of transparency, chaos and power struggles.

(2) *Differentiation phase*: during this phase, the organization has to deal with increasing complexity, manageability and control. Specialization and formalization emerge, and it is necessary to define functions and departments. Rules and workflow processes along with quality certifications contribute to standardization. Subject and target orientation are in the foreground, with order, structure and rationality. Major risks are diverging ways of thinking and working, increased bureaucracy and a loss of shared work experience among employees due to growth.

(3) *Integration phase*: this phase combines the improvisation of the pioneer phase with the rationality of the differentiation phase. The headquarters do not control and regulate, but offer supporting and advisory services. Visions and values are developed, and the purpose of the organization is explicitly defined. Cooperation is based on personal responsibility and self-organization. The organization tends to be self-centred and to neglect external stakeholders such as customers, suppliers and partner companies.

(4) *Association phase*: this phase considers the entire value chain and opens the organizational boundaries to external stakeholders. The organization is considered as an ecosystem which includes other organizations, people, the wider society and ecological issues. Social networks, digitalization and decentralized structures play a central role. The intensive relationships with other stakeholders lead to the exchange of experiences and strategy development. Major risks are asymmetrical power relationships and networks or partners striving for monopoly positions.

The process model of organizational development, proposed by Sackmann (2017), focuses on corporate culture and differentiates five phases:

(1) *Start-up phase* (foundation of the organization): basic strategies and structures are formed, and socio-cultural values of the founder play a pivotal role.

(2) *Development phase* (growth of the organization): proven practices are improved and expanded. Subcultures develop and a cultural knowledge base emerges along with implicit and explicit rules and standards.

(3) *Maturity phase* (consolidation of the organization): implicit and explicit rules and standards that determine the scope of behaviour consolidate. Rites, rituals and ceremonies emerge, and so does bureaucratization.

(4) *Crisis phase* (re-orientation of the organization): procedures and behaviours that no longer prove to be successful require a rethinking of the organization.

(5) *Renewal phase or decline* (re-invention or decline of the organization): an adaptation to external pressures and internal demands takes place (renewal). If the organization fails to adapt, it will not survive. If the organization succeeds, it will be able to reorient its practices and processes, and move to the renewal phase.

3.2   Structural Model of Organizational Development

Structural models of organizational development take into account influencing factors for constructive change and their interrelationships. Glasl et al. (2020) developed a structural model which considers three subsystems covering seven key elements which are central for constructive organizational development:

(1)   The cultural subsystem is the mental pole of the organization: it embraces the two key elements *identity* and *strategy*.
(2)   The social subsystem refers to the psychological dimension of the organization: it includes the three key elements *structure, people* and *functions*.
(3)   The technical and instrumental subsystem is the physical (or material) pole of the organization: it contains the two key elements *processes* and *resources*.

If organizations strive to develop, they must consider the three systems and the associated key elements, which are likely to influence each other (Glasl et al., 2020). In the social subsystem, negotiation of (new) practices takes place between individuals, and their interests, desires and goals. Constructive intercultural organizational development attaches particular importance to the cultural subsystem and the background of people: it is only when their respective values, characteristics and goals are taken into account that processes can be developed at the organizational level.

The seven key elements for constructive intercultural organizational development change with the strategic orientation of organizations. In terms of Perlmutter's (1969) classification scheme, the *ethnocentric* orientation is most likely to be found at the pioneer (or start-up) phase. The *polycentric* orientation is most often associated with the differentiation (or) development phase. The *geocentric* orientation requires network thinking as well as an understanding of interdependence between parent and subsidiary companies, and it can develop at the earliest in the integration (or maturity) phase. The association (or renewal) phase offers room for numerous intercultural networking, also in the sense of fluid and multiple cultures. The intercultural organizational development matrix describes the way organizations may deal with internationalization and cultural plurality (Table 12.5).

3.3   Constructively Designing Intercultural Organizational Development

To design intercultural organizational development constructively and effectively, it is necessary to consider the strategic orientation of the organization, based on Perlmutter's (1969) classification (Chapter 2). Accordingly, managers and employees must select and apply suitable methods and instruments, as indicated in Table 12.5. In ethnocentric organizations, intercultural organizational development tends to be a top-down process imposed by the headquarters; in polycentric organizations, the process is rather decentralized and takes place in subsidiaries; in geocentric organizations, which are often structured as networks, there is coordination and mutual exchange between headquarters and subsidiaries.

Table 12.5 Intercultural organizational development matrix

Elements	Ethnocentric organization 'One size fits it all'	Polycentric organization 'Both-and'	Geocentric organization 'Hybrid'
Identity	Values and principles of the parent company apply to all subsidiaries.	Subsidiaries develop their own values and principles independently.	Values and principles of the parent *and* subsidiary companies are integrated.
Strategy	Strategy is developed at the parent company.	Subsidiaries develop their own strategies within general framework conditions.	Strategy is developed jointly in an interactive and negotiated process.
Structure	The organizational structure of subsidiaries reflects the structure of the parent company.	Subsidiaries have their own organizational structures.	Network structures result from the possibilities and potentials of the different entities.
People	Uniform leadership and communication culture defined by the parent company.	Subsidiaries have their own management and communication cultures.	Through *best practices*, new (shared) leadership and communication cultures develop.
Functions	Cross-border projects are managed centrally.	Projects are initiated and managed on a site-specific basis.	Projects are distributed according to available resources and managed jointly.
Processes	Parent company designs work processes; centralized information and knowledge management.	Subsidiaries have their own work processes; information and knowledge are available locally.	Process optimization is achieved through mutual exchange of experience and recognition of strengths.
Resources	Standards and systems are developed in the parent company and transferred to subsidiaries.	Local standards and systems are applied within the frame of budget constraints; problems are solved where they arise.	Standards and systems are selected jointly to be locally meaningful and globally applicable.

Source: Adapted from Barmeyer (2018, pp. 278–281).

Constructive intercultural organizational development – adapted to geocentric organizations – aims at developing a *hybrid* culture that is shaped by *all* actors whatever their cultural background. This approach follows the principle of mutual and regular exchange between the participants. The organizational culture that results from these exchange processes is ideally applicable to different cultural contexts and levels (for example, national, regional, professional and departmental cultures). Organizational processes should therefore facilitate effective, conflict-free and synergetic intercultural cooperation.

In the sense of an emerging new, hybrid culture, it is essential to consider various tools of intercultural organizational development to ensure that they:

- are not implemented purely as top-down measures,
- are compatible with the actors' cultural backgrounds,
- promote an equal dialogue between the different parties,
- consider intercultural synergy as a source of value creation.

Boxes 12.3 and 12.4 present two tools for organizational development that can be used constructively in a culturally sensitive way: appreciative inquiry and 360° feedback.

BOX 12.3 APPRECIATIVE INQUIRY AS A CONSTRUCTIVE TOOL OF INTERCULTURAL ORGANIZATIONAL DEVELOPMENT

Appreciative inquiry aims at developing and fostering strengths within organizations rather than identifying and solving problems. The goal is to overcome resistance to change by building on individual competencies, linking the old and known to the new and unknown. It is based on a circular process covering four stages:

1. Discover strengths and competences
2. Dream and envision the future and the objectives
3. Design and plan the steps to reach the objectives
4. Deliver: implement the steps.

Source: Cooperrider et al. (2008).

BOX 12.4 CULTURALLY ADAPTED IMPLEMENTATION OF 360° FEEDBACK

Implemented as a common organizational development intervention method in many Anglo-Saxon and German organizations, the 360° feedback method aims at enhancing processes and/or products through feedback from several stakeholders, such as leaders, colleagues, or even customers or suppliers. The 360° feedback generally requires values such as openness to discuss errors (in terms of low-context communication), honesty and open-mindedness towards change, as it allows identifying and analysing past errors or steps that went wrong within groups or organizations. The following case exemplifies how the 360° feedback was adapted to cultural values in France and Germany:

A globally operating medium-sized company with headquarters in Switzerland and subsidiaries in Germany and France decided to conduct an employee survey on the topic of values and leadership. 360° feedback was used as an instrument in Switzerland, and Germany and France were selected as pilot countries. The German subsidiary managed and supervised the project. During the preparation, it became clear that the elaborated procedure and questionnaire could not be used in France because the feedback culture was not well developed, and different norms and laws applied with regard to personal rights.

The project lead noticed that the feedback process had to be adapted to the French context. In the feedback process in France, it was expected that the top management made a first pass, in which they collected feedback from each other and from the higher hierarchical levels. The top management was accompanied, especially with regard to the horizontal discussion among colleagues. Giving feedback to lower hierarchical levels usually provoked problems. Subsequently, all managers were included. A consultant, who was accompanying the organization for a longer period, carried out a 60-minute coaching session with all participants. Subjective questions towards more personal topics (including values such as loyalty and trust) had to be formulated in a culturally appropriate way, otherwise it may have occurred that trade unions blocked the process.

Source: Barmeyer et al. (2015, p. 79).

An interesting approach from a constructive perspective is the so-called innovation-inspired positive organizational development, which builds on organizational innovation to enable organizations to use their strengths to innovate:

> The idea of positivity becomes not just an end state to which we should aspire, but rather a catalytic resource for framing organizational change from the outset and a means for creating change. This new form of OD [organizational development] posits that change is not simply about moving from a '–7' to a neutral '0' but is also about a qualitatively different kind of change that moves us from a '+2' to a plus '+20' or '+200'. (Cooperrider & Godwin, 2011, p. 740)

Instead of focusing on solving problems, this approach focuses on creating solutions that positively benefit the organization and its environment. The dynamic process is called 'transformational positivity' and covers three phases, which lead to innovation and creativity (Cooperrider & Godwin, 2011):

(1) *Elevating strengths:* identifying and assessing the strengths of all members of the team/ organization, that are to be developed;
(2) *Magnifying strengths:* selecting and aligning strengths that serve the goal of the organiza-tion and amplifying individual strengths;
(3) *Refracting:* discovering, designing and establishing new and positive behaviours while leaving behind the old, outdated ones, which do not serve the spirit of innovation.

Transferred to an intercultural context, this approach allows combining strengths of indi-viduals from different cultural backgrounds, for example language competences, cultural knowledge, value orientations and perspectives of interpretation. For organizations operating in intercultural settings, it is important to recognize and identify the respective strengths, value orientations and competences of all members that contribute to synergistic outcomes (Jensen, 2015). For magnifying strengths, managers and team members need to choose the strengths needed, highlight their importance, appreciate them and foster their development in the sense of 'amplifying'. Lastly, with the activated energy by recognition and appreciation, individuals are willing, motivated and able to establish new products, practices or business models. However, this process is only possible if relationships among members are extended and fostered, and if the strengths are constantly valued by 'appreciative inquiry' (Cooperrider et al., 2008) (Box 12.3).

The approach highlights three characteristics that must be met by individuals and organiza-tions in order to succeed (Cooperrider & Godwin, 2011):

(1) 'A spirit of inquiry': the willingness to share perspectives and opinions among individu-als affected by change and the openness to converse.
(2) 'A collaborative design approach': the commitment of individuals to contribute to change; each individual is considered as an 'expert' who knows best which change prac-tices work and which do not work.
(3) 'A positive view of humankind': the assumption that individuals are willing to work and interested in constructive human development.

Along with these 'constructive factors', organizational culture plays a major role in the constructive development of organizations and individuals. Box 12.5 provides an example of Mexican immigration to the US, which reveals the relevance of organizational culture to successfully integrate and acculturate individuals.

BOX 12.5 HOW ORGANIZATIONAL CULTURE FACILITATES THE ACCULTURATION OF IMMIGRANTS

The constructive design of intercultural organizational development facilitates the process of acculturation, which refers to the adjustment in the host culture. Organizations can play an important role in influencing the acculturation of foreigners, which in turn may influence organizational outcomes. A survey of Mexican immigrants working in the United States indicates that the organizational climate significantly affects acculturation strategies adopted by immigrants. Their acculturation strategies in the workplace can take the form of biculturalism, assimilation and separation. It is interesting to note that the majority of immigrants adopted biculturalism strategies, thus adapting to the host culture while retaining their original culture. Their acculturation was facilitated in workplace settings with a high intercultural group climate, that is, in groups where cultural differences were valued and accepted. Such climates can be fostered by training and orientation sessions as well as socialization tactics, which allow addressing diversity issues and increasing perceptions of inclusion. The adopted acculturation strategies in turn increased the organizational fit perceived by Mexican immigrants. Due to their adjustment in the host culture, immigrants with contrasting cultural orientations were thus able to perceive high levels of fit within their workplace and could thus positively contribute to organizational outcomes.

Source: Based on Valenzuela et al. (2020).

Moreover, intercultural organizational development should be moderated by people who have experienced multiple cultures through an intercultural background and study (or work) experience abroad. As 'boundary spanners', these individuals are able to understand different contexts and perspectives. They contribute to organizational dynamics as active 'change agents' (Barner-Rasmussen et al., 2014). In business practice, their behaviour remains often weakly recognized as helpful and useful by other employees. Multinationals should therefore communicate on the importance of boundary spanning and publicly acknowledge the key role of boundary spanners in intercultural organizational development (Mäkelä et al., 2019).

In summary, the following factors facilitate intercultural organizational development from a *constructive intercultural management* perspective (Bradford & Burke, 2005; Cooperrider & Srivastava, 1987):

(1)   Consider organizations as ecosystems, not as machines.
(2)   Take on a positive view on humankind and assume that organizations and people can develop constructively together despite their cultural differences.
(3)   Align individual goals and interests with organizational goals and interests.

(4)   Foster organizational learning, and motivate individuals to learn and to bring in their competences and potentials.
(5)   Consider the relevance of organizational culture and climate, and foster collaboration instead of competition.
(6)   Pursue change from the bottom, instead of imposed top-down.
(7)   Talk openly about conflicts rather than ignoring them to enhance constructive collaboration, and foster openness and honesty.
(8)   Apply methods such as 'appreciative inquiry' or '360° feedback' to leverage synergy potential in multicultural organizations: recognize and utilize strengths rather than discussing problems.
(9)   Consider cultural differences (values, beliefs, interpretations and behaviours) between individuals and their respective strengths, and do not underestimate their impact on collaborative behaviour.
(10) Use boundary spanners to mediate between culturally different groupings and to drive constructive intercultural organizational development.

SUMMARY

In this chapter, we have emphasized the predominant role played by culture for the development of organizations in the global VUCA world. Organizational development concerns the designing of change processes. The aim is to create a favourable environment within organizations in order to respond to external and internal pressure for change, to foster organizational learning and to provide opportunities for future development. It appears that conceptions of organizational development show significant differences across cultures, and it is essential to adopt appropriate instruments, methods and practices to meet local expectations. Intercultural organizational development focuses on the integration of cultural aspects to shape interculturality in a constructive way.

DISCUSSION QUESTIONS

1. Why does culture play a key role for organizational development in a globalized world?
2. Which metaphors can be used for characterizing cultural conceptions of organizations?
3. How can process and structural models be applied for intercultural organizational development?
4. What are the benefits associated with the constructive implementation of intercultural organizational development?

13
Towards constructive interculturality in organizations

Constructive intercultural management shows that organizations, departments and teams can interact *successfully* with people from different cultural backgrounds. The reasons for successful collaboration have rarely been explored, and the conscious design of constructive interculturality is still a grey spot in research and practice (Barmeyer & Franklin, 2016; Barmeyer & Davoine, 2019). We consider that interculturality as a dynamic process of adaptation, learning and development, negotiated by individuals from diverse contexts, can – when managed in an appropriate way – lead to complementarity and synergy. This concluding chapter provides a systemic framework and aims to summarize key factors that contribute to the *constructive* design of interculturality in organizations.

1. A SYSTEMIC FRAMEWORK FOR CONSTRUCTIVE INTERCULTURALITY

The theoretical frames, models, concepts and empirical findings presented in the different chapters of this book allow us to elaborate a systemic framework with key factors that contribute to intercultural complementarity and synergy (Figure 13.1). We consider that actors often play a major role in the design of *constructive interculturality* and position them in the upper part of the framework. They actively shape the organization's strategies, structures, processes and cultures. These actors can be intercultural individuals and leaders, boundary spanners and multilingual individuals who bring in their multifaceted abilities and competences, such as intercultural and linguistic competences. We therefore develop their role and functions in more detail. Institutions are positioned in the lower part of the framework because they build the fundamentals of the system, in which actors and organizations are embedded. Institutions correspond to local laws, regulations and societal norms, industrial relations, embedded networks and ecosystems as well as educational systems. They remain relatively stable over time, even if they can evolve under the pressure of actors and organizations.

The systemic framework assumes that actors actively build and change the organization's capacity to deal constructively with interculturality. Their actions can concern four organizational elements: cultures, strategies, structures and processes (Barmeyer & Mayrhofer, 2016; Galbraith, 1995). It is important to mention that all six elements (actors, cultures, strategies, structures, processes and institutions) of the framework are systemically connected: they influence each other, and the interplay of their elements build a whole for *constructive intercultural*

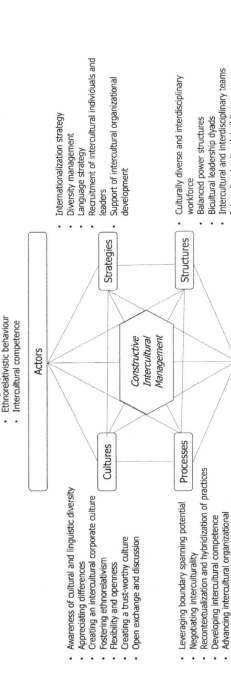

Figure 13.1   A systematic framework for constructive intercultural management

management. In the following, we will present the four elements and propose questions that organizations can reflect on to successfully implement *constructive intercultural management*. We will then depict facilitating factors of these four elements in a matrix along with the three-level model (Chapter 4), which categorizes facilitating factors on micro-, meso- and macro-levels.

Culture is a system of values, meanings and solution-finding abilities, which influences individuals and groups at the micro-, meso- and macro-levels, and which in turn is marked by strategy, structures and processes. So, for example, strategy influences organizational culture, which also shapes individual behaviour within organizations. Intercultural complementarity and synergy arise from the dynamic combination of different values, meanings and solution-finding orientations (Chapter 3), which complement each other through negotiated interculturality. With regard to culture, organizations should raise the following questions:

- Which cultures and languages are represented? Is there an awareness of cultural and linguistic diversity?
- Does the organization draw on the rich pool of professional, cultural and linguistic knowledge?
- Is there an open, trusting organizational culture that contributes to constructive interculturality?
- (How) Can the (sometimes diverging) respective values and strengths of individuals and groups be combined to form a new and complementary whole?
- How far do leaders and employees leverage cultural diversity by negotiating interculturality?
- Do leaders promote intercultural learning and development processes on both an individual and organizational level?
- Are employees motivated to learn and develop?
- What are the scopes of action for cultural adaptation and development processes at the micro-, meso-, and macro-levels?

Despite the evidence to consider mainly cultural factors when practising *constructive intercultural management*, it is important to take into account all factors that, at a first glance, are not related to cultures, such as the actors' personalities and identities as well as the situational context, as proposed by the three-factor model (Chapter 4). Moreover, actors influence and are influenced by strategies, structures and processes.

Strategies relate to the organization's visions and goals, which lead to the organization's emergence, development and survival. When aligned in an appropriate way with individual and collective interests (connection between strategies and actors), the organization's strategy can support the development of intercultural complementarity and synergy. This, in turn, will have effects on organizational structures and processes. In this regard, the following questions can be raised:

- Which strategy does the organization pursue? Is the strategic orientation ethnocentric, polycentric, regiocentric or geocentric?

- To what extent do leaders and employees recognize, operationalize and promote interculturality as a strategic resource that contributes to the creation of competitive advantages?
- To what extent is the strategy suitable for promoting intercultural synergy?
- Does the organization implement cultural and linguistic diversity management?
- Does the organization incentivize the recruitment of intercultural employees?
- Does the organization pursue a language strategy? Which languages are represented within the organization? Is this language accepted and fluently spoken by all members?
- Does the organization give room for intercultural learning and development? Which measures of individual and organizational development are available?
- Do leaders and employees work explicitly with interculturality? Is culture a topic?

Structures refer to arrangements and ordering of interrelated elements, whether they are people, tasks or positions, and whose interactions form a whole, that is, the organization. Structures influence organizations and individuals, but also reflect organizational cultures, strategies and processes. To build complementarity and synergy, structures must be aligned to fit the desired goals. In terms of *constructive intercultural management*, the following questions could be asked:

- Do leaders implement structurally the cultural and linguistic pluralism and the interdisciplinary enrichment that prevail within the organization?
- Do leaders create interculturally balanced structures that enable the development of intercultural complementarity?
- Does the organization encourage intercultural or cross-functional teams and bicultural leadership dyads?
- Are boundary spanners and their core competencies used at the right positions?
- Does the organization promote network-building and exchange? How does the organization utilize knowledge and skills of these diverse networks?
- Are sufficient and appropriate communication structures available within the organization (infrastructure, digital platforms, spaces and places for exchange)?

Processes include the pathways and approaches by which tasks within an organization are achieved. They refer to forms of collaborating, problem-solving and organizing and are reflected in practices and routines. Processes are embedded within a cultural, organizational and institutional context, and this is why they must be thoroughly reflected when designing interculturality constructively. The following questions may support reflection:

- Do leaders promote, support and leverage the communication and cooperation of boundary spanners, intercultural and cross-functional teams?
- Does the organization promote negotiated interculturality within teams and departments?
- Are cultural differences consciously leveraged through exchange, discussions and learning processes?
- Which methods and formats are applied to support cooperation (for example, regular meetings, feedback, events and activities)?

- Are actors in different cultural contexts allowed to recontextualize or hybridize working practices?
- Is language pluralism practised within the organization? How does the organization promote multilingualism? How is information translated?

Cultures, strategies, structures and processes together form the organization as a whole, influenced by institutions and actively shaped by individuals, and a harmonization of their interplay is important for creating intercultural complementarity and synergy. With regard to structures and processes, Nancy Adler (1980, p. 173) highlights: 'a cultural synergistic organization is one in which structures and processes reflect the best aspects of all members' cultures without violating the norms of any single culture'. Table 13.1 summarizes facilitating factors for *constructive intercultural management*, which have been identified throughout this book. They can be completed and adapted to the organizational context.

Table 13.1 Facilitating factors for constructive intercultural management

	Strategies Definition and implementation of goals and visions	**Cultures** System of values, meanings and solution-finding	**Structures** Balance of interests and power	**Processes** Negotiation and innovation
Individual Micro-level	Selection and recruitment of experts and managers Use of resources and core competences Development of intercultural competences Employee exchange and assignments	Intercultural attitude, experience and sensitivity (ethnorelativism) Consciously dealing with stereotypes Intercultural competence and cultural intelligence Language skills	Intercultural networks Bicultural leadership dyads Use of intercultural individuals as boundary spanners	Negotiated identities Multilingualism Intercultural interaction Intercultural competence development Boundary spanning
Organization Meso-level	Balance of interests and power Geocentric orientation Appreciation and promotion of (cultural) diversity	Trusting and appreciative organizational culture that encourages innovation Organizational learning	Make cooperation rules explicit Management and leadership of intercultural teams	Negotiated culture, hybrid culture, dilemma theory Team development Organizational development Transfer and recontextualization
Society Macro-level	Sustainability Multiculturality in society	Effective institutions Values such as trust, openness and ability to cooperate	Structure of economic system Multiculturality, interculturality and transculturality	Transfer and exchange encouraging innovation, hybridization and learning

To constructively combine and further develop the various factors, individual and organizational learning processes are required, which are initiated, promoted and accompanied by intercultural competence and organizational development.

2. A SPECIAL FOCUS ON INDIVIDUALS AS BOUNDARY SPANNERS

In addition to the contextual and organizational factors, the individual level is of particular importance in *constructive intercultural management*. Individuals who have intercultural competences and experiences have the ability to recognize and implement intercultural complementarity and synergy in the work context (Lee, 2010).

Intercultural individuals (Chapter 2), who have internalized more than one linguistic and cultural system, play a central role for constructive interculturality. Due to their multicultural and multilingual identities (Lee et al., 2018), they are able to easily switch the 'codes' and the 'frames' of situations, and adapt to the languages and underlying meaning systems within and across organizations. They identify with different systems of meaning and can thus better adopt neutral meta-positions than people who have been socialized in a monocultural context.

Intercultural individuals and their identification with multiple cultures might bear fruitful insights and effects for *constructive intercultural management*. Their affiliation to more than one culture, either to national cultures or other subcultures, can – when managed in an appropriate way – bring about boundary functions to organizations. Intercultural individuals can take on roles as boundary spanners within and between organizations, which lead to enhanced information exchange, translation capabilities, (social) network-building and problem-solving (Barner-Rasmussen et al., 2014; Barmeyer et al., 2020). By integrating several cultural knowledge systems, language competences and the ability to switch perspectives (Brannen & Thomas, 2010), intercultural individuals show greater social capital and more intercultural skills (Fitzsimmons et al., 2017), as well as a higher degree of well-being and empathy. The breadth of knowledge, skills and competencies can then be used to fulfil important functions within and across organizations which can lead to positive outcomes in intercultural work settings.

Especially *third-culture nationals* (TCN) reveal particular competences and assume important mediating functions for intercultural exchange at the interfaces between organizational units (Barmeyer et al., 2020): they operate as intercultural *boundary spanners* between different language, cultural, and organizational and management systems (Table 13.2).

Table 13.2 Third-culture nationals as boundary spanners

Domains	Language systems Meaning, sense and interpretation	Cultural systems Values and identities, norms and practices	Organizational and management systems Strategies, structures, processes and systems
Competence	Language competence	Intercultural competence	Management expertise
Function of third culture nationals	Translation of work-related content Creating trust through common language use	Mediation between different cultural systems Creation of mutual understanding	Arbitration in conflicts between employees of different organizational units

Source: Based on Barmeyer and Eberhardt (2017, p. 15).

As mentioned in the structural element and in Chapter 6, *bicultural leadership dyads* refer to the staffing of management positions with two persons of different cultural origins (Barmeyer & Davoine, 2019). There are several advantages associated with bicultural leadership dyads: (1) they combine diverse and specialized expertise, which a single person cannot reveal in depth and width; (2) they share roles and responsibilities, for example in administrative, strategic or operational activities; (3) partners can share and use their respective social networks as a common resource; (4) they are able to communicate constructively with employees from two (or more) cultures and thus to (5) involve multiple perspectives in decision-making processes. Moreover, (6) leadership dyads allow a constant dialogical negotiation and alignment of the organization's goals, tasks and practices between the partners. This enables the partners to explain facts and situations, and to solve problems more efficiently. However, it is necessary to choose a balanced symmetrical distribution of power. Moreover, mutual trust and respect are as important as regular communication between the partners. Box 13.1 reveals the advantages of bicultural leadership dyads.

BOX 13.1   ADVANTAGES OF BICULTURAL LEADERSHIP DYADS

- Combine different perspectives on challenges
- Bring in different cultural values, interpretations and solution-finding abilities
- Possess a higher language repertoire and are thus able to communicate with employees from different linguistic backgrounds
- Divide responsibilities, functions and tasks
- Share and use wider social networks
- Reveal higher sensitivity and empathy towards employees from different backgrounds
- Act as strategic (knowledge) bridges between headquarters and subsidiaries
- Integrate not only different cultural views, but also functional and professional backgrounds
- Learn from each other through observation, exchange, feedback and common experiences

Source: Based on Barmeyer and Davoine (2019).

Intercultural leaders and employees can be boundary spanners in organizations that take into account new and fast-changing social contexts and multiple dynamic cultures (Fitzsimmons et al., 2013; Mendenhall et al., 2018). They are likely to be aware of their own and foreign cultural imprints and know how to combine these respective peculiarities in a synergistic way. In general, intercultural leaders are able to influence others and to diffuse a shared vision that enables *constructive interculturality* by developing individuals and organizations, even in turbulent and uncertain times as described by the VUCA (Volatility, Uncertainty, Complexity and Ambiguity) world (Mendenhall et al., 2018). In this way, they can control and develop a complex organizational system which requires a high degree of accepting and valuing otherness, that is to say to perceive different cultural characteristics as a strength.

Through *constructive intercultural management*, organizations with an international orientation can strategically draw on the competences of intercultural leaders and employees as a resource for organizational learning and development (Box 13.2).

BOX 13.2 HOW ORGANIZATIONS CAN BENEFIT FROM INTERCULTURAL EMPLOYEES

1. Recruiting intercultural employees and maximizing their ability to use their skills
2. Promoting employees with intercultural competences in leadership positions
3. Encouraging the development and use of multiple language skills
4. Developing intercultural skills through assignments, experiential programmes, language classes and intercultural trainings
5. Creating visible signs to value multiculturalism
6. Organizing platforms and events where employees can exchange their intercultural knowledge and experience
7. Mentoring new intercultural employees by senior-level multicultural role models
8. Favouring intercultural employees for international assignments
9. Leveraging the knowledge and competences of expatriates after their stay abroad
10. Initiating organizational learning through knowledge exchange.

Source: Based on Fitzsimmons et al. (2011, p. 204).

3. NEW WAYS FOR DESIGNING CONSTRUCTIVE INTERCULTURALITY

Aligned with the presented goals of this book in the introduction (Table 1.1), Figure 13.2 shows how organizations can increase their creative and synergetic outcomes in eight steps.

Constructive intercultural management is based on a multitude of combined and interdependent factors. We have explained and illustrated these factors throughout this book by selected theoretical frameworks and empirical studies. The new integrative and systemic framework presented in this chapter provides the opportunity to identify factors of complementary and synergetic cooperation, and whenever possible, to develop them.

Both research and practice need to deal increasingly with constructive interculturality in the future. Organizations are confronted with life-long learning processes, which often have no clear beginning and no clear end, but represent phases and cycles. *Constructive intercultural management* will always be asked to give new ideas and impulses, and to encourage further individual and organizational development. We hope that our book can help organizations to successfully design and implement constructive interculturality!

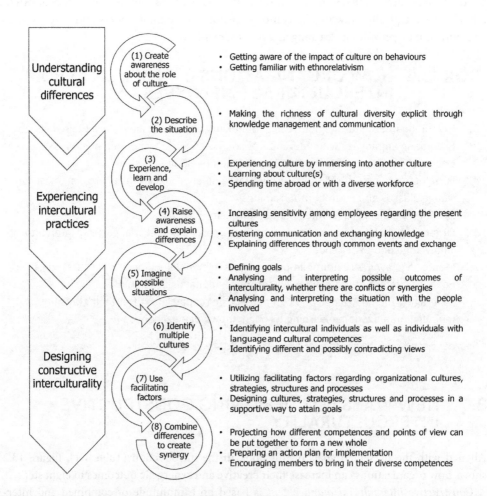

Figure 13.2 Eight steps for leveraging constructive interculturality in organizations

REFERENCES

Abbas, J. A. (1996). Organizational development in the Arab world. *Journal of Management Development, 15*(5), 4–21.

Abodohoui, A. & Su, Z. (2020). Influence of Chinese managerial soft power on African skills development. *International Business Review, 29*(5), forthcoming.

Adler, N. J. (1980). Cultural synergy: The management of cross-cultural organizations. In W. W. Burke & L. D. Goodstein (Eds.), *Trends and issues in organizational development: Current theory and practice* (pp. 163–184). University Associates.

Adler, N. J. (1983). Cross-cultural management research: The ostrich and the trend. *Academy of Management Review, 8*(2), 226–232.

Adler, N. J. & Aycan, Z. (2018). Cross cultural interaction: What we know and what we need to know. *Annual Review of Organizational Psychology & Organizational Behavior, 5*, 307–333.

Adler, N. J. & Gundersen, A. (2008). *International dimensions of organizational behavior*. Thomson South-Western.

Adler, N. J. & Osland, J. S. (2016). Women leading globally: What we know, thought we knew, and need to know about leadership in the 21st century. In J. S. Osland, M. Li & M. E. Mendenhall (Eds.), *Advances in global leadership* (vol. 9, pp. 15–56). Emerald.

Aichhorn, N. & Puck, J. (2017). Bridging the language gap in multinational companies: language strategies and the notion of company-speak. *Journal of World Business, 52*(3), 386–403.

Amado, G., Faucheux, C. & Laurent, A. (1991). Organizational change and cultural realities: Franco-American contrasts. *International Studies of Management & Organization, 21*(3), 62–95.

Anderson, D. L. (2019). *Organization development: The process of leading organizational change*. Sage.

Ang, S. & van Dyne, L. (2015). *Handbook of cultural intelligence: Theory, measurement, and applications*. Routledge.

Angouri, J. & Piekkari, R. (2018). Organising multilingually: Setting an agenda for studying language at work. *European Journal of International Management, 12*(1-2), 8–27.

Angué, K. & Mayrhofer, U. (2010). International R&D cooperation: The effects of distance on the choice of the country of partners. *M@n@gement, 13*(1), 1–37.

Argyris, C. (1971). *Management and organizational development: The path from XA to YB*. McGraw Hill.

Backmann, J., Kanitz, R., Tian, A. W., Hoffmann, P. & Hoegl, M. (2020). Cultural gap bridging in multinational teams. *Journal of International Business Studies, 51*(8), 1283–1311.

Bandeira-de-Mello, R., Ghauri, P., Mayrhofer, U. & Meschi, P.-X. (2015). Theoretical and empirical implications for research on South–South and South–North expansion strategies. *M@n@gement, 18*(1), 1–7.

Barenboim, D. & Said, W. E. (2002). *Parallels and paradoxes: Explorations in music and society*. Vintage.

Barmeyer, C. (1996). *Interkulturelle Qualifikationen im deutsch-französischen Management kleiner und mittelständischer Unternehmen*. Röhrig Universitätsverlag.

Barmeyer, C. (2000). *Interkulturelles Management und Lernstile*. Campus.

Barmeyer, C. (2002). Interkulturelles coaching. In C. Rauen (Ed.), *Handbuch Coaching* (pp. 199–231). Hogrefe.

Barmeyer, C. (2010). Das Passauer 3-Ebenen-Modell. Von Ethnozentrismus zu Ethnorelativismus durch kontextualisierte interkulturelle Organisationsentwicklung. In C. Barmeyer & J. Bolten (Eds.), *Interkulturelle Personal- und Organisationsentwicklung. Methoden, Instrumente und Anwendungsfälle* (pp. 31–56). Wissenschaft & Praxis.

Barmeyer, C. (2011a). Kultur in der Interkulturellen Kommunikation. In C. Barmeyer, P. Genkova & J. Scheffer (Eds.), *Interkulturelle Kommunikation und Kulturwissenschaft. Grundbegriffe, Wissenschaftsdisziplinen, Kulturräume* (pp. 13–35). Karl Stutz.

Barmeyer, C. (2011b). Interkulturalität. In C. Barmeyer, P. Genkova & J. Scheffer (Eds.), *Interkulturelle Kommunikation und Kulturwissenschaft. Grundbegriffe, Wissenschaftsdisziplinen, Kulturräume* (pp. 37–77). Karl Stutz.

Barmeyer, C. (2012a). *Taschenlexikon Interkulturalität*. UTB/Vandenhoeck & Ruprecht.

Barmeyer, C. (2012b). 'Context matters': Zur Bedeutung von Rekontextualisierung für den internationalen Transfer von Personalmanagementpraktiken. In V. Stein & S. Müller (Eds.), *Aufbruch des strategischen Personalmanagements in die Dynamisierung* (pp. 101–115). Nomos.

Barmeyer, C. (2013). Kulturspezifische und kulturvergleichende Perspektiven auf Führung und Organisation in deutschen und französischen Kooperationen. Eine Anwendung des Passauer Drei-Ebenen Modells. In D. Wawra (Ed.), *European Studies – Interkulturelle Kommunikation und Kulturvergleich* (pp. 255–282). Peter Lang.

Barmeyer, C. (2018). *Konstruktives Interkulturelles Management.* Vandenhoeck & Ruprecht.

Barmeyer, C., Bausch, M. & Moncayo, D. (2019a). Cross-cultural management research: Topics, paradigms, and methods – a journal-based longitudinal analysis between 2001 and 2018. *International Journal of Cross Cultural Management, 19*(2), 218-244.

Barmeyer, C. & Davoine, E. (2006). International corporate cultures: From helpless global convergence to constructive European divergence. In C. Scholz & J. Zentes (Eds.), *Strategic management – New rules for old Europe* (pp. 227–245). Gabler.

Barmeyer, C. & Davoine, E. (2011). The intercultural challenges in the transfer of codes of conduct from the USA to Europe. In H. Primecz, L. Romani & S. Sackmann (Eds.), *Cross-cultural management in practice. Culture and negotiated meanings* (pp. 53–63). Edward Elgar Publishing.

Barmeyer, C. & Davoine, E. (2019). Facilitating intercultural negotiated practices in joint ventures: The case of a French–German railway organization. *International Business Review, 28*(1), 1–11.

Barmeyer, C., Davoine, E. & Stokes, P. (2019b). When the 'well-oiled machine' meets the 'pyramid of people': Role perceptions and hybrid working practices of middle managers in a binational organization – ARTE. *International Journal of Cross Cultural Management, 19*(3), 251–272.

Barmeyer, C. & Eberhardt, J. (2017). Interkulturelle Brückenbauer: Die Funktion des Drittkultur-Managers. *Wirtschaftspsychologie aktuell, 24*(2), 13–15.

Barmeyer, C. & Franklin, P. (Eds.) (2016). *Intercultural management. A case-based approach to achieving complementarity and synergy.* Palgrave Macmillan.

Barmeyer, C., Ghidelli, E., Haupt, U. & Piber, H. (2015). Organisationsentwicklung im interkulturellen Raum. Ein Orientierungsmodell für Organisationsberater. *OrganisationsEntwicklung, 4*(15), 75–81.

Barmeyer, C. & Haupt, U. (2007). Interkulturelles Coaching. In J. Straub, A. Weidemann & D. Weidemann (Eds.), *Handbuch Interkulturelle Kommunikation und Kompetenz* (pp. 784–793). Metzler.

Barmeyer, C. & Haupt, U. (2016). Future+: Intercultural challenges and success factors in an international virtual project team. In C. Barmeyer & P. Franklin (Eds.), *Intercultural management: A case-based approach to achieving complementarity and synergy* (pp. 204–216). Palgrave Macmillan.

Barmeyer, C. & Mayer, C.-H. (2020). Positive intercultural management in the fourth industrial revolution: Managing cultural otherness through a paradigm shift. *International Review of Psychiatry, 32*(7–8), 638–650.

Barmeyer, C. & Mayrhofer, U. (2008). The contribution of intercultural management to the success of international mergers and acquisitions: An analysis of the EADS Group. *International Business Review, 17*(1), 28–38.

Barmeyer, C. & Mayrhofer, U. (2014). How has the French cultural and institutional context shaped the organization of the Airbus Group?. *International Journal of Organizational Analysis, 22*(4), 426–448.

Barmeyer, C. & Mayrhofer, U. (2016). Strategic alliances and intercultural organizational change: The Renault–Nissan case. In C. Barmeyer & P. Franklin (Eds.), *Intercultural management: A case-based approach to achieving complementarity and synergy* (pp. 303–317). Palgrave Macmillan.

Barmeyer, C. & Mayrhofer, U. (2020). Contextualizing intercultural competencies: Genesis, concepts and research agenda. In B. Grasser, S. Loufrani-Fedida & E. Oiry (Eds.), *Managing competences: Research, practice and contemporary issues* (pp. 233–251). Taylor & Francis.

Barmeyer, C., Mayrhofer, U. & Würfl, K. (2019c). Informal information flows in organizations: The role of the Italian coffee break. *International Business Review, 28*(4), 796–801.

Barmeyer, C. & Schirrmacher, U. (2013). Interkulturelle Kompetenzentwicklung durch (Unternehmens-) Planspiele als Instrumente für ganzheitliches Lernen an Hochschulen. In K. von Helmolt, G. Berkenbusch & W. Jia (Eds.), *Interkulturelle Lernsettings. Konzepte, Formate. Erfahrungen* (pp. 217–240). Ibidem.

Barmeyer, C., Stein, V. & Eberhardt, J. M. (2020). Third-country nationals as intercultural boundary spanners in multinational corporations. *Multinational Business Review, 28*(4), 521–547.

Barner-Rasmussen, W. (2015). What do bicultural-bilinguals do in multinational corporations. In N. Holden, S. Michailova & S. Tietze (Eds.), *The Routledge companion to cross-cultural management* (pp. 142–150). Routledge.

Barner-Rasmussen, W. & Björkman, I. (2007). Language fluency, socialization and inter-unit relationships in Chinese and Finnish subsidiaries. *Management and Organization Review, 3*(1), 105–128.

Barner-Rasmussen, W., Ehrnrooth, M., Koveshnikov, A. & Mäkelä, K. (2014). Cultural and language skills as resources for boundary spanning within the MNC. *Journal of International Business Studies, 45*(7), 886–905.

Barner-Rasmussen, W. & Langinier, H. (2020). Exploring translanguaging in international business. Towards a comparison of highly context-embedded practices. In S. Horn, P. Lecomte & S. Tietze (Eds.), *Managing multilingual workplaces: Methodological, empirical and pedagogic perspectives* (pp. 105–121). Routledge.

Bartel-Radic, A. & Giannelloni, J.-L. (2017). A renewed perspective on the measurement of cross-cultural competence: An approach through personality traits and cross-cultural knowledge. *European Management Journal, 35*(5), 632–644.

Bartunek, J. M. & Woodman, R. W. (2012). The spirits of organization development, or why OD lives despite its pronounced death. In K. Cameron & G. Spreitzer (Eds.), *The Oxford handbook of positive organizational scholarship* (pp. 727–736). Oxford University Press.

Bass, B. M. & Riggio, R. E. (2006). *Transformational leadership.* Psychology Press.

Batchelder, D. (1993). Using critical incidents. In T. Gochenour (Ed.), *Beyond experience. The experiential approach to cross-cultural education* (pp. 101–112). Intercultural Press.

Bausch, M., Barmeyer, C. & Mayrhofer, U. (2020). Cultural challenges and quality management practices of a German multinational in Brazil. In B. Amann & J. Jaussaud (Eds.), *Cross-cultural challenges in international management* (pp. 74–93). Routledge.

BBC (2020, 5 November). Ethical veganism is philosophical belief, tribunal rules. https://www.bbc.com/news/uk-50981359 [last accessed 2 December 2020].

Beddi, H. & Mayrhofer, U. (2013). Headquarters–subsidiaries relationships of French multinationals in emerging markets. *Multinational Business Review, 21*(2), 174–194.

Beeler, B. & Lecomte, P. (2017). Shedding light on the darker side of language: A dialogical approach to cross-cultural collaboration. *International Journal of Cross Cultural Management, 17*(1), 53–67.

Bekker, C. J. (2008). Finding the other in Southern African business leadership. *Regent Global Business Review,* 18–21. https://www.regent.edu/acad/global/publications/rgbr/vol2iss1/2008%20April_Ubuntu-Kenosis_Bekker.pdf [last accessed 2 December 2020].

Benedict, R. (1934). *Patterns of culture.* Houghton-Mifflin.

Bennett, J. M. (1993). Cultural marginality: Identity issues in intercultural training. In R. M. Paige (Eds.), *Education for the intercultural experience* (pp. 109–135). Intercultural Press.

Bennett, M. J. (1986). A developmental approach to training for intercultural sensitivity. *International Journal of Intercultural Relations, 10*(2), 179–198.

Bennett, M. J. (2017). Developmental model of intercultural sensitivity. In Y. Y. Kim (Ed.), *The international encyclopedia of intercultural communication.* Wiley.

Bennett, N. & Lemoine, G. J. (2014). What VUCA really means for you. *Harvard Business Review, 92*(1/2). https://ssrn.com/abstract=2389563.

Bergareche, B. C. (1993). Lingua franca y lengua de moros. *Revista de Filología Española 73*(3), 417–426.

Bergé, J.-S., Harnay, S., Mayrhofer, U. & Obadia, L. (Eds.) (2018). *Global phenomena and social sciences. An interdisciplinary and comparative approach.* Springer.

Berger, P. & Luckmann, T. (1966). *The social construction of reality: A treatise in the sociology of knowledge.* Doubleday.

Bhawuk, D. P. (2017). Culture assimilator. In Y. Y. Kim (Ed.), *The international encyclopedia of intercultural communication.* Wiley.

Bhawuk, D. & Triandis, H. (1996). The role of culture theory in the study of culture and intercultural training. In D. Landis & R. S. Bhagat (Eds.), *Handbook of intercultural training* (pp. 17–34). Sage.

Bird, A. (2018). Mapping the content domain of global leadership competencies. In M. E. Mendenhall, J. Osland, A. Bird, G. R. Oddou, M. J. Stevens, M. Maznevski & G. K. Stahl (Eds.), *Global leadership: Research, practice, and development* (pp. 119–142). Routledge.

Bird, A. & Mendenhall, M. E. (2016). From cross-cultural management to global leadership: Evolution and adaptation. *Journal of World Business, 51*(1), 115–126.

Bjerregaard, T., Lauring, J. & Klitmøller, A. (2009). A critical analysis of intercultural communication research in cross-cultural management introducing newer developments in anthropology. *Critical Perspectives on International Business, 5*(3), 207–228.

Blazejewski, S. (2006). Transferring value infused organizational practices in multinational companies. In M. Geppert & M. Mayer (Eds.), *Global, national and local practices in multinational companies* (pp. 63–104). Palgrave Macmillan.

Blunt, P. & Jones, M. L. (1997). Exploring the limits of Western leadership theory in East Asia and Africa. *Personnel Review, 26*(1/2), 6–23.

Bolten, J. (2015). *Einführung in die Interkulturelle Wirtschaftskommunikation.* UTB.

Bouncken, R., Brem, A. & Kraus, S. (2016). Multi-cultural teams as sources for creativity and innovation: The role of cultural diversity on team performance. *International Journal of Innovation Management, 20*(1), 1–34.

Bradford, D. L. & Burke, W. W. (Eds.) (2005). *Reinventing organization development: New approaches to change in organizations.* Wiley.

Brannen, M. Y. (1992). Organizational culture in a binational context: a model of negotiated culture. *Anthropology of Work Review, 13*(2), 9–11.

Brannen, M. Y. (1998). Negotiated culture in binational contexts: A model of culture change based on a Japanese/American organizational experience. *Anthropology of Work Review, 18*(2/3), 6–17.

Brannen, M. Y. (2004). When Mickey loses face: Recontextualization, semantic fit, and the semiotics of foreignness. *Academy of Management Review, 29*(4), 593–616.

Brannen, M. Y., Garcia, D. & Thomas, D. C. (2009). Biculturals as natural bridges for intercultural communication and collaboration. In S. Fussell, P. Hinds & T. Ishida (Eds.), *Proceedings of the 2009 international workshop on intercultural collaboration* (pp. 207–210). Association for Computing Machinery.

Brannen, M. Y. & Mughan, T. (Eds.) (2017). *Language in international business: Developing a field.* Palgrave Macmillan.

Brannen, M. Y., Piekkari, R. & Tietze, S. (2017). The multifaceted role of language in international business: Unpacking the forms, functions and features of a critical challenge to MNC theory and performance. In M. Y. Brannen & T. Mughan (Eds.), *Language in international business* (pp. 139–162). Palgrave Macmillan.

Brannen, M. Y. & Salk J. E. (2000). Partnering across borders: Negotiating organizational culture in a German–Japanese joint venture. *Human Relations, 53*(4), 451–487.

Brannen, M. Y. & Thomas, D. C. (2010). Bicultural individuals in organizations: Implications and opportunity. *International Journal of Cross Cultural Management, 10*(1), 5–16.

Brimm, L. (2010). *Global cosmopolitans. The creative edge of difference.* Palgrave Macmillan.

Brinkmann, U. & van Weerdenburg, O. (2014). *Intercultural readiness. Four competences for working across cultures.* Palgrave Macmillan.

Brislin, R. (1986). A culture general assimilator: Preparation for various types of sojourns. *International Journal of Intercultural Relations, 10*(2), 215–234.

Buckley, P. (2014). *The multinational enterprise and the emergence of the global factory.* Palgrave Macmillan.

Buckley, P. & Ghauri, P. (Eds.) (2015). *International business strategy. Theory and practice.* Routledge.

Burns, J. M. (1978). *Leadership.* Harper & Row.

Cagiltay, K., Bichelmeyer, B. & Akilli, G. K. (2015). Working with multicultural virtual teams: critical factors for facilitation, satisfaction and success. *Smart Learning Environments, 2*(11), 1–16.

Caligiuri, P. (2012). *Cultural agility: Building a pipeline of successful global professionals.* Wiley.

Caligiuri, P. (2013). Developing culturally agile global business leaders. *Organizational Dynamics, 3*(42), 175–182.

Caligiuri, P., Mencin, A., Jayne, B. & Traylor, A. (2019). Developing cross-cultural competencies through international corporate volunteerism. *Journal of World Business, 54*(1), 14–23.

Caligiuri, P. & Tarique, I. (2016). Cultural agility and international assignees' effectiveness in cross-cultural interactions. *International Journal of Training and Development, 20*(4), 280–289.

Cameron, K. (2017). Cross-cultural research and positive organizational scholarship. *Cross Cultural & Strategic Management, 24*(1), 13–32.

Cameron, K. S. & Spreitzer, G. M. (2011). What is positive about positive organizational scholarship? In K. S. Cameron & G. M. Spreitzer (Eds.), *The Oxford handbook of positive organizational scholarship* (pp. 1–14). Oxford University Press.

Canney-Davison, S. & Ward, K. (2021). *Leading international teams: A guide to the new world order.* Taylor & Francis.

Carson, B. (2015). 14 words you understand only if you work at Google. *Businessinsider*. https://www .businessinsider.com/14-words-you-only-understand-if-you-work-inside-google-2015-9?r=DE&IR= T [last accessed 2 December 2020].

Casmir, F. (1993). Third-culture building: A paradigm shift for international and intercultural communication. *Annals of the International Communication Association*, *16*(1), 407–428.

Casmir, F. (1999). Foundations for the study of intercultural communication based on a third-culture building model. *International Journal of Intercultural Relations*, *23*(1), 91–116.

Cavusgil, S. T. & Knight, G. (2009). *Born global firms: A new international enterprise*. Business Expert Press.

Cavusgil, S. T., Knight, G. & Riesenberger, J. (2019). *International business. The new realities* (5th ed.). Pearson.

Chalençon, L., Colovic, A., Lamotte, O. & Mayrhofer, U. (2017). Reputation, e-reputation and value creation of mergers-acquisitions. *International Studies of Management and Organization*, *47*(1), 4–22.

Chalençon, L. & Mayrhofer, U. (2018). Do cross-border mergers-acquisitions in mature and emerging markets create similar value?. *Journal of Organizational Change Management*, *31*(4), 944–958.

Chanlat, J. F. (2013). Intercultural analysis and the social sciences. In J. F. Chanlat, E. Davel & J. P. Dupuis (Eds.), *Cross-cultural management: Culture and management across the world* (pp. 11–40). Routledge.

Chen, Y., Friedman, R., Yu, E., Fang, W. & Lu, X. (2009). Supervisor-subordinate guanxi: Developing a three-dimensional model and scale. *Management and Organization Review*, *5*(3), 375–399.

Chevrier, S. (2003). Cross-cultural management in multinational project groups. *Journal of World Business*, *38*(2), 141–149.

Chevrier, S. (2009). Empowerment: a practice embedded in cultural contexts. A comparison between the United States and France. In C. Hansen & Y. T. Lee (Eds.), *Culture and human resource development* (pp. 77–89). Palgrave Macmillan.

Chevrier, S. (2011). Exploring the cultural context of Franco–Vietnamese development projects: Using an interpretative approach to improve the cooperation process. In H. Primecz, L. Romani & S. Sackmann (Eds.), *Cross-cultural management in practice: Culture and negotiated meanings* (pp. 41–52). Edward Elgar Publishing.

Chevrier, S. (2013). Managing multicultural teams. In J. F. Chanlat, E. Davel & J. P. Dupuis (Eds.), *Cross-cultural management: Culture and management across the world* (pp. 203–223). Routledge.

Chevrier, S. (2016). A tough day for a French expatriate in Vietnam: The management of a large international infrastructure project. In C. Barmeyer & P. Franklin (Eds.), *Intercultural management: A case-based approach to achieving complementarity and synergy* (pp. 228–239). Palgrave Macmillan.

Chevrier, S. & Viegas-Pires, M. (2013). Delegating effectively across cultures. *Journal of World Business*, *48*(3), 431–439.

Chhotray, S., Sivertsson, O. & Tell, J. (2018). The roles of leadership, vision, and empowerment in born global companies. *Journal of International Entrepreneurship*, *16*(1), 38–57.

Chidlow, A., Plakoyiannaki, E. & Welch, C. (2014). Translation in cross-language international business research: Beyond equivalence. *Journal of International Business Studies*, *45*(5), 562–582.

Chreim S. (2015). The (non)distribution of leadership roles: Considering leadership practices and configurations. *Human Relations*, *68*(4), 517–543.

Chua, R. & Jin, M. (2020). Across the great divides: Gender dynamics influence how intercultural conflict helps or hurts creative collaboration. *Academy of Management Journal*, *63*(3), 903–934.

Church-Morel, A. & Bartel-Radic, A. (2016). Skills, identity, and power: The multifaceted concept of language diversity. *International Management*, *21*(1), 12–24.

Cirque du Soleil (2020a). History. https://www.cirquedusoleil.com/about-us/history [last accessed 2 December 2020].

Cirque du Soleil (2020b). Creative process. https://www.cirquedusoleil.com/about-us/creative-process [last accessed 2 December 2020].

Ciuk, S., James, P. & Śliwa, M. (2019). Micropolitical dynamics of interlingual translation processes in an MNC subsidiary. *British Journal of Management*, *30*(4), 926–942.

Claes, M. T. (2019). Pizza Hut Vietnam: Adapting a global code of conduct. In C. Prange & R. Kattenbach (Eds.), *Management practices in Asia* (pp. 153–166). Springer.

Comfort, J. & Franklin, P. (2014). *The mindful international manager: How to work effectively across cultures*. Kogan Page.

Cooperrider, D. L. & Godwin, L. (2011). Positive organization development: Innovation-inspired change in an economy and ecology of strengths. In K. S. Cameron & G. M. Spreitzer (Eds.), *Oxford handbook of positive organizational scholarship* (pp. 737–750). Oxford University Press.

Cooperrider, D. L. & Srivastava, S. (1987). Appreciative inquiry in organizational life. In W. Pasmore & W. Woodman (Eds.) *Research in organizational change and development: An annual series featuring advances in theory, methodology and research* (vol. 1) (pp. 129–169). JAI Press.

Cooperrider, D., Whitney, D. D., Stavros, J. M. & Stavros, J. (2008). *The appreciative inquiry handbook: For leaders of change.* Berrett-Koehler.

Cramton, C. D. & Hinds, P. J. (2014). An embedded model of cultural adaptation in global teams. *Organization Science, 25*(4), 1056–1081.

Crouch, C. (2010). Complementarity. In G. Morgan, J. Campbell, C. Crouch, O. K. Pedersen & R. Whitley (Eds.), *Comparative institutional analysis* (pp. 117–137). Oxford University Press.

Crozier, M. & Friedberg, E. (1979). *Macht und Organisation: Zwänge Kollektiven Handelns.* Athenäum.

Cuervo-Cazurra, A. & Ramamurti, R. (Eds.) (2015). *Understanding multinationals from emerging markets.* Cambridge University Press.

Czinkota, M., Ronkainen, I. & Gupta, S. (2021). *International business* (9th ed.). Cambridge University Press.

d'Iribarne, P. (1994). The honour principle in the bureaucratic phenomenon. *Organization Studies, 15*(1), 81–97.

d'Iribarne, P. (2009). National cultures and organisations in search of a theory: An interpretative approach. *International Journal of Cross Cultural Management, 9*(3), 309–332.

d'Iribarne, P. (2010). In China, between guanxi and the celestial bureaucracy. *Gérer & Comprendre, 100*(2), 37–47.

d'Iribarne, P. (2012). *Managing corporate values in diverse national cultures. The challenge of differences.* Routledge.

d'Iribarne, P., Chevrier, S., Henry, A., Segal, J.-P. & Tréguer-Felten, G. (2020). *Cross-cultural management revisited.* Oxford University Press.

d'Iribarne, P. & Henry, A. (2007). *Successful companies in the developing world: Managing in synergy with cultures.* Agence Française de Développement.

Danone (2020). https://www.danone.com [last accessed 2 December 2020].

Davoine, E. & Ravasi, C. (2013). The relative stability of national career patterns in European top management careers in the age of globalisation: A comparative study in France/Germany/Great Britain and Switzerland. *European Management Journal, 31*(2), 152–163.

Day, P. (2015, 9 June). Entrepreneur of the year: a Bedouin turned businessman. https://www.bbc.com/news/business-33068445 [last accessed 2 December 2020].

Delmestri, G. & Walgenbach, P. (2005). Mastering techniques or brokering knowledge? Middle managers in Germany, Great Britain and Italy. *Organization Studies, 26*(2), 197–220.

de Saussure, F. (1916[2011]). *Course in general linguistics.* Columbia University Press.

de Waal, M. F. & Born, M. P. (2020). Growing up among cultures: Intercultural competences, personality, and leadership styles of third culture kids. *European Journal of International Management, 14*(2), 327–356.

Dheer, R., Lenartowicz, T. & Peterson, M. (2015). Mapping India's regional subcultures: Implications for international management. *Journal of International Business Studies. 46*(4), 443–467.

Dickson, M. W., Castaño, N., Magomaeva, A. & Den Hartog, D. N. (2012). Conceptualizing leadership across cultures. *Journal of World Business, 47*(4), 483–492.

Di Marco, M. K., Taylor, J. E. & Alin, P. (2010). Emergence and role of cultural boundary spanners in global engineering project networks. *Journal of Management in Engineering, 26*(3), 123–132.

DiStefano, J. J. & Maznevski, M. L. (2000). Creating value with diverse teams in global management. *Organizational Dynamics, 29*(1), 45–63.

Dominguez, N. & Mayrhofer, U. (2017). Internationalization stages of traditional SMEs: Increasing, decreasing and re-increasing commitment to foreign markets. *International Business Review, 26*(6), 1051–1063.

Dominguez, N. & Mayrhofer, U. (Eds.) (2018a). *Key success factors of SME internationalisation: A cross-country perspective.* Emerald.

Dominguez, N. & Mayrhofer, U. (2018b). *Mixel Agitators: An SME's intercultural experience in China.* Centrale de Cas et de Médias Pédagogiques (French Case Clearing House).

Dominguez, N., Mayrhofer, U. & Obadia, C. (2017). The antecedents of information exchange in export business networks. *M@n@gement*, *20*(5), 463–491.

Dörrenbächer, C. & Geppert, M. (2017). *Multinational corporations and organization theory: Post millennium perspectives*. Emerald.

Duarte, F. (2006). Exploring the interpersonal transaction of the Brazilian jeitinho in bureaucratic contexts. *Organization*, *13*(4), 509–527.

Earley, P. C. & Ang, S. (2003). *Cultural intelligence: Individual interactions across cultures*. Stanford University Press.

Ehnert, I. & Claes, M. T. (2014). Global leadership for sustainable development. In B. Gehrke & M. T. Claes (Eds.), *Global leadership practices: A cross-cultural management perspective* (pp. 149–168). Palgrave Macmillan.

Ellenrieder, L. & Kammhuber, S. (2009). *Beruflich in Chile: Trainingsprogramm für Manager, Fach-und Führungskräfte*. Vandenhoeck & Ruprecht.

ESCP Europe (2020). Moving tomorrow. http://escpeurope-centreinterculturalmanagement.eu/ learning/moving-tomorrow/ [last accessed 2 December 2020].

Ethnologue (2020). https://www.ethnologue.com/ [last accessed 2 December 2020].

Evans, P., Lank, E. & Farquhar, A. (1989). Managing human resources in the international firm. In P. Evans, Y. Doz & A. Laurent (Eds.), *Human resource management in international firms* (pp. 113–125). Palgrave Macmillan.

Fang, T. (2006). From 'onion' to 'ocean': Paradox and change in national cultures. *International Studies of Management and Organization*, *35*(4), 71–90.

Fang, T. (2012). Yin yang: A new perspective on culture. *Management and Organization Review*, *8*(1), 25–50.

Festing, M. & Maletzky, M. (2011). Cross-cultural leadership adjustment – a framework based on the theory of structuration. *Human Resource Management Review*, *21*(3), 186–200.

Fitzsimmons, S. R. (2013). Multicultural employees: A framework for understanding how they contribute to organizations. *Academy of Management Review*, *38*(4), 525–549.

Fitzsimmons, S. R., Lee, Y. T. & Brannen, M. Y. (2012). Marginals as global leaders: Why they might just excel. *European Business Review*, November–December, 7–10.

Fitzsimmons, S. R., Lee, Y. T. & Brannen, M. Y. (2013). Demystifying the myth about marginals: Implications for global leadership. *European Journal of International Management*, *7*(5), 587–603.

Fitzsimmons, S. R., Liao, Y. & Thomas, D. C. (2017). From crossing cultures to straddling them: An empirical examination of outcomes for multicultural employees. *Journal of International Business Studies*, *48*(1), 63–89.

Fitzsimmons, S. R., Miska, C. & Stahl, G. (2011). Multicultural employees: Global business' untapped resource. *Organizational Dynamics*, *40*(3), 199–206.

Flaherty, J. E. (2015). The effects of cultural intelligence on team member acceptance and integration in multinational teams. In S. Ang & L. van Dyne (Eds.), *Handbook of cultural intelligence: Theory, measurement, and applications* (pp. 210–223). Routledge.

Flanagan, J. (1954). The critical incident technique. *Psychological Bulletin*, *51*(4), 327–358.

Fowler, S. & Blohm, J. (2004). An analysis of methods for intercultural training. In D. Landis, J. Bennett & M. Bennett (Eds.), *Handbook of intercultural training* (pp. 37–84). Sage.

Fowler, S. M. & Pusch, M. D. (2010). Intercultural simulation games: A review (of the United States and beyond). *Simulation & Gaming*, *41*(1), 94–115.

Fredriksson, R., Barner-Rasmussen, W. & Piekkari, R. (2006). The multinational corporation as a multilingual organization. *Corporate Communications: An International Journal*, *11*(4), 406–423.

French, W. & Bell, C. (1978). *Organizational development: Behavior science interventions for organizational improvement*. Prentice Hall.

Friel, D. & de Villechenon, F. P. (2018). Adapting a lean production program to national institutions in Latin America: Danone in Argentina and Brazil. *Journal of International Management*, *24*(3), 284–299.

Galbraith, J. R. (1995). *Designing organizations: An executive briefing on strategy, structure, and process*. Jossey-Bass.

Gannon, M. J. & Pillai, R. (2016). *Understanding global cultures: Metaphorical journeys through 34 nations, clusters of nations, continents, and diversity*. Sage.

Gao, H., Knight, J. G., Yang, Z. & Ballantyne, D. (2014). Toward a gatekeeping perspective of insider–outsider relationship development in China. *Journal of World Business*, *49*(3), 312–320.

Geertz, C. (1973). *The interpretation of culture*. Basic Books.

Gehrke, B. (2014). Global leadership: Engaging people across cultures. In B. Gehrke & M. T. Claes (Eds.), *Global leadership practices: A cross-cultural management perspective* (pp. 132–148). Palgrave Macmillan.

Gehrke, B. & Claes, M. T. (Eds.) (2014). *Global leadership practices: A cross-cultural management perspective*. Palgrave Macmillan.

Gelles, D. (2020, 10 November). The husband-and-wife team behind the leading vaccine to solve Covid-19. *New York Times*. https://www.nytimes.com/2020/11/10/business/biontech-covid-vaccine .html [last accessed 2 December 2020].

Gereffi, G. (2018). *Global value chains and development – redefining the contours of 21st century capitalism*. Cambridge University Press.

Gertsen, M. C. (1990). Intercultural competence and expatriates. *International Journal of Human Resource Management, 1*(3), 341–362.

Gertsen, M. C. & Zølner, M. (2012). Recontextualization of the corporate values of a Danish MNC in a subsidiary in Bangalore. *Group & Organization Management, 37*(1), 101–132.

Gessler, M. (2017). Educational transfer as transformation: A case study about the emergence and implementation of dual apprenticeship structures in a German automotive transplant in the United States. *Vocations and Learning, 10*(1), 71–99.

Gibson, C. B. & Gibbs, J. L. (2006). Unpacking the concept of virtuality: The effects of geographic dispersion, electronic dependence, dynamic structure, and national diversity on team innovation. *Administrative Science Quarterly, 51*(3), 451–495.

Glasl, F., Kalcher, T. & Piber, H. (2020). *Professionelle Prozessberatung: Das Trigon-Modell der sieben OE-Basisprozesse*. Haupt.

Glasl, F. & Lievegoed, B. (2011). *Dynamische Unternehmensentwicklung. Wie Pionierbetriebe und Bürokratien zu schlanken Unternehmen werden*. Haupt.

GLOBE (2020). Global leadership and organizational behavior effectiveness, https://globeproject.com/ [last accessed 2 December 2020].

Goethe, J. W. v. (1810). *Zur Farbenlehre*. Cotta.

Goethe, J. W. v. (1819). *West-Östlicher Divan*. Cottaische Buchhandlung.

Google (2020). Distributed work playbooks. http://services.google.com/fh/files/blogs/distributedwor kplaybooks.pdf [last accessed 2 December 2020].

Grandin, G. (2009). *Fordlandia: The rise and fall of Henry Ford's forgotten jungle city*. Metropolitan Books.

Granovetter, M. (1983). The strength of weak ties: A network theory revisited. *Sociological Theory, 1*, 201–233.

Hall, E. T. (1981). *The silent language*. Doubleday.

Hall, E. T. (1983). *The dance of life: The other dimension of time*. Anchor Books.

Hall, E. T. & Hall, M. (1990). *Understanding cultural differences. Germans, French, and Americans*. Intercultural Press.

Halliday, J. (2020, 15 November). BioNTech vaccine scientist says jab could halve Covid transmission. *The Guardian*. https://www.theguardian.com/world/2020/nov/15/biontech-vaccine-scientist-says -jab-could-halve-covid-transmission-pfizer [last accessed 2 December 2020].

Hampden-Turner, C. (1990). *Charting the corporate mind*. Free Press.

Hampden-Turner, C. (1992). *La culture d'entreprise. Des cercles vicieux aux cercles vertueux*. Seuil.

Hampden-Turner, C. & Trompenaars, F. (1993). *The seven cultures of capitalism*. Doubleday.

Hampden-Turner, C. & Trompenaars, F. (2000). *Building cross-cultural competence: How to create wealth from conflicting values*. Wiley.

Hampden-Turner, C. & Trompenaars, F. (2006). Cultural intelligence: Is such a capacity credible? *Group & Organization Management, 31*(1), 56–63.

Hampden-Turner, C. & Trompenaars, F. (2020). *Riding the waves of culture – understanding diversity in global business* (4th ed.). McGraw Hill.

Hang, T. T. (2008). Women's leadership in Vietnam: Opportunities and challenges. *Signs: Journal of Women in Culture and Society, 34*(1), 16–21.

Hassan, I., Ghauri, P. & Mayrhofer, U. (2018). Merger and acquisition motives and outcome assessment. *Thunderbird International Business Review, 60*(4), 709–718.

Headland, T., Pike, K. & Harris M. (1990). *Emic and etic. The insider/outsider-debate*. Sage.

Henderson, L. S., Stackman, R. W. & Lindekilde, R. (2018). Why cultural intelligence matters on global project teams. *International Journal of Project Management*, 36(7), 954–967.

Herd, A. & Lowe, K. (2020). Cross-cultural comparative leadership studies: A critical look to the future. In B. Szkudlarek, L. Romani, D. V. Caprar & J. S. Osland (Eds.) *The Sage handbook of contemporary cross-cultural management* (pp. 357–374). Sage.

Hernandez Bark, A. S., Escartín, J. & van Dick, R. (2014). Gender and leadership in Spain: A systematic review of some key aspects. *Sex Roles*, 70(11), 522–537.

Hertrich, S., Kalika, M. & Mayrhofer, U. (2016). *Danone: A world leader of the food-processing industry.* Centrale de Cas et de Médias Pédagogiques (French Case Clearing House).

Hill, C. W. L. & Hult, G. T. M. (2020*). International business. Competing in the global market place* (13th ed.). McGraw Hill.

Hinds, P. J., Neeley, T. B. & Cramton, C. D. (2014). Language as a lightning rod: Power contests, emotion regulation, and subgroup dynamics in global teams. *Journal of International Business Studies*, 45(5), 536–561.

Hofstede, G. (2002). Dimensions do not exist: A reply to Brendan McSweeney. *Human Relations*, 55(11), 1355–1361.

Hofstede, G. H., Hofstede, G. J. & Minkov, M. (2010). *Cultures and organizations: Software of the mind. Intercultural cooperation and its importance for survival.* McGraw Hill.

Holden, N. J. & Michailova, S. (2014). A more expansive perspective on translation in IB research: Insights from the Russian handbook of knowledge management. *Journal of International Business Studies*, 45(7), 906–918.

Holden, N. J. & von Kortzfleisch, H. F. (2004). Why cross-cultural knowledge transfer is a form of translation in more ways than you think. *Knowledge and Process Management*, 11(2), 127–136.

Hoppe, M. H. (2004). Cross-cultural issues in the development of leaders. In C. D. McCauley & E. van Velsor (Eds.), *The center for creative leadership handbook of leadership development* (pp. 331–360). Jossey-Bass.

Hoppe, M. H. & Bhagat, R. S. (2007). Leadership in the United States of America: The leader as cultural hero. In J. S. Chhokar, F. C. Brodbeck & R. J. House (Eds.), *Culture and leadership across the world: The GLOBE book of in-depth studies of 25 societies* (pp. 475–543). Lawrence.

Horn, S., Lecomte, P. & Tietze, S. (Eds.) (2020). *Managing multilingual workplaces: Methodological, empirical and pedagogic perspectives.* Routledge.

House, R. J., Dorfmann, P. W., Javidan, M., Hanges, P. J. & Sully de Luque, M. (2014). *Strategic leadership across cultures: Globe study of CEO leadership behavior and effectiveness in 24 countries.* Sage.

House, R. J., Hanges, P. J., Javidan, M., Dorfman, P. W. & Gupta, V. (Eds.) (2004). *Culture, leadership and organizations: The GLOBE study of 62 societies.* Sage.

Hrenyk, J., Szymanski, M., Kar, A. & Fitzsimmons, S. R. (2016). Understanding multicultural individuals as ethical global leaders. In J. S. Osland, M. Li & M. E. Mendenhal (Eds.), *Advances in global leadership* (vol. 9, pp. 57–78). Emerald.

Inglehart, R. (2018). *Culture shift in advanced industrial society.* Princeton University Press.

International Organization for Migration (2019). World migration report 2020. https://publications.iom .int/system/files/pdf/wmr_2020.pdf [last accessed 2 December 2020].

Janssens, M. & Steyaert, C. (2014). Re-considering language within a cosmopolitan understanding: Toward a multilingual franca approach in international business studies. *Journal of International Business Studies*, 45(5), 623–639.

Javidan, M. & Bowen, D. (2013). The 'global mindset' of managers. *Organizational Dynamics*, 42(2), 145–155.

Jensen, K. R. (2015). Global innovation and cross-cultural collaboration: The influence of organizational mechanisms. *International Management*, 19(special issue), 101–116.

Johansen, B. (2007). *Get there early. Sensing the future to compete in the present.* Berrett-Koehler.

Johanson, J. & Vahlne, J.-E. (2009). The Uppsala internationalization process model revisited: From liability of foreignness to liability of outsidership. *Journal of International Business Studies*, 40(9), 1411–1431.

Joiner, B. (2019). Leadership agility for organizational agility. *Journal of Creating Value*, 5(2), 139–149.

Kaplan, R. B. (1966). Cultural thought patterns in inter-cultural education. *Language Learning*, 16(1-2), 1–20.

Kashubskaya-Kimpelainen, E., Festing, M., Maletzky, M. & Frank, F. (2009). Encadrer des équipes russes. *Expansion Management Review, 134*, 74–87.

Kempf, C. & Holtbrügge, D. (2020). Moderators and mediators of cross-cultural training effectiveness: Literature review and development of a conceptual model. *European Journal of International Management, 14*(2), 293–326.

Kempf, M. & Franklin, P. (2016). Adidas and Reebok: What expatriate managers need to manage M&As across cultures. In C. Barmeyer & P. Franklin (Eds.), *Intercultural management: A case-based approach to achieving complementarity and synergy* (pp. 148–166). Palgrave Macmillan.

Kieser, A. & Walgenbach, P. (2010). *Organisation*. Schäffer-Poeschl.

Klitmøller, A. & Lauring, J. (2013). When global virtual teams share knowledge: Media richness, cultural difference and language commonality. *Journal of World Business, 48*(3), 398–406.

Kluckhohn, C. (1953). Universal categories of culture. In A. L. Kroeber (Eds.), *Anthropology today* (pp. 507–524). University of Chicago Press.

Kluckhohn, F. R. & Strodtbeck, F. L. (1961). *Variations in value orientations*. Greenwood Press.

Kohls, R. (1994). On becoming a foreigner. In F. Luce (Ed.), *The French-speaking world* (pp. 42–56). NTC.

Kostova, T. (1999). Transnational transfer of strategic organizational practices: A contextual perspective. *Academy of Management Review, 24*(2), 308–324.

Koveshnikov, A., Barner-Rasmussen, W., Ehrnrooth, M. & Mäkelä, K. (2012). A framework of successful organizational practices in Western multinational companies operating in Russia. *Journal of World Business, 47*(3), 371–382.

Kroeber, A. L. & Kluckhohn, C. (Eds.) (1954). *Culture. A critical review of concepts and definitions*. Random House.

Lakshman, C. (2013). Biculturalism and attributional complexity: Cross-cultural leadership effectiveness. *Journal of International Business Studies, 44*(9), 922–940.

Laloux, F. (2014). *Reinventing organizations: A guide to creating organizations inspired by the next stage in human consciousness*. Nelson Parker.

Lee, Y-T. (2010). Home versus host – identifying with either, both or neither? The relationship between dual cultural identities and intercultural effectiveness. *International Journal of Cross Cultural Management, 10*(1), 55–76.

Lee, Y.-T., Masuda, A., Fu, X. & Reiche, B. S. (2018). Navigating between home, host, and global: Consequences of multicultural team members' identity configurations. *Academy of Management Discoveries, 4*(2), 180–201.

Lervik, J. E. (2008). Knowledge management and knowledge transfer in multinational enterprises. Cultural and institutional perspectives. In P. B. Smith, M. F. Peterson & D. C. Thomas (Eds.), *Handbook of cross-cultural management research* (pp. 301–317). Sage.

Li, C., Brodbeck, F. C., Shenkar, O., Ponzi, L. J. & Fisch, J. H. (2017). Embracing the foreign: Cultural attractiveness and international strategy. *Strategic Management Journal, 38*(4), 950–971.

Lisak, A. & Erez, M. (2015). Leadership emergence in multicultural teams: The power of global characteristics. *Journal of World Business, 50*(1), 3–14.

Lisak, A., Erez, M., Sui, Y. & Lee, C. (2016). The positive role of global leaders in enhancing multicultural team innovation. *Journal of International Business Studies, 47*(6), 655–673.

LOHAS (2020). http://www.lohas.com.au [last accessed 2 December 2020].

Lønsmann, D. (2017). Embrace it or resist it? Employees' reception of corporate language policies. *International Journal of Cross Cultural Management, 17*(1), 101–123.

Lowe, S., Kainzbauer, A. & Hwang, K. S. (2019). Exploring culture as a paradox: Complementary QUEUE analysis of cultural values and practices. *Journal of Organizational Change Management, 33*(1), 127–142.

Luiz, J. M. (2015). The impact of ethno-linguistic fractionalization on cultural measures: Dynamics, endogeneity and modernization. *Journal of International Business Studies, 46*(9), 1080–1098.

Lutz, D. (2009). African, *Ubuntu* philosophy and global management. *Journal of Business Ethics, 84*(3), 313–328.

Machkova, H. & Mayrhofer, U. (2018). *Market entry strategies of car manufacturers in the Czech Republic*. Centrale de Cas et de Médias Pédagogiques (French Case Clearing House).

Magnani, G., Mayrhofer, U. & Zucchella, A. (2018). *ATOM, a small multinational company*. Centrale de Cas et de Médias Pédagogiques (French Case Clearing House).

Mahadevan, J. (2011). Engineering culture(s) across sites: Implications for cross-cultural management of emic meanings. In H. Primecz, L. Romani & S. Sackmann (Eds.), *Cross-cultural management in practice: Culture and negotiated meanings* (pp. 89–100). Edward Elgar Publishing.

Mäkelä, K., Barner-Rasmussen, W., Ehrnrooth, M. & Koveshnikov, A. (2019). Potential and recognized boundary spanners in multinational corporations. *Journal of World Business, 54*(4), 335–349.

Makimoto, T. & Manners, D. (1997). *Digital nomad*. Wiley.

Maletzky, M. (2010). *Kulturelle Anpassung als Prozess interkultureller Strukturierung. Eine strukturations-theoretische Betrachtung kultureller Anpassungsprozesse deutscher Auslandsentsendeter in Mexiko*. Rainer Hampp.

March, J. G. & Simon, H. A. (1958). *Organizations*. Wiley.

Marcus, J., Kahraman, F., Su, S. & Fritzsche, B. (2019). Capturing intranational cultural variation in international business research: Microsocietal differences in collectivism across Turkey. *Journal of World Business, 54*(6), forthcoming.

Marschan, R., Welch, D. & Welch, L. (1997). Language: The forgotten factor in multinational management. *European Management Journal, 15*(5), 591–598.

Maslow, A. (1954). *Motivation and personality*. Harper & Row.

Maslow, A. (1964). Synergy in the society and in the individual. *Journal of Individual Psychology, 20*(2), 153–164.

Maslow, A. & Honigmann, J. (1970). Synergy: some notes of Ruth Benedict. *American Anthropologist, 72*(2), 320–333.

Mayer, C. H., Boness, C. M. & Louw, L. (2017). Perceptions of Chinese and Tanzanian employees regarding intercultural collaboration. *SA Journal of Human Resource Management, 15*(1), 1–11.

Mayer, C. H., Louw, L. & Boness, C. M. (Eds.) (2019). *Managing Chinese-African business interactions: Growing intercultural competence in organizations*. Springer.

Mayrhofer, U. (Ed.) (2013). *Management of multinational companies: A French perspective*. Palgrave Macmillan.

Mayrhofer, U. (2017). *Management interculturel. Comprendre et gérer la diversité culturelle*. Vuibert.

Mayrhofer, U., Didi Alaoui, M. & Papetti, C. (2020). *PocketConfidant AI. Digital self-coaching powered by artificial intelligence*. Centrale de Cas et de Médias Pédagogiques (French Case Clearing House).

Maznevski, M. L. & Athanassiou, N. A. (2003). Designing the knowledge-management infrastructure for virtual teams: Building and using social networks and social capital. In C. B. Gibson & S. G. Cohen (Eds.), *Virtual teams that work: Creating conditions for virtual team effectiveness* (pp. 196–213). Wiley.

Maznevski, M. L. & Chudoba, K. M. (2000). Bridging space over time: Global virtual team dynamics and effectiveness. *Organization Science, 11*(5), 473–492.

Maznevski, M. L. & Chui, C. (2018). Leading global teams. In M. Mendenhall, J. Osland, A. Bird, G. Oddou, M. Stevens, M. Maznevski & G. K. Stahl (Eds.), *Global leadership: Research, practice, and development* (pp. 273–301). Taylor & Francis.

Maznevski, M. L. & DiStefano, J. J. (2000). Global leaders are team players: Developing global leaders through membership on global teams. *Human Resource Management, 39*(2–3), 195–208.

McSweeney, B. (2009). Dynamic diversity: Variety and variation within countries. *Organization Studies, 30*(9), 933–957.

Mendenhall, M. (2018). Leadership and the birth of global leadership. In M. E. Mendenhall, J. Osland, A. Bird, G. R. Oddou, M. J. Stevens, M. Maznevski & G. K. Stahl (Eds.), *Global leadership: Research, practice, and development* (pp. 3–27). Routledge.

Mendenhall, M. E., Osland, J., Bird, A., Oddou, G. R., Stevens, M. J., Maznevski, M. & Stahl, G. K. (2018). *Global leadership: Research, practice, and development*. Routledge.

Miao, C., Humphrey, R. H. & Qian, S. (2018). A cross-cultural meta-analysis of how leader emotional intelligence influences subordinate task performance and organizational citizenship behavior. *Journal of World Business, 53*(4), 463–474.

Milliot, E. (2016). The pivotal role of guanxi for economic intelligence in the People's Republic of China. *International Management, 20*(4), 133–145.

Moalla, E. & Mayrhofer, U. (2020). How does distance affect market entry mode choice? Evidence from French companies. *European Management Journal, 38*(1), 135–145.

Mohamed, A. A. & Mohamad, S. (2011). The effect of wasta on perceived competence and morality in Egypt. *Cross Cultural Management, 18*(4), 412–425.

Moore, A. M. & Barker, G. G. (2012). Confused or multicultural: Third culture individuals' cultural identity. *International Journal of Intercultural Relations, 36*(4), 553–562.

Moore, F. (2016). *Transnational business cultures: Life and work in a multinational corporation.* Routledge.

Moore, F. (2020). Multiple interpretations of 'national culture' and the implications for international business: The case of Taiwan. *Journal of World Business, 55*(5), forthcoming.

Morgan, J. (2015, 13 July). The 5 types of organizational structures: Part 3, Flat organizations. *Forbes.* https://www.forbes.com/sites/jacobmorgan/2015/07/13/the-5-types-of-organizational-structures-part-3-flat-organizations/?sh=6119ffc36caa [last accessed 2 December 2020].

Morrison, E., Hutcheson, S., Nilsen, E., Fadden, J. & Franklin, N. (2019). *Strategic doing: Ten skills for agile leadership.* Wiley.

Nakhle, S. F. & Davoine, E. (2016). Transferring codes of conduct within a multinational firm. The case of Lebanon. *EuroMed Journal of Business, 11*(3), 1–19.

Nathan, G. (2015). A non-essentialist model of culture: Implications of identity, agency and structure within multinational/multicultural organizations. *International Journal of Cross Cultural Management, 15*(1), 101–124.

Nazarkiewicz, K. (2018). Was ist interkulturelles Coaching? 20 Jahre und (k)ein bisschen Klarheit. *Organisationsberatung, Supervision, Coaching, 25,* 21–39.

Neeley, T. (2017). *The language of global success: How a common tongue transforms multinational organizations.* Princeton University Press.

Newburger, E. (2020, 15 March). LVMH will use its perfume and cosmetics factories to manufacture free hand sanitizer for France. *CNBC News.* https://www.cnbc.com/2020/03/15/lvmh-will-use-its-perfume-and-cosmetics-factories-to-manufacture-free-hand-sanitizer.html [last accessed 2 December 2020].

Nkomo, S. (2011). A postcolonial and anti-colonial reading of 'African' leadership and management in organization studies: tensions, contradictions and possibilities. *Organization, 18*(3), 365–386.

Northouse, P. G. (2018). *Leadership: Theory and practice.* Sage.

Osland, J. S. & Bird, A. (2000). Beyond sophisticated stereotyping: Cultural sensemaking in context. *Academy of Management Perspectives, 14*(1), 65–77.

Özbilgin, M. & Chanlat, J. F. (2018). *Management and diversity. Perspectives from different national contexts.* Emerald.

Pananond, P., Gereffi, G. & Pedersen, T. (2020). An integrative typology of global strategy and global value chains: The management and organization of cross-border activities. *Global Strategy Journal, 10*(3), 421–443.

Parsons, T. (1952). *The social system.* Free Press.

Parsons, R. (2008). We are all stakeholders now: The influence of western discourses of 'community engagement' in an Australian Aboriginal community. *Critical Perspectives on International Business, 4*(2/3), 99–126.

Paulus, P. B., van Der Zee, K. I. & Kenworthy, J. (2016). Cultural diversity and team creativity. In V. P. Glavenau (Ed.), *The Palgrave handbook of creativity and culture research* (pp. 57–76). Palgrave Macmillan.

Peltokorpi, V. (2015). Language-oriented human resource management practices in multinational companies. In N. Holden, S. Michailova & S. Tietze (Eds.), *The Routledge companion to cross-cultural management* (pp. 161–180). Routledge.

Perlmutter, H. V. (1969). The tortuous evolution of the multinational corporation. *Columbia Journal of World Business, 4*(1), 9–18.

Perlmutter, H. V. & Heenan, D. A. (1979). *Multinational organization development: A social architectural perspective.* Addison-Wesley Publishing.

Perry-Smith, J. E. & Shalley, C. E. (2014). A social composition view of team creativity: The role of member nationality-heterogeneous ties outside of the team. *Organization Science, 25*(5), 1434–1452.

Piekkari, R. (2008). Language and careers in multinational corporations. In S. Tietze (Ed.), *International management and language* (pp. 128–137). Routledge.

Piekkari, R., Welch, D. & Welch, L. S. (2014). *Language in international business: The multilingual reality of global business expansion.* Edward Elgar Publishing.

Pike, K. (1954). *Language in relation to a unified theory of the structure of human behavior.* Mouton.

Pinho, A. S. (2015). Intercomprehension: A portal to teachers' intercultural sensitivity. *The Language Learning Journal, 43*(2), 148–164.

Pollock, D., van Reken, R. & Pfüger, G. (2003). *Third culture kids: Aufwachsen in mehreren Kulturen*. Francke.

Ralston, D. A. (2008). The crossvergence perspective: Reflections and projections. *Journal of International Business Studies, 39*(1), 27–40.

Rathje, S. (2007). Interkulturelles consulting. In J. Straub, A. Weidemann & D. Weidemann (Eds.), *Handbuch Interkulturelle Kommunikation und Kompetenz* (pp. 800–808). Metzler.

Ray, P. & Anderson, S. R. (2000). *The cultural creatives: How 50 million are changing the world*. Harmony Books.

Raz, A. E. (2009). Transplanting management: Participative change, organizational development, and the glocalization of corporate culture. *The Journal of Applied Behavioral Science, 45*(2), 280–304.

Reckwitz, A. (2020). *Society of singularities*. Wiley.

Redding, G. (2005). The thick description and comparison of societal systems of capitalism. *Journal of International Business Studies, 36*(2), 123–155.

Reiter-Palmon, R., Wigert, B. & de Vreede, T. (2012). Team creativity and innovation: The effect of group composition, social processes, and cognition. In M. D. Mumford (Ed.), *Handbook of organizational creativity* (pp. 295–326). Elsevier.

Renault–Nissan–Mitsubishi (2020). About us. https://www.alliance-2022.com/about-us [last accessed 2 December 2020].

Rework (2020). Introduction. https://rework.withgoogle.com/guides/understanding-team-effectiveness/steps/introduction [last accessed 2 December 2020].

Rigby, D. K., Sutherland, J. & Takeuchi, H. (2016). Embracing agile. *Harvard Business Review, 94*(5), 40–50.

Robertson, B. J. (2015). *Holacracy: The new management system for a rapidly changing world*. Henry Holt and Company.

Romani, L. & Szkudlarek, B. (2014). The struggles of the interculturalists: Professional ethical identity and early stages of codes of ethics development. *Journal of Business Ethics, 119*(2), 173–191.

Romero, M., Usart, M. & Ott, M. (2015). Can serious games contribute to developing and sustaining 21st century skills?. *Games and Culture, 10*(2), 148–177.

Rosa, B., Gugler, P. & Verbeke, A. (2020). Regional and global strategies of MNEs: Revisiting Rugman & Verbeke (2004). *Journal of International Business Studies, 51*(7), 1045–1053.

Rose, E., van Tulder, R., Verbeke, A. & Wei, Y. (Eds.) (2021). *The multiple dimensions of institutional complexity in international business research*. Emerald.

Rosenberg, M. J. & Hovland, C. I. (1960). Cognitive, affective, and behavioural components of attitudes. In C. I. Hovland & M. J. Rosenberg (Eds.), *Attitude organisation and change: An analysis of consistency among attitude components* (pp. 1–14). Yale University Press.

Rosinski, P. (2003). *Coaching across cultures. New tools for leveraging national, corporate & professional differences*. Nicholas Brealey.

Rudolph, C. W., Rauvola, R. S. & Zacher, H. (2018). Leadership and generations at work: A critical review. *The Leadership Quarterly, 29*(1), 44–57.

Sackmann, S. A. (2017). *Unternehmenskultur: Erkennen-Entwickeln-Verändern*. Springer.

Sackmann, S. A. & Phillips, M. E. (2004). Contextual influences on culture research: Shifting assumptions for new workplace realities. *International Journal of Cross Cultural Management, 4*(3), 370–390.

Saldanha, F. P., Cohendet, P. & Pozzebon, M. (2014). Challenging the stage-gate model in crowdsourcing: The case of Fiat Mio in Brazil. *Technology Innovation Management Review, 4*(9), 28–35.

Samdanis, M. & Özbilgin, M. (2020). The duality of an atypical leader in diversity management: The legitimization and delegitimization of diversity beliefs in organizations. *International Journal of Management Reviews, 22*(2), 101–119.

Samovar, L. A. & Porter, R. E. (Eds.) (1991). *Intercultural communication*. Wadsworth.

Sarala, R., Vaara, E. & Junni, P. (2019). Beyond merger syndrome and cultural differences: New avenues for research on the 'human side' of global mergers and acquisitions (M&As). *Journal of World Business, 54*(4), 307–321.

Schein, E. H. (1986 [2016]). *Organizational culture and leadership* (5th ed.). Jossey-Bass.

Schein, E. H. (1989). Organization development: science, technology, or philosophy?. *Sloan School of Management*, MIT.

Scherm, M. (1998). Synergie in Gruppen – mehr als eine Metapher? In E. Ardelt-Gattinger, H. Lechner & W. Schlögl (Eds.), *Gruppendynamik. Anspruch und Wirklichkeit der Arbeit in Gruppen* (pp. 62–70). Verlag für Angewandte Psychologie.

Schmid, S., Grosche, P. & Mayrhofer, U. (2016). Configuration and coordination of international marketing activities. *International Business Review, 25*(2), 535–547.

Schneider, S., Barsoux, J. L. & Stahl, G. K. (2014). *Managing across cultures* (3rd ed.). Pearson.

Scholz, C. & Stein, V. (2013). *Interkulturelle Wettbewerbsstrategien*. Vandenhoeck & Ruprecht.

Schuler (2013). Schuler supports vocational training in Mexico. https://www.schulergroup.com/major/us/unternehmen/presse/pressemeldungen/archiv/2013/2013_06_21_mexiko/index.html [last accessed 2 December 2020].

Schwab, K. (2017). *The fourth industrial revolution*. Crown Business.

Scott, W.R. (2014). *Institutions and organizations*. Sage.

Selmier, W., Newenham-Kahindi, A. & Oh, C. (2015). Understanding the words of relationships: Language as an essential tool to manage CSR in communities of place. *Journal of International Business Studies, 46*(2), 153–179.

Shim, W. S. & Steers, R. M. (2012). Symmetric and asymmetric leadership cultures: A comparative study of leadership and organizational culture at Hyundai and Toyota. *Journal of World Business, 47*(4), 581–591.

Sidani, Y. M. (2008). Ibn Khaldun of North Africa: An AD 1377 theory of leadership. *Journal of Management History, 14*(1), 73–86.

Smith, P. B., Andersen, J. A., Ekelund, B., Graversen, G. & Ropo, A. (2003). In search of Nordic management styles. *Scandinavian Journal Management, 19*(4), 491–507.

Smither, R., Houston, J. & McIntire, S. (2016). *Organization development: Strategies for changing environments*. Routledge.

Søderberg, A. M. (2015). Recontextualising a strategic concept within a globalising company: A case study on Carlsberg's 'winning behaviours' strategy. *The International Journal of Human Resource Management, 26*(2), 231–257.

Spencer-Oatey, H. & Franklin, P. (2009). *Intercultural interaction. A multidisciplinary approach to intercultural communication*. Palgrave Macmillan.

Spitzberg, B. H. & Changnon, G. (2009). Conceptualizing intercultural competence. In D. Deardorff (Ed.), *The Sage handbook of intercultural competence* (pp. 2–52). Sage.

Stahl, G. K., Maznevski, M., Voigt, A. & Jonsen, K. (2010). Unraveling the effects of cultural diversity in teams: A meta-analysis of research on multicultural work groups. *Journal of International Business Studies, 41*(4), 690–709.

Stahl, G. K. & Tung, R. L. (2015). Towards a more balanced treatment of culture in international business studies: The need for positive cross-cultural scholarship. *Journal of International Business Studies, 46*(6), 391–414.

Stahl, G. K., Tung, R. L., Kostova, T. & Zellmer-Bruhn, M. (2016). Widening the lens: Rethinking distance, diversity, and foreignness in international business research through positive organizational scholarship. *Journal of International Business Studies, 47*(6), 621–630.

Stein, V. (2010). Interkulturelle Kreativität. In C. Barmeyer & J. Bolten (Eds.), *Interkulturelle Personal- und Organisationsentwicklung. Methoden, Instrumente und Anwendungsfälle* (pp. 65–77). Wissenschaft und Praxis.

Steyaert, C., Ostendorp, A. & Gaibrois, C. (2011). Multilingual organizations as 'linguascapes': Negotiating the position of English through discursive practices. *Journal of World Business, 46*(3), 270–278.

Stoermer, S., Davies, S. & Froese, F. J. (2021). The influence of expatriate cultural intelligence on organizational embeddedness and knowledge sharing: The moderating effects of host country context. *Journal of International Business Studies, 52*(3), 432–445.

Strauss, A. L. (1978). *Social negotiations: Varieties, contexts, processes and social order*. Jossey-Bass.

Strauss, A. L. (1982). Interorganizational negotiation. *Urban Life, 11*(3), 350–368.

Stumpf, C. (2021). *From the old into the new. How an international practice transfer fostered an organization's intercultural organizational development*. PhD thesis, University of Munich.

Su, N. (2015). Cultural sensemaking in offshore information technology service suppliers: A cultural frame perspective. *MIS Quarterly, 39*(4), 959–983.

Szkudlarek, B., Osland, J. S., Nardon, L. & Zander, L. (2020). Communication and culture in international business – moving the field forward. *Journal of World Business, 55*(6), forthcoming.

Szymanski, M. (2018). Biculturals: Cultural chameleons or a brand new species? *Global network for advanced management*. https://globalnetwork.io/perspectives/2018/07/biculturals-cultural-chameleons-or-brand-new-species [last accessed 2 December 2020].

Tenzer, H. & Pudelko, M. (2015). Leading across language barriers: Managing language-induced emotions in multinational teams. *The Leadership Quarterly, 26*(4), 606–625.

Tenzer, H., Pudelko, M. & Harzing, A. W. (2014). The impact of language barriers on trust formation in multinational teams. *Journal of International Business Studies, 45*(5), 508–535.

Thomas, D. C. & Inkson, K. C. (2017). *Cultural intelligence: Surviving and thriving in the global village*. Berrett-Koehler.

Thompson, B. Y. (2019). The digital nomad lifestyle: (Remote) work/leisure balance, privilege, and constructed community. *International Journal of the Sociology of Leisure, 2*(1–2), 27–42.

Tietze, S. (2008). *International management and language*. Routledge.

Tietze, S. & Piekkari, R. (2020). Languages and cross-cultural management. In B. Szkudlarek, L. Romani, D. V. Caprar & J. S. Osland (Eds.), *The Sage handbook of contemporary cross-cultural management* (pp. 181–195). Sage.

Ting-Toomey, S. & Dorjee, T. (2018). *Communicating across cultures*. Guilford Press.

Tréguer-Felten, G. (2017). The role of translation in the cross-cultural transferability of corporate codes of conduct. *International Journal of Cross Cultural Management, 17*(1), 137–149.

Triandis, H. C. (1972). *The analysis of subjective culture*. Wiley.

Triandis, H. C. (1995). *Individualism and collectivism*. Westview Press.

Triki, D. & Mayrhofer, U. (2016). Do initial characteristics influence IJV longevity? Evidence from the Mediterranean region. *International Business Review, 25*(4), 795–805.

Trompenaars, F. (2003). *Did the pedestrian die?*. Capstone.

Trompenaars, F. & Hampden-Turner, C. (2004). *Managing people across cultures*. Capstone.

Trompenaars, F. & Hampden-Turner, C. (2011). *Riding the waves of culture: Understanding diversity in global business*. Nicholas Brealey.

Tuckman, B. W. & Jensen, M. A. (1977). Stages of small-group development revisited. *Group and Organization Studies, 2*(4), 419–427.

UNCTAD (2020). World investment report 2020. https://unctad.org/system/files/official-document/wir2020_en.pdf [last accessed 2 December 2020].

United Nations (2019). Population facts. https://www.un.org/en/development/desa/population/publications/pdf/popfacts/PopFacts_2019-6.pdf [last accessed 2 December 2020].

Usunier, J. C. (2011). Language as a resource to assess cross-cultural equivalence in quantitative management research. *Journal of World Business, 46*(3), 314–319.

Usunier, J. C. (2019). *Intercultural business negotiations. Deal-making or relationship building*. Routledge.

Usunier, J. C., van Herk, H. & Lee, J. A. (2017). *International and cross-cultural business research*. Sage.

Valentino, A., Caroli, M. & Mayrhofer, U. (2018). Establishment modes and network relationships of foreign subsidiaries. *International Business Review, 27*(6), 1250–1258.

Valenzuela, M. A., Flinchbaugh, C. & Rogers, S. E. (2020). Can organizations help adjust? The effect of perceived organizational climate on immigrants' acculturation and consequent effect on perceived fit. *Journal of International Management, 26*(3), forthcoming.

Valve (2012). Handbook for new employees. https://steamcdn-a.akamaihd.net/apps/valve/Valve_NewEmployeeHandbook.pdf [last accessed 2 December 2020].

Vora, D. & Kainzbauer, A. (2020). Humanistic leadership in Thailand: A mix of indigenous and global aspects using a cross-cultural perspective. *Journal of Cross Cultural & Strategic Management, 27*(4), 665–687.

Vora, D., Martin, L., Fitzsimmons, S. R., Pekerti, A. A., Lakshman, C. & Raheem, S. (2019). Multiculturalism within individuals: A review, critique, and agenda for future research. *Journal of International Business Studies, 50*(4), 499–524.

Walther, M. (2014). *Repatriation to France and Germany: A comparative study based on Bourdieu's theory of practice*. Springer.

Wang, Q., Clegg, J., Gajewska-De Mattos, H. & Buckley, P. (2020). The role of emotions in intercultural business communication: Language standardization in the context of international knowledge transfer. *Journal of World Business, 55*(6), forthcoming.

Weber, M. (1949[2017]). *Methodology of social sciences*. Free Press.

Weber, M. (1963). *The sociology of religion*. Beacon.

West-Eastern Divan Orchestra (2020). West-Eastern Divan Orchestra. https://west-eastern-divan.org/divan-orchestra [last accessed 2 December 2020].

Whitley, R. (1999). *Divergent capitalism. The social structuring and change of business systems.* Oxford University Press.

Wiener, N. (1948). *Cybernetics or control and communication in the animal and the machine.* Technology Press.

Wiggins, B. E. (2017). Intercultural games and simulations. In Y. Y. Kim (Ed.), *The international encyclopedia of intercultural communication.* Wiley.

Witt, M. A. (2008). Crossvergence 10 years on: Impact and further potential. *Journal of International Business Studies, 39*(1), 47–52.

Wolf, E. R. (1982). *Europe and the people without history.* University of California Press.

World Values Survey (2020). http://www.worldvaluessurvey.org [last accessed 2 December 2020].

WorldWork (2020). International profiler. https://worldwork.global/international-profiler/ [last accessed 2 December 2020].

Xing, Y., Liu, Y., Tarba, S. Y. & Cooper, C. L. (2016). Intercultural influences on managing African employees of Chinese firms in Africa: Chinese managers' HRM practices. *International Business Review, 25*(1), 28–41.

Yagi, N. & Kleinberg, J. (2011). Boundary work: An interpretive ethnographic perspective on negotiating and leveraging cross-cultural identity. *Journal of International Business Studies, 42*(5), 629–653.

Yanaprasart, P. (2015). Multilinguaculturing. Making an asset of multilingual human resources in organizations. In N. Holden, S. Michailova & S. Tietze (Eds.), *The Routledge companion to cross-cultural management* (pp. 112–130). Routledge.

Ybema, S. B. & Byun, H. (2009). Cultivating cultural differences in asymmetric power relations. *International Journal of Cross Cultural Management, 9*(3), 339–358.

Youssef, C. M. & Luthans, F. (2012). Positive global leadership. *Journal of World Business, 47*(4), 539–547.

Yu, H. C. & Miller, P. (2005). Leadership style: The X generation and baby boomers compared in different cultural contexts. *Leadership and Organization Development Journal, 26*(1), 35–50.

Zaidman, N. & Cohen, H. (2020). Micro-dynamics of stress and coping with cultural differences in high tech global teams. *Journal of International Management, 26*(3), forthcoming.

Zander, L. & Butler, C. L. (2010). Leadership modes: Success strategies for multicultural teams. *Scandinavian Journal of Management, 26*(3), 258–267.

Zander, L., Mockaitis, A. I. & Butler, C. L. (2012). Leading global teams. *Journal of World Business, 47*(4), 592–603.

Zander, L. & Romani, L. (2004). When nationality matters. A study of departmental, hierarchical, professional, gender and age-based employee groupings' leadership preference across 15 countries. *International Journal of Cross Cultural Management, 4*(3), 291–315.

INDEX